*Praise for Lawrence James*

'Lawrence James is the doyen of Empire historians'
Philip Hensher, *Spectator*

'James writes with energy and flair'            *The Times*

'Illuminating... a highly readable summary of the Chinese encounter with the whole of the modern world'
*Literary Review*

'Pithy, eminently accessible... What helps it to stand out is its brevity and brisk pace'            *Daily Telegraph*

'Wonderfully concise... James tells the story from the times of the Opium Wars to those of Xi Jinping with his customary panache... A copy of this book should be in the Christmas stocking of all British diplomats and politicians who are concerned with the future of their relationship with Xi's China'
A. N. Wilson, *Times Literary Supplement*

'Judicious and never dull... essential reading'
John Keay, author of *China: A History*

'James's writing is always full of energy and animation; he has an excellent eye for revealing detail, and yet is not afraid to attempt the broad, magisterial sweep'
William Dalrymple, *Sunday Times*

LAWRENCE JAMES was a founding member of the University of York and then took a research degree at Merton College, Oxford. After a distinguished teaching career he became a full-time writer in 1985 and has emerged as one of the outstanding narrative historians of his generation for works including *The Rise and Fall of the British Empire* and *Churchill and Empire*.

Also by Lawrence James

*The Golden Warrior: The Life and Legend of Lawrence of Arabia*

*The Iron Duke: A Military Biography of Wellington*

*Imperial Warrior: The Life and Times of Field-Marshal Viscount Allenby 1861–1936*

*The Rise and Fall of the British Empire*

*The Illustrated Rise and Fall of the British Empire*

*Raj: The Making and Unmaking of British India*

*Warrior Race: A History of the British at War*

*The Middle Class: A History*

*Churchill and Empire: A Portrait of an Imperialist*

*Empires in the Sun: The Struggle for the Mastery of Africa, 1830–1980*

*Aristocrats: Power, Grace, and Decadence: Britain's Great Ruling Classes from 1066 to the Present*

# THE LION AND THE DRAGON

Britain and China:
A History of Conflict

## LAWRENCE JAMES

WEIDENFELD & NICOLSON

First published in Great Britain in 2023 by Weidenfeld & Nicolson
This paperback edition published in 2024 by Weidenfeld & Nicolson,
an imprint of The Orion Publishing Group Ltd
Carmelite House, 50 Victoria Embankment
London EC4Y 0DZ

An Hachette UK Company

1 3 5 7 9 10 8 6 4 2

A CIP catalogue record for this book is
available from the British Library.

ISBN (Mass Market Paperback) 978 1 4746 1020 9
ISBN (eBook) 978 1 4746 1021 6
ISBN (Audio) 978 1 4091 8289 4

Typeset at The Spartan Press Ltd,
Lymington, Hants

Printed and bound in Great Britain by Clays Ltd,
Elcograf S.p.A.

www.weidenfeldandnicolson.co.uk
www.orionbooks.co.uk

*To the memory of Tranter, a springer spaniel.*

# CONTENTS

## PART THREE: COLD WAR AND PEACE, 1946–2022

# INTRODUCTION

This book is about one of history's reversals of fortune. In less than 200 years, China has been transformed from a fading empire under Britain's thumb to a global superpower on track to become the world's largest economy. In the same period, Britain has undergone a reverse process: it has shed its empire, status as a world superpower and economic pre-eminence, and it has been overtaken economically by China.

The story begins in 1839 when Britain, then an arriviste, enterprising and ruthless power, went to war with China. The issue was trade: for over 150 years, China had exported ceramics, fine fabrics and tea to Britain – all highly desirable, particularly among the wealthy – and re-exported to the Continent. British exports were unwelcomed in China. Two trade missions in 1793 and 1817 had been curtly dismissed: China could do without the products of Britain's industrial revolution. High-grade British opium cultivated in Bengal was a different matter, for Chinese users could not get enough of it. The balance of trade began to swing against China, and its government feared that the country would soon be drained of silver and slide into bankruptcy. An embargo was imposed on all imported opium.

Britain protested and a one-sided war followed. China promised to open its markets to British imports, chiefly cheap, machine-produced cotton wares. Within twenty years, the Chinese would be purchasing steam engines, iron ships and other products of Britain's industrial revolution. Britain also annexed Hong Kong island as a naval base and business hub.

Breaking into the Chinese market was a part of Britain's wider economic success story. The profits accumulated from technical innovation and a dominance of global markets were invested in foreign ventures. By 1900, Britain had become banker to the world and China was one of its major clients. Today, China is deploying her accumulated capital to fund overseas enterprises. Many are situated in Britain, where in 2023 Chinese investment totals £1.4 billion.

The history of Anglo-Chinese relations also contains many warnings. The most obvious are the dangers of hubris and racial stereotypes. Early Victorian Britain saw itself as a progressive nation leading the world in scientific innovation, economic energy and moral reform via Christianity. Britain treated China as an empire captive to its illustrious past and on the verge of deliquescence. The Chinese saw things differently: they were the heirs of an ancient and sophisticated civilisation, disdainful of other countries, of which they knew little and cared less. Educated Chinese regarded Britain as a faraway and inferior state inhabited by barbarians. Chinese emperors enjoyed the 'mandate of heaven' and ruled as benevolent autocrats quarantined from criticism and served by mandarins steeped in Confucian tradition and hostile to change. China was sufficient unto itself and wished to remain so. This proved impossible, since she could not defend herself against the weaponry of the recent European scientific and technological renaissance.

Britain believed that the war with China was a catalyst for the country's regeneration. It would profit from the achievements of the Western enlightenment, enjoy its fruits and open up to Christian missionaries who would uproot superstition and overturn false gods. Local reactions oscillated between delight and wonder – the Chinese enjoyed railway journeys and were entranced by photography – and resentment against patronising foreigners and their alien religion. These reactions, and their consequences, are a thread which runs through the early parts of this book.

Britain celebrated her forceful penetration of the Chinese market as a victory for progress, even though further campaigns were needed between 1857 and 1860 to convince the Chinese of their new destiny. At its heart lay a surrender of power which then and later kindled lasting resentment against Britain. Defeats had forced China's emperors to submit to treaties which curtailed their authority and made many of their coastal and inland cities enclaves where all foreigners enjoyed privileges, including exemption from Chinese laws which were considered unreliable and inferior.

Accumulated impositions by foreigners rankled and the iniquities of what the Chinese called the 'unequal' treaties were blamed on Britain. The transfer of sovereignty in Hong Kong in 1997 was celebrated in China as a belated righting of a historic injustice. It also stirred memories of a humiliating past in which the warships of Britain and other powers steamed up China's rivers to coerce and chastise. Alien presumption became a focus for indigenous nationalism; modern Chinese politicians still refer to the unfairness of 'unequal' treaties and single out Britain as their architect and prime beneficiary.

Memories of past intimidation and injustice run deep in China and this forms one enduring thread in this book. However, the Chinese experience of Britain was not all negative. The Victorian and subsequent British statesmen and businessmen saw themselves as the creators of a new China who were harnessing its human and physical resources to create a modern and prosperous capitalist state. This could only be achieved from the top downwards and so Britain did all in its power to uphold the authority of the Qing emperors and nudge them towards the Western world. Britain was China's guardian and trustee.

Britain's position in China was never unshakeable or exclusive. It had required substantial French assistance to win the 1860 war and Britain allowed the United States and European powers to secure the same concessions that were enjoyed by her own subjects. To have done otherwise would have been a heretical rejection of the British faith in competition and the free market. Nor was British power in China absolute, although British control of her customs services provided the means for the collection and dispersal of revenues without corrupt leakages.

After 1890 Britain's primacy in China was being jeopardised. Other powers, hungry for a slice of the Chinese cake, were jealous of British supervision of China's economy. A spirit of predatory imperialism now pervaded the foreign ministries of Russia, France, Germany and China's near neighbour, the newly industrialised Japan. All regarded China as a land mass to be partitioned and shared out in the same way as contemporary Africa. Britain was reluctantly sucked into the complex geopolitics of great-power empire-building in the Far East. Continental rivalries and tensions were exported to China, where both Russia and Germany were staking claims. The Chinese resisted: at the very close of the century, populist insurgents known as Boxers demanded the expulsion of all foreigners and converged on Beijing. An armada of European and American warships descended on Tianjin, troops came ashore, and the Boxers were crushed.

Among the troops rushed to China in 1900 was a Russian army, carried by the recently built Trans-Siberian Railway. Britain and Russia were rivals in Asia, and by this date, Russia was pressing her claim to Manchuria which was rich in minerals and open spaces for Russian immigrant farmers. Britain strongly objected, but the row was settled by diplomacy, as were other international arguments over disputed territory and spheres of influence in Africa. Henceforward, Britain became increasingly anxious about her future in China. An immediate response was to bolster her influence through an alliance with Japan, signed in 1902. It proved a Faustian pact, for while it provided security against Russian regional penetration, Tokyo's strategists were soon laying plans to extend Japanese influence in China at Britain's expense.

Anglo-Chinese relations in the first half of the twentieth century were shaped by the chronic instability within China. The troubles had begun in the winter of 1911 to 1912, when a revolution spearheaded by the Chinese army deposed the Qing dynasty and established a republic. The revolutionaries were nationalists, but there was no consensus as to how and by what principles the country would be governed. For fifty years, educated Chinese had absorbed Western political theories and debated the pros and cons of democracy, liberalism, socialism and Communism. None filled the vacuum left by the Qings. Instead, as Mao Zedong observed, power flowed from the barrel of a gun. China fragmented as warlords seized control of large areas; there was a civil war between Chiang Kai-shek's Nationalists and Mao's Communists; and in 1937 Japan invaded and within three years had overrun vast areas of northern and southern China.

The Soviet Union exploited China's chaos: it supplied arms to warlords, Nationalists and Communists and was willing to fight limited campaigns to impede the Japanese in Manchuria. It did so as part of wider ideological policy designed to undermine the British Empire throughout Asia.

Britain watched these events nervously while its investments in China soared: they totalled £1.2 million in 1936. But these assets and British commerce were imperilled by Japan's war, which aimed simultaneously to secure economic paramountcy and to extirpate British influence throughout China.

Japan's war against China had far-reaching repercussions. Britain had to balance her Far Eastern interests with the acquisitive ambitions of Hitler and Mussolini in Europe. At the same time, there was the local upsurge of anti-imperial nationalism in India, Burma and Malaya, all of which were receiving covert Japanese encouragement. In 1938 Neville Chamberlain's government was prepared to extend credit and military supplies to Chiang Kai-shek's Nationalist army, which were delivered overland from Burma. Russia too engaged in a proxy war against China, sending desperately needed aircraft to Chiang Kai-shek's outnumbered air force.

The harsh truth was that Britain was militarily overstretched and unable to salvage her former position in China. Her only hope was to enlist America, which had the wherewithal to tilt the balance against Japan and fund Chinese resistance. How this was achieved is described in the chapters covering the Second World War in the Far East. They cover the precipitate collapse of British, French and Dutch colonies in the region, and the mixed fortunes of Britain's ally China.

Britain and America were at loggerheads over China's future. President Roosevelt sympathised with Chinese aspirations and believed that an independent China, allied with and guided by the United States, would be central to the post-war dispensation of world power. Yet America treated China as a junior partner in the Allied war effort. Chiang Kai-shek did not attend the wartime 'Big Three' conferences in which Churchill, Roosevelt and Stalin hammered out grand strategy and agreed the blueprint for the balance of global power in the post-war world. China was again a country to which things happened, for it was agreed that the Soviet Union would invade and occupy Manchuria once the war had been won in Europe. Nonetheless, American pressure persuaded Britain to negotiate the revoking of the old unequal treaties.

Their disappearance was integral to Roosevelt's vision of a new China fulfilling her natural role as a great power well disposed towards America. Churchill disagreed trenchantly: he refused to believe that China could ever achieve parity with the West and was determined to retain Hong Kong after Japan's defeat. Unlike the president, the prime minister considered an intact British Empire vital for the new world order. These fundamental differences led to the hitherto little-known attempt by Chiang Kai-shek to seize Hong Kong by force in the closing days of the war. This *coup de main* was backed by senior American advisers to Chiang, but details of this conspiracy were leaked to the British who planned a swift *coup de main* against Hong Kong. President Truman gave his blessing to the plan and the American 5th Fleet co-operated with an unopposed landing which secured the colony.

At the same time, British and Indian forces were reoccupying Malaya, French Indo-China and the Dutch East Indies. The age of empires was not over, for America now needed them in order to hold its own in a new conflict: the Cold War.

The last section of this book traces Anglo-Chinese relations during the Cold War. It is a history of China's bloody internal upheavals; her economic miracle and emergence as a global superpower; and her intermittent contests with her two rivals: the United States and the Soviet Union. The narrative also follows the eclipse of British influence in the Far East, the loss of Britain's land empire and her efforts to find a role in the world as a subordinate partner of America. This would be defined as the 'special relationship', but it has never been a harmonious one, particularly when it came to devising a common policy towards China. Washington's hawks considered British reservations as symptoms of limp-wristed appeasement.

Clashes occurred over Britain's recognition of the Communist regime which won power in 1949 and, during the 1950s, over America's willingness to deploy atomic weapons against China during the Korean War and during the confrontations between China and Taiwan. Taiwan, annexed by Japan in 1895 and retaken in 1945, was the refuge of Chiang Kai-shek's Nationalists. In American eyes, the island was an embattled outpost of the Free World of capitalism and democracy. For China it was and still is a province lost to foreigners whose recovery was a matter of national pride and prestige.

Like Taiwan, Hong Kong was another reminder of past humiliations. From 1842 it was a British colony which had prospered beyond the dreams of avarice, and this book charts its progress and the commercial ethos encouraged by its rulers. Communist China chose to let it thrive as a valuable conduit for trade and investment. Hong Kong was exempted from the post-1945 policy of preparing colonies for self-government. It remained a tight ship, with the colonial authorities clamping down rigorously on political dissent.

The last section of this book covers the wrangling that led up to the transfer of power in Hong Kong in 1997. At the same time, it traces the emergence of the new China, her astonishing economic revolution and its consequences for her people and the world. These developments, which began in the 1970s, have coincided with a reversal of roles between China and Britain. The former is now a global superpower with a vast network of trade and investment agreements (the 'Belt and Road' system), formidable armed forces and a string of naval bases.

Above all, China now believes that its new strength gives it the right to make the rules of trade and diplomacy, just as Britain had done in the nineteenth century. As for Britain, its land empire has disappeared and, as Kipling had predicted, it is now 'one with Nineveh and Tyre'. Her people are richer and live longer than their ancestors, but the future of the economy generates unease and foreboding. They are also somewhat afraid that their addiction to the products of Chinese ingenuity and the demand for Chinese investment has left them vulnerable. Just as the Chinese had once feared that cameras could steal their subjects' souls, there have been newspaper rumours that Chinese components in household refrigerators could somehow spy on their British owners.

## Part One

---

## Lion Rampant, 1830–1912

# 1

## Barbarians: The Origins of the First Opium War, 1830–1839

Hubris rather than opium led to the war between Britain and China in 1839. Each was an imperial power intoxicated by assumptions of moral, political and military superiority. The Chinese were in thrall to a metaphysical view of the world which elevated their country and its emperors to an abstract sovereignty over all other nations. This boast was supported by the belief that over the past 2,000 years China had evolved a perfect culture, society and system of government. The British were equally consumed by a sense of innate superiority in every form of human endeavour which qualified them to bring political, moral, economic and scientific enlightenment to the rest of the world.

The small British mercantile community in Guangzhou (Canton), who were officially licensed to trade with China, believed this and fuelled their convictions with champagne, brandy, whisky and sherry. All flowed decadently during regular parties which reminded hosts and guests that Britain was a strong, enterprising nation whose expanding territorial empire straddled the world. The annual anniversary of the 1815 Battle of Waterloo on 18 June was remembered with pride and gusto: the rest of the foreign community were invited to dinners during which their hosts sang patriotic songs and proposed multiple toasts to the heroes of the battle. Similar carouses celebrated Queen Victoria's accession in 1837 and her subsequent birthdays. Her 158 subjects made up just over a half of Guangzhou's foreign population and included sixty-two Parsi merchants from Bombay.[1] Over the past 100 years, Britain's conquests in India had made her a formidable Asian power and an equal match to her closest rivals, Russia and China.

All but a few of the revellers were engaged in the import of opium, which the Chinese used as a narcotic, restorative, stimulant and medicine. Discerning consumers craved the purest Bengali opium, which was supplied by British and Indian merchants for whom the 1830s was a decade of rich rewards due to demand outrunning supplies. An alarmed government in Beijing feared that this upsurge could lead to mass, uncontrollable opium addiction.

Raising a glass in honour of the Duke of Wellington reassured British traders at a time when their presence in China was precarious and their future uncertain. The Chinese Empire regarded the presence of all foreigners as an unwelcome, possibly dangerous necessity and treated them with a blend of disdain and misgiving. Anxiety flowed downwards from the Qing emperors who, in 1757, had confined all Europeans to Guangzhou and imposed strict rules on their movements and transactions. This quarantine favoured China, for it provided an outlet for the exports of tea, fine ceramics and textiles that were prized in Europe.

This Chinese hostility rankled and the response was impatience and contempt. One merchant considered the Chinese as strangers to 'the arts of civilised life' and 'ignorant of science and politics', while another looked forward to a time when Britain would 'liberate' the masses from the Qing dynasty. The notion of conquering China was fantastic and would remain so. Most of the British community simply wanted the Chinese to treat their country with the respect it deserved, to adopt free trade and acquiesce to the laws of supply and demand. These aims were strongly supported at home, particularly by the manufacturers of mass-produced textiles who dreamed of clothing millions of Chinese.

The Chinese Empire profited from the arrangement, but the good times gradually turned to bad thanks to an upsurge in the demand for Bengali opium which, during the 1830s, was draining China of roughly £1 million a year. China was facing a trade deficit which, if not reversed, would trigger an economic crisis. Opium imports were paid for in silver and so the continuing loss of currency threatened to weaken the economy and the authority of the Qing dynasty. Less silver meant fewer silver *taels*, the basic unit of currency, which, in turn, meant a fall in imperial revenues. The emperor would be unable to pay the bureaucrats who ran his empire and the soldiers who pro-tected it against internal and external enemies. Opium also threatened China with long-term economic debility. Illegal addiction could sap the numbers and energy of the peasant farmers and artisans whose labour sustained the nation and whose taxes paid for its governance. Under Qing rule, China had undergone an agricultural revolution marked by land reclamation, crop diversification and improved farming techniques. The upshot had been a steady rise in population which, by 1830, was estimated at 400 million.

Early in 1839, and in order to stave off an economic crisis, Emperor Daoguang instructed Lin Zexu, the governor-general of Hunan and Hubei provinces, to confiscate all opium stocks held by the foreign merchants in Guangzhou and to forbid further imports. Soon after his arrival, Lin, a man of high principles, excused his actions on moral rather than economic grounds. In an open letter to Queen Victoria, he insisted that China no longer wanted to exchange 'poison' for tea and porcelain. His master in Beijing, who occasionally smoked opium, was a pragmatist primarily concerned with financial stability and dynastic security.

Daoguang's distrust of foreigners, irrespective of why they were in his empire, was understandable. The Qings were also incomers, Manchus from Manchuria who had seized power in 1644 and were therefore outsiders in the eyes of the majority of Han Chinese who were concentrated in the middle and eastern parts of the country. This alien dynasty asserted its absolute authority and ethnic ascendancy by compelling the Han to wear pigtails and forbidding them to ride horses. The coercive power of the Qing state was embodied in the Bannermen, a loyal reserve army of Manchu cavalry and infantry scattered in garrisons across the empire. By the early nineteenth century, these soldiers were often little more than idlers who enjoyed an easy life.

Given their origins, the Qing emperors were always uneasy about their own and their empire's vulnerability to foreigners. Europeans illicitly at large in China were free to gather intelligence about her geography, population, resources and defences. Even more disturbing was the potential infiltration of novel ideas that might become an explosive force which could shatter the quietist Confucian ideology and traditions that were foundations of the Qing autocracy.

Imperial power was rooted in the ancient Confucian concept of 'all under heaven' (*Tianxia*), which placed China and its emperors above a world whose various states theoretically submitted to their divinely ordained sovereignty. This concept of China as an overarching entity set the pattern of her relations with the representatives of foreign states: they were supplicants from distant tributaries. Geography contributed to China's world view, for it was confined by the physical boundaries of the China Sea, the Himalayan mountains and deserts of Central

Asia. On the edges of these natural frontiers was a periphery of loose dependencies – Manchuria, Mongolia, Korea and Tibet. At the close of the eighteenth century, two subordinate states, Vietnam and Burma, had detached themselves from China's control and, revealingly, Britain began to absorb the latter into her Indian empire in the 1820s. Beyond the eastern Asian land mass and the China Sea lay other polities about which China knew very little beyond the fact that they were inferior and within her divine, imperial orbit.[2]

The spiritual impulses which guided China and her rulers were the teachings of Confucius (551–479 BCE), who had instructed the Chinese on how best to conduct their personal, family and public lives. His advice was complemented by Buddhism, which was concerned with the heart and mind, and Taoism, which encouraged the cultivation of the body. All faiths coexisted, although a profound knowledge of Confucian doctrines was the basis for the examinations for entry into the imperial civil service. When Lin rebuked the British for the opium trade, he was invoking the Confucian axiom 'Do not to others what you would not have others do to you.'

Chinese notions of the divine ordering of the world and their relative geographical ignorance beyond their immediate sphere of influence resulted in a similarly naive political world view. This was noted as such by the British trade missions to Beijing in 1793 and 1816. Each was treated as if it had been sent by some subordinate Mongol khan and the first was dismissed by the Emperor Qianlang, who curtly told the emissaries: 'We possess all things. I set no value on objects strange and ingenious and have no use for your manufactures.' King George III, the ruler of Canada, Australia and a substantial swathe of India, and whose navy dominated the oceans of the world, counted for nothing in China's self-contained and introverted universe.

Yet the imperial government in Beijing was aware of the expansion of British power in India and its slow encroachment on Chinese influence over Tibet. Nepal's conquest by the East India Company's army in 1816 detached the mountain kingdom from China's orbit and placed neighbouring Sikkim (now a state in north-east India) within Britain's. Soon after, the company's army occupied Lower Burma, hitherto part of another tributary state.[3] These losses on the far periphery of the Chinese Empire did not unduly trouble Beijing, nor, significantly, did imperial intelligence agencies fail to link British forward policies in the tributary kingdom of Burma with the activities of Guangzhou merchants. Overall, the emperor and his ministers had yet to understand the spread of British power in Asia, the aggressive impulses behind it, and how it might affect China. For them, the outbreak of war was a severe shock.

The British commercial community in Guangzhou were intensely sensitive to their lowly status, which was commonly expressed in insults. In 1834 Lord Napier, the British superintendent of trade, was enraged when he discovered that a local mandarin dismissed him as '*yimu*', that is, 'barbarian eye'. Worse still for a naval officer and veteran of Trafalgar, his fellow countrymen were derided as '*yi*', which meant 'barbarian'.[4] Alternative but equally unfavourable translations were 'stranger' or a tribesman from the fringes of China. Other terms of contempt commonly used by officials in Guangzhou were '*fahren*' ('uncultured people') and '*fanqui*' ('foreign devils'). The implication of barbarity infuriated the British, who would later demand its removal from the Chinese lexicon. Some Chinese scholars justified this arrogance on the grounds that Europeans were a different species. They possessed four testicles, were addicted to sodomy, and were martyrs to intestinal distempers that could only be cured by imports of Chinese tea and rhubarb.[5]

Foremost among Guangzhou's barbarians were two dynamic and ruthless businessmen, James Matheson and William Jardine. They were products of the eighteenth-century Scottish Enlightenment, Scotland's advanced educational system and the work ethic preached by the Presbyterian kirk. Both were taught that individual endeavour and industry were good for the soul, pleasing to God and deserving of earthly rewards. Each graduated from Edinburgh University at the age of eighteen, Jardine with a medical degree and Matheson with one in the arts and medicine. Family connections secured each a post in the East India Company and through diligence, hard graft and a knack for spotting market opportunities they flourished and formed a partnership. The pair moved to Guangzhou in the 1820s and concentrated on the import of Bengali opium. Both were mistrusted by the Chinese, who nicknamed Jardine 'the iron-headed old rat'.[6]

Jardine and Matheson were also consummate political operators who knew how to manipulate the levers of power in Britain. Their objective was to persuade the government that it was in the national interest to compel the stubborn Chinese to open their ports to foreign traders, allow them to buy and sell as they wished, and show a proper deference to Britain. Both men were convinced that such a reversal of policy would require the surgical application of overwhelming force. They believed a short, decisive war would produce a pliant and co-operative China.

Domestic political circumstances were advantageous, for the 1832 Reform Act had transformed Britain's political landscape, creating a new electorate dominated by the middle classes, a crop of new constituencies in the industrial regions and a Whig government responsive to the wishes of manufacturers and exporters. It was to the commercial lobbies that Jardine and Matheson appealed, and they got a sympathetic response. In 1836 the Manchester Chamber of Commerce reminded Parliament that the China trade was worth £4 million annually and warned that British assets in Guangzhou were threatened with confiscation by Chinese officials. Glaswegian businessmen complained that the obtuse Chinese were rejecting the benefits of free trade. The dignity as well as the prosperity of Britain was also at stake: Liverpool merchants informed Parliament about the Chinese disdaining Europeans as 'barbarians' and, most shameful of all, a 'degraded race'.[7]

As well as whipping up indignation in Britain's industrial heartlands, Matheson secretly prepared for a conflict with China which he believed was inevitable and desirable. He employed local Chinese sources to gather geographical and political intelligence that would be invaluable if, as he hoped, the British government decided to take up the cudgels on behalf of the China merchants.[8]

Jardine and Matheson had rightly judged the prevailing temper of their countrymen at home and in China. Britain in the 1830s was a self-confident nation, proud of its native genius and dedicated to the creation of wealth. When the expatriates in Guangzhou raised their glasses to Waterloo, they were celebrating a battle that marked the debut of Britain as the world's first industrial power and the first global superpower. British engineers led the way in applying steam technology to manufacturing industry and transport. Britain's merchant fleet dominated the world's shipping. And the counting houses of the City of London were creating an invisible but immensely influential empire of investment, brokerage and insurance.

The early Victorians were proud of these achievements and convinced themselves that their present and future success was a result of a Divine Providence which recognised and blessed a morally virtuous and devout nation. The modern Britain of the mechanised factory, steamship and railway engine was a force for the physical and moral regeneration of mankind, a process that would include the eventual conversion of large areas of the world to Christianity. These enterprises depended upon the global acceptance of free trade. Its principles derived from Adam Smith's *The Wealth of the Nations* (1776). He advocated unrestricted markets for all resources and goods (including labour), free competition between businesses and nations, and the ascendancy of the natural laws of supply and demand. These were, of course, the conditions that suited a country which, by 1850, possessed over a half of the world's manufacturing capacity.

A revealing insight into the free trade mind was provided by Arthur Cunynghame, a junior army officer who, in 1840, found himself bound for China, where he would risk his life compelling the Chinese to adopt the teachings of Adam Smith. Cunynghame sincerely believed that he was fighting for a just cause and he never missed a chance to illuminate the blessings of free trade in the journal of his voyage. He was excited by the progress he witnessed in Britain's new colony of Singapore, which, he predicted, was about to become a regional economic powerhouse. He noted the commercial enterprise of Chinese immigrants, 'who enjoy more freedom than in their much boasted Celestial Empire'. Like so many of his countrymen, Cunynghame was convinced that free trade fostered the unrestricted movement of labour and, in doing so, released human talents.

In another fledgling colony, Sarawak (now part of Malaysia), Cunynghame encountered Dyak peoples mining antimony, which was shipped to Britain, where it was used to produce mock-silver cutlery for middle-class dinner tables. In return for their labour, the indigenous people were given wages which they spent on 'Manchester goods and other European manufactures'. At the close of his narrative, Cunynghame offered his vision of the new and better world which Britain was creating: 'The love of science and enterprise under the much-loved banner, the Union Jack, go hand-in-hand to the uttermost parts of the world.'[9]

Jardine and Matheson, their fellow merchants in Guangzhou and their allies in Britain's industrial cities would have applauded these sentiments. They also knew that Britain possessed the necessary muscle with which to impose the tenets of free trade on the governments of countries such as China. Since 1815 Britain had enjoyed a position of pre-eminence on every sea and ocean in the world and a string of strategic bases to shelter, refit and victual her men-o'-war. Unfortunately, Royal Navy warships seldom appeared off Guangzhou, and when they did they were unimpressive small sloops rather than formidable line-of-battle ships. The equivalent of HMS *Victory* would have generated wonder and fear among the Chinese, who might have grasped something of British power.

This deficiency was remedied in 1839 by the directors of the East India Company, who decided to pre-empt an expected Chinese ban on Indian opium imports. Fearful of the loss of revenues, they secretly commissioned a warship designed specifically for minatory coastal and riverine operations in China. The *Nemesis* was a 660-ton, iron-built, shallow-draught paddle-steamer with ample storage space for coal and a formidable armament including two sixty-pound cannon. It was completed within three months by Lairds of Birkenhead and, having passed its sea trials, the *Nemesis* began its eight-month journey to China in March 1840.

When Emperor Daoguang and the provincial governor Lin Zexu impounded the Guangzhou stocks of opium in an attempt to terminate the trade in the winter of 1838–39, the resulting war was one that was long expected (and desired) by Jardine, Matheson and the directors of the East India Company. Daoguang's only alternative would have been to legalise opium and impose a tax on consumers, and perhaps this is the route he would have chosen if he had realised that war would be the outcome of his decision. Qishan, another imperial adviser, had dissented and warned that the opium embargo would provoke British retaliation. But Daoguang was unperturbed and willing to go further. Subsequent imperial instructions to Lin included a suggestion that he might recruit Guangzhou's 'best divers and swimmers' and order them to board foreign ships at anchor and 'massacre' all on board. Intelligence of this scheme reached Captain Charles Elliot, the chief superintendent of British trade in China.

After a sixty-day trek from Beijing, Lin arrived at Guangzhou and, on 15 March 1839, informed the foreign business community that the opium trade was now forbidden and all stocks stored in their warehouses would be confiscated and burned. The announcement was a shocking affront to which Elliot reacted with characteristic rashness. He urged all foreigners to leave the city and find refuge in the Portuguese settlement at Macao and promised that Britain would extract compensation of between £2 million and £2.5 million from the Chinese. This was tantamount to a threat of war and was presumptuous insofar as it forced the hand of Prime Minister Lord Melbourne's ministry. In May, Jardine embarked on a 114-day voyage to England, where he gave ministers an account of recent events, steadied their nerves and suggested how China could be brought in line.

## Energetic Measures:
## The First Opium War, 1839–1842

The First Opium War began without a formal declaration of war from either side. For Lin, the enforcement of Chinese laws on foreigners in Guangzhou was a domestic matter and, therefore, not the concern of the British government. The impact of his open letter to Queen Victoria outlining the ethical reasons for outlawing the opium trade was somewhat diminished by his addressing her as a king, but it did, unbeknown to Lin, cause a political row in Britain nonetheless. The opium trade was repugnant to the powerful humanitarian lobby, which quickly mobilised to vilify it and condemn a government which was about to wage war on its behalf. Evangelical Christians, liberals and radicals cherished a vision of Britain as a godly nation dedicated to the uprooting of evil and injustice throughout the world. The formidable temperance and missionary lobbies added their protests. It was unthinkable that a humane nation already engaged in a global war against slavery should condone, let alone actively encourage, drug addiction.

Paradoxically, opium consumption was legal in Britain, where it was a prime ingredient in commercial curatives devised, among other things, for calming over-active infants. In 1830 Britain imported 30,000 pounds of mostly Turkish-grown opium, a total which doubled over the next thirty years.[1] Drawing attention to this moral discrepancy, Jardine dismissed opponents of the Chinese opium trade as 'the rigidly righteous'.[2] Ranged against the philanthropists were the pragmatists, who were loosely attached to the idea of Britain as a moral beacon but were unwilling to allow it to impede the nation's commercial interests. Lord Melbourne's government took this view and treated the seizure and destruction of the property of British subjects as a declaration of war.

Not that the Cabinet had much room for diplomatic manoeuvre, after Elliot had publicly pledged that Britain would secure compensation for the incinerated opium. Implicit in his demand was the threat of a military response if the Chinese did not comply, and this was understood by Lin and Guangzhou's foreign community. Melbourne publicly admitted that he had no faith in Elliot as a negotiator, but was forced to support him to uphold British prestige.[3] Moreover, the prime minister was conscious of the growing pressure from commercial lobbies who wanted condign retaliation as a means of asserting the global primacy of free trade, at least among those countries unable to resist.

During the winter of 1839 to 1840, the Cabinet, taking on board Jardine's advice on the geography of China, the effectiveness of her armed forces and Britain's overall strategy, agreed that a limited war was feasible and winnable. Force would be used to compel the emperor to open China's ports to free trade, pay compensation for the incinerated opium and foot the bill for the war. This indemnity would preserve the Whigs' reputation as a party which did not squander public funds. Apart from Hong Kong, which had been earmarked as a future naval base and commercial centre, no annexations were planned.

The foreign secretary, Viscount Palmerston, had been easily persuaded. He was a cocksure, combative and shrewd aristocrat whose forthright patriotism and readiness to use sea power to coerce those foreign governments which flouted British interests won popular support. Another enthusiast for punitive operations against China was the secretary at war, Thomas Babington Macaulay, a passionate if verbose champion of Britain's civilising imperial mission. A few years before he had introduced a British-style educational system to India as the foundation of a programme to bring progress and what he believed to be superior European enlightenment to the subcontinent. Like Palmerston, Macaulay was adept at beating the patriotic drum: during one Parliamentary debate on the Chinese war, he reminded MPs that Britain was 'a country unaccustomed to defeat, to submission, or to shame'.

Palmerston and Macaulay were confident that Britain had sufficient naval and military muscle to overawe China, despite two contemporary crises involving Britain's historic rivals, France and Russia. Imagined Russian intrigues in Afghanistan had led to its invasion by an Anglo-Indian army in December 1839, and French backing for anti-Turkish forces in the Levant had prompted British naval and military intervention there during 1840. Critics of the government were fearful that three wars at once might lead to naval and military overstretch which would tempt France and Russia to challenge British interests elsewhere.

Partisan political preoccupations also helped shape foreign policy at that time. The Tories loathed free trade and were initially disinclined to back a war waged in its name. They were a party dominated by landowners and therefore did everything in their power to protect agriculture, for if free trade was taken to its limits and produce could be freely imported, incomes from farming would fall. On the other hand, untaxed imported food, particularly grain, would keep down the cost of living which, in turn, would suppress wages to the advantage of industry and commerce. Moreover, the Tories were angered by the government pursuing its China policy in a hugger-mugger fashion without consulting Parliament. Details of the preparations for the expedition to the Far East were revealed in the British and French newspapers: in February 1840 the 74-gun battleship HMS *Blenheim*, the future flagship of the China expedition, was reported as refitting at Portsmouth for service in the 'East Indies'.[4]

The Tory Opposition smelled a rat and secured a debate at the beginning of March and another early in April. The first opened with a Tory demand that ministers should declare whether Britain was actually at war with China and, if so, how it could be justified. Lord John Russell, the home secretary, prevaricated by assuring the Commons that the ministry was taking measures in response to the recent 'insults and injuries' suffered by the Guangzhou merchants. He then muddied the waters by stating that warlike preparations were also being undertaken by the East India Company.[5] This was true, for the orders to muster an expeditionary force had been sent by Palmerston to the governor-general of India, Lord Auckland, the previous November.[6]

The Tories were dissatisfied with Whig evasiveness and in the April debate turned their fire on the government's handling of the crisis. Sir James Graham MP criticised the headstrong actions of Elliot, who had left his superiors with little diplomatic leeway. Other Opposition speakers played the moral card and emphasised what one called the 'danger and shame' of the opium trade. As to the results of the war, one Tory feared that Britain was about to acquire an onerous liability, for if the 'corrupt' and 'despotic' Qing Empire were to collapse then Britain would have to fill a power vacuum 'like that in India'.[7] Early Victorian pride in empire was always tempered by anxieties that it might expand to unmanageable proportions.

In response, Palmerston told the House that vigorous action was imperative, since 'trade with China can no longer be conducted with security to life and property'. Macaulay attempted to blur the moral issue by claiming that opium was a beneficial curative and analgesic and rightly observed that the Chinese emperor was more fearful of the haemorrhage of silver than of the spread of addiction. In an effort to rally commercial interests, he told the House that the principles of free trade were at stake. 'No machinery, however powerful', he declared, could deny the Chinese those 'luxuries' for which there was a valid demand.[8] Although a Tory, the Duke of Wellington reminded the Lords that local Chinese officials took bribes and had long connived at the opium trade. The duke also raised the issue of national prestige: the contemptuous treatment of Elliot, 'a person of high station in another country', had been intolerable.[9]

Tory arguments eroded the Whig Commons majority, which fell from 112 to 9. The war would go ahead and the *Blenheim* continued sailing southwards to the Cape.[10] Jardine then decided to strengthen the voice of the Chinese lobby by entering Parliament in the general election of June 1841. He was returned unopposed by the 230 voters of Ashburton, a pliable borough in south Devon, on a Whig/free trade ticket. He spoke once and briefly in the Commons in March 1842 in support of compensation for the Guangzhou merchants.[11] His partner Matheson replaced him as MP for Ashburton in a by-election in 1843 and he was succeeded by his son, Thomas, in the 1847 general election. All three were beneficiaries of the Great Reform Act, which had produced an abundance of small, urban constituencies that well-funded businessmen could secure to promote their special interests.

Command of the forces in China was placed in the hands of two capable and experienced officers, General Sir Hugh Gough and Admiral Sir Humphrey Le Fleming Senhouse, both in their sixties and veterans of the Napoleonic Wars. Each was familiar with the nature of the kind of warfare that would bring China to her knees and which Britain had used to her advantage in the imperial campaigns fought over the last 100 years. Flotillas of warships bombarded shore defences and landing parties of marines, infantrymen and sailors were rowed ashore in boats to storm the battered fortifications. These amphibious assaults were backed by artillery and, after 1800, by Congreve rocket batteries.

Like so many soldiers who pushed back the frontiers of empire, Gough's background was the Anglo-Irish gentry, a caste with plenty of experience of disciplining Britain's restless Celts. Ireland's lords and squires were often out of pocket and so they welcomed military careers overseas as an honourable and, on occasions, profitable occupation for younger sons with limited prospects at home. Gough was a tough, pugnacious commander with an imposing presence enhanced by bushy sideburns and a fine aquiline nose. He believed himself to be under the protection of Providence, spoke with a strong Irish brogue, was as fearless as a lion and cared for his men with a paternal affection.[12] At heart, he was always a daring and brave subaltern who led from the front and by example, sharing the risks of battle with the men he commanded. During the siege of Guangzhou in May 1841, he waded ashore ahead of landing parties while 'matchlock balls whizzed over and around him, cannonballs ploughed up paddy fields'. He never ducked. During the attack on a fortified position on an island off Xiamen, he led the assault and escalade.[13] Gough's tactical philosophy was simple: set an example of courage; trust in the grit and valour of the British soldier; and get to grips with the enemy as soon as possible, even if this required full-frontal bayonet charges. His modern, fictional counterpart was Evelyn Waugh's Brigadier Ritchie-Hook, for whom war was about 'biffing' the enemy.

Admiral Humphrey Le Fleming Senhouse, meanwhile, embodied the physical and mental spirit of Nelson's navy, in which he had served with distinction. He was of the opinion that audacity and a faith in the professional pride, seamanship and bravery of officers and men won battles. The official despatches of Gough and Senhouse were full of the qualities they (and civilians at home) expected and contained many references to the zeal, daring, gallantry and stamina of the men they commanded.

Elliot remained responsible for diplomatic contacts with the Chinese, and the commanders found him irresponsible and too willing to make concessions. Gough thought him 'as whimsical as a shuttlecock' and, during the siege of Guangzhou in May 1841, his efforts to procure a truce prompted Senhouse to comment that 'as usual' Elliot was 'acting on the spur of the moment'.[14] The admiral died a few days later from fever and sunstroke brought on by his exertions during the recent fighting, in which he had been in the forefront of the action. He was replaced by Sir William Parker, another veteran of the Napoleonic Wars whose bravery had won him the admiration of Nelson.

Local misgivings about Elliot's fitness for dealing with the Chinese were shared by Palmerston, who ordered his recall. In August 1841 Elliot was superseded by Sir Henry Pottinger, another sprig of the Irish gentry. He was a steady and unwavering negotiator who had proved his mettle as a soldier and administrator in India and who rubbed along well with Gough and Parker. On disembarkation at Hong Kong (now the British operational base) he relayed Palmerston's instructions, which were to take 'energetic measures' to expose further China's vulnerability and so compel the emperor to seek terms from a position of weakness.

During the eight weeks which it had taken Pottinger to reach Hong Kong, a general election had been held which returned a Tory ministry under Sir Robert Peel. His party was now committed to a war that was under way and, in the Queen's Speech, the new government promised to bring it 'to a satisfactory conclusion'. This would be achieved when the Chinese emperor recognised the 'justice' of British demands.[15] The alternative of cutting and running would of course have been political suicide.

From the start, the war in China was an unequal contest. A pre-war intelligence report on the Chinese armed forces described its war junks as 'ridiculous', while the infantry depended upon bladed weapons and bows and arrows. The only firearms were antiquated matchlocks with a slow and unreliable rate of fire. Chinese artillery was also outdated, cumbersome and relied on coarse gunpowder which burned slowly.[16] One cannon, captured at Zhoushan, was an imported piece with markings that revealed it had been originally cast for the arsenal of Queen Elizabeth I.[17]

Chinese military technology had ground to a halt in the seventeenth century, while Europe's had undergone a revolution. Applied chemistry and physics coupled with precision engineering and industrial manufacturing techniques equipped the British soldier and sailor with a formidable armoury. Mass-produced muskets and rifles outranged the Chinese matchlock and had a faster rate of fire. The disparity was even greater in artillery, for the British deployed mobile and accurate cannon and war rockets which fired explosive shells and missiles. For those involved in the development of the new military technology, the war was a potential laboratory. Captain William Hall, the commander of the *Nemesis* and a specialist in the application of steam power, looked forward to the China campaign as 'an admirable field for experiments'.[18]

The results were encouraging and, for some, horrifying. On sea and land, British firepower dominated the battlefield. During the fighting in the approaches of Guangzhou early in 1841, Hall described how a Congreve rocket launched from the *Nemesis* struck a war junk which exploded 'like the mighty rush of fire from a volcano'. A further ten junks were sunk during this engagement. When the city's defences were assaulted, concentrated canister and grape shot and musketry cut swathes through defenders. 'Those who stuck it out... drew down on themselves indiscriminate slaughter.' The disparity of arms was reflected in the casualties: British losses during the assault on Guangzhou in the last week of May were fourteen dead and ninety-one wounded, whereas the Chinese losses were calculated at between 500 and 1,000 dead with 1,500 wounded.[19]

Hand-to-hand combat was uncommon. During the fighting in Guangzhou, a marine officer 'got several pokes in the ribs' and 'a spear in his side'. He ran one assailant 'through the cheek', whereupon the man lunged at a sergeant who killed him with his bayonet'.[20] Whenever they were able to wield their swords and spears, Chinese skill and tenacity impressed their adversaries. But these qualities did not overcome the terror created by unfamiliar and devastating weapons. During the early bombardment of the outer defences of Guangzhou, an officer of the *Nemesis* noted that 'The Chinese no sooner saw the black snout of our craft... than they deserted their guns and fled in great confusion.'[21] They called his vessel the 'Devil Ship' and the 'Pirate'.

Systematically applied terror was the basis of British strategy. The capture and occupation of Guangzhou at the end of May 1841 (after which it was opened to international trade) was followed by a sequence of amphibious attacks on Chinese ports and a riverine offensive against Nanjing. What followed was a fourteen-month campaign of attrition in which British forces took Xiamen, Ningbo, Zoushan (Chusan), Shanghai and Nanjing. Pottinger would have liked to have gone further and urged a policy of systematic looting of captured ports. Gough was appalled: he wanted to impress on the Chinese that the British were 'not only a brave, but a just, a liberal and honest people'. Furthermore, an autocratic government would take little heed of the sufferings of its subjects.[22] The general also tried to clamp down on private looting, but with limited success.

Daoguang and his advisers reacted to the events with a mixture of incredulity and frenzy. In theory, the emperor could raise 800,000 fighting men to oppose an invasion force of 10,000. The trouble was that China's administrative machine was not up to the task of concentrating forces scattered across vast areas and sending them where they were needed. Moreover, the central government was often ill informed how many soldiers were actually available. When warships appeared off Tianjin in May 1840, 1,800 men of the 2,400-strong garrison were nowhere to be found.[23]

Muddle and inertia hindered China's mobilisation at every level. Both were encountered by Ching Chao Fei, a soldier's son whose father had urged him to enlist and presented him with a sword with which to behead a 'foreign chieftain'. Utterly inexperienced in such matters, Fei was placed in charge of the manufacture of mortars and rockets, but he managed as best he could, guided by a seventeenth-century artillery handbook entitled the *Firedragon Book*. None of the weapons he produced ever saw action. The patriotic Fei was dismayed by disobedient soldiers, bribery and bogus victories claimed by ambitious commanders.[24] Misinformation added to the confusion at the top. In May 1842, when his empire was suffering reverse after reverse, Daoguang asked why the British were selling opium and what Indians were doing in their army.[25] His questions revealed the extent to which he and his ministers were ignorant of reverses on the battlefield, Western technical advances and, closer to home, of the growth of British power in India. The first was understandable given the over-optimistic despatches of his commanders, while the latter two indicated a failure to comprehend or even investigate changes beyond China's frontiers.

A few Chinese grasped realities. Yang Fang, the general who succeeded the sacked Lin in Guangzhou early in 1841, succinctly summed up the situation: 'The foreigners' cannon always strike us, but ours cannot strike them back. We live on solid ground, while the foreigners float back and forth on the waves. We are the hosts, they are the guests – why have they been so successful against us? They must have been using the dark arts.'[26] Such candour was rare and unwelcome in Beijing. Other generals knew this and reported fictitious successes laced with disingenuous observations about their opponents' shortcomings. One remarked that the British have 'no other skill than trade' and that their 'legs were so stiff that if they fell over they could not get up'.[27]

By the spring of 1842 China was losing an unequal war. Fortified cities were falling like ninepins, armies were routed, the costs of the war soared, casualties multiplied and generals exaggerated the numbers of their enemies to excuse their defeats.[28] The loss of Shanghai and Nanjing in June and July threatened China's internal and seaborne trade and food distribution systems. There was also disturbing evidence that loyalty to the Qing dynasty was dissolving in areas under British control, where Chinese were selling food to British forces and hiring themselves out as labourers. A report to the emperor, found on the corpse of a mandarin in March, claimed that 'The mass of the people remain neutral, for these rebellious barbarians issue edict after edict to tranquillise them. They do not oppress the villages, and we have therefore lost our hold upon the fears and hopes of their inhabitants.'[29] An alien Manchu dynasty was already being blamed for its failure to protect its Chinese subjects.[30]

In Beijing the moment had arrived for a painful reappraisal of China's predicament. The result was a change of policy: resistance was replaced by vacillation and appeasement with the removal of British forces as the overriding objective. Tentative negotiations began in June and concluded at the end of August with the signing of the Treaty of Nanjing on board a British battleship. From the start, China was negotiating from a position of weakness, for, in the brutal words of one British officer, 'we have now the whip hand of the Chinese' and have 'taught them a lesson in humility'.[31]

This lesson in humility had enormous significance: by seeking terms from China's invaders, Daoguang was admitting that his once over-arching empire now enjoyed 'equality' with Britain and her empire. This theoretic equality was not apparent in the terms of the Nanjing Treaty. The emperor's diplomats agreed a war indemnity of £5.6 million to be paid within three years, delivered Hong Kong to Britain in perpetuity and established Guangzhou, Xiamen, Fuzhou (Foochow), Ningbo and Shanghai as ports open to international trade. In each of these 'Treaty' ports, a British consul oversaw trade and had the right to try to punish British subjects according to British laws. This clause was particularly galling for the Chinese, since it rested on the assumption that their laws and courts were inferior and could not therefore be trusted to uphold justice as it was understood in Britain.

Other clauses of the treaty emphasised Chinese incapacities. Whenever necessary, the consuls could summon British warships to protect foreigners and their property and maintain public order. China forfeited the right to impose or adjust tariffs, which were henceforward fixed at 5 per cent and, in time, would be administered by British officials. A subsequent agreement gave Britain a 'most favoured nation' status in trade, a privilege later extended to France and the United States. In return, British forces were withdrawn from China, although a garrison remained in Hong Kong to safeguard the Royal Navy's new Far Eastern base.

The First Opium War and the Nanjing Treaty were a turning point in Chinese and world history. They changed the balance of power in Asia to Britain's advantage and China's loss. From her power base in India and with an army that included 7,000 Indian sepoys, Britain had inflicted severe damage on the Chinese Empire and compelled its emperor to adopt policies that had hitherto been considered unthinkable and diminished his dynasty's status and authority.

# 3

## *Shi Yizhi:*
## Reactions to the Opium War

Britain celebrated the Treaty of Nanjing as a resounding victory: the government had secured its aims and China had settled the bill for the war. Queen Victoria and Prince Albert were so overwhelmed by the acquisition of a new colony that they briefly considered naming their firstborn child the Princess of Hong Kong. Sir Henry Pottinger received a hero's welcome, first in Bombay, where grateful merchants presented him with a silver plate, and then in the industrial cities of Britain. The Manchester Chamber of Commerce cheered him to the rafters and the lord mayor thanked him for his part in the advancement of a 'superior enlightenment'. He added, to laughter, that 'all the mills we have here' would be hard pressed to satisfy the demands of 400 million new customers for textiles.[1] A trade revolution was under way. By 1867 British machine-made cotton accounted for 20 per cent of China's imports and Indian cotton manufacturers enjoyed a share of this expanding market. Chinese customers preferred the smooth finish of the foreign products, which compared favourably with the coarser local textiles.[2] Meanwhile, the flow of Bengali opium continued and by the end of the century made up 14 per cent of India's revenues.[3] The trade only ceased in 1931.

However, a war fought to safeguard the opium trade continued to provoke outrage at home. Appalled by reports of one-sided battles, the *Spectator* condemned the fighting as 'sheer butchery'.[4] After the terms of the Nanjing Treaty had been announced, the Wesleyan, Baptist and London missionary societies petitioned Parliament to outlaw the opium trade. Their demands were presented by the Tory humanitarian and philanthropist Lord Ashley (later the Earl of Shaftesbury), who said that now the 'sad war' was over China was open to 'honourable and lucrative commerce'. He was glad that cotton imports were rising but saddened that nothing had yet been done to end a commerce that 'destroys the man, both body and soul'.[5] No vote was taken, and in any case opium remained freely available in Britain too until 1911.

Matheson had vainly hoped that Daoguang would soon legalise opium and so legitimise the trade. Nevertheless, the Treaty of Nanjing offered a bright future for his enterprises and he was quick to use it to diversify his business. In 1844 Jardine and Matheson moved their headquarters from Guangzhou to Hong Kong, where the company had already acquired real estate and was soon engaged in finance, shipping, insurance, commercial property and, later, railways. Risks remained, for there was evidence that the Chinese authorities would endeavour to hinder the enforcement of a treaty which had been imposed on them by force of arms. Palmerston understood this and in 1847 observed with typical bluntness that 'The Chinese must learn and be convinced that if they attack our people and our factories they will be shot.'[6]

Chinese pirates were killed in large numbers. Piracy, an over-romanticised crime that embraced murder, rape and theft, had been endemic in Chinese waters for at least 1,000 years and still persists, but the increase in European shipping during the eighteenth century saw a corresponding rise in the practice. It was a well-organised business: in the early 1800s a short-lived confederation of pirate chiefs was formed whose members owned fifty junks and commanded more than 20,000 men.[7] In some coastal regions, pirate captains often controlled one or more villages and were to all intents and purposes the proprietors of private estates. While they resolutely resisted Qing efforts to eliminate them, the pirates were apolitical parasites who wished only to be left alone to grow rich.[8]

Free trade encompassed the freeing of trade from maritime pred-ators, and China agreed to accept assistance from the Royal Navy in the war against piracy under the terms of the Nanjing Treaty. British men-o'-war, based in Hong Kong, began operations to suppress coastal and riverine piracy that would continue until the 1930s, when carrier-based Swordfish aircraft strafed and bombed pirate junks on the lower Yangtze.[9] It was a slow war of attrition fought against elusive adversaries whose junks sheltered in tiny inlets and creeks, often on small, remote islands. Intelligence as to their whereabouts came from local mandarins, the pirates' victims and peasants under the thumbs of pirate overlords.

The navy responded well, for the zeal of officers and ratings was sharpened by the lure of bounty money paid by the Admiralty. The going rate, fixed by British law, was £20 for each pirate killed or cap-tured, with the money distributed to crews according to rank. Prisoners were delivered to the Chinese authorities for trial and execution, which was also the penalty for piracy in Britain until 1860. There were good pickings for the vigilant and daring. In 1849 the crew of the paddle-sloop HMS *Medea* amassed £1,900, with a bonus of livestock given by grateful Chinese peasants and fishermen after a series of actions in the waters off Hong Kong. In one engagement against a pirate flotilla of nineteen well-armed junks, including several in excess of 500 tons, the guns of the *Medea* sank thirteen and killed more than 200 pirates for no loss.[10] This was exceptional: between 1858 and 1860 the crews of sixteen vessels on the China station received an average of £850 in bounties. Payments were, however, delayed: the crews of the splendidly named HMS *Rattler* and *Spartan* waited four years for head money earned in 1854.[11]

The delegation of coastal and riverine policing to the Royal Navy was a reminder that for the time being Britain was the predominant foreign power in China. Yet her primacy was not assured, for the war had aroused acquisitive ambitions in Paris and St Petersburg. For Russia, the penetration and piecemeal acquisition of China's western and north-eastern provinces and zones of influence were a natural outcome of its eastward expansion in Central Asia. Land, minerals and settlement by native Russians were the objectives rather than trade, for pre-industrial Russia knew that it could not compete with British manufactures.[12] Early moves were tentative and often taken on the initiative of local commanders. A military geographical survey was the cover for the occupation and annexation of Chinese territory at the mouth of the Amur River and Sakhalin island in 1855. Two years later Russia was covertly assisting Uyghur Muslim rebels in the historically restless Xinjiang province.

France's Far Eastern imperial gambit was the result of the policies of the Orléanist monarchy and its successor, the Second Empire. Each attempted to win the hearts and votes of their Roman Catholic sub-jects, and Napoleon III hoped to repeat the transient but intoxicating triumphs of his uncle and namesake. In 1844 China granted France similar privileges to those recently obtained by Britain and the uncon-ditional return of all the property of Catholic missions commandeered in 1724 when the emperor had banned 'perverse sects and sinister doctrines'.[13] This was a significant concession, for it became the basis of France's official protectorate not only of its missions, but for its Chinese converts too. The maltreatment of Catholic missionaries in China's tributary state, Vietnam, was the pretext for a French punitive expeditionary force in 1858. Saigon was annexed along with three coastal provinces.

Chinese reactions to the war and its outcome were complex and contradictory. The recent war had literally blown to smithereens China's mystic global supremacy, but her cultural and religious institutions and their philosophical and religious foundations remained intact. Insofar as war has always been a test of a nation's will and administrative machinery, China had failed. Some Chinese recognised this and concluded that in order to survive, the Qing state needed to regenerate itself, assimilate fresh ideas from abroad and adapt to a new international environment. Others disagreed vehemently, and so the official, commercial and intellectual elites split into two camps. One was profoundly conservative, defiant and determined to evade or frustrate the terms of the Nanjing Treaty and so preserve its country's traditions. Hanging on would not be easy, for China's internal sovereignty had been diluted and the mystique and authority of the Qing dynasty had been shaken. Conservatives treated these setbacks as temporary and reversible.

Opponents of the traditionalists preferred enlightened pragmatism to stubborn reaction. China's future salvation lay in what came to be known as the policy of *Shi Yizhi* – that is, gaining and learning from the wisdom of foreigners. The investigation and absorption of Western knowledge would give China the mental and physical wherewithal to transform and strengthen herself, preserve her independence and become an equal in a world now dominated by the West. *Shi Yizhi*'s advocates argued that the necessary processes of regeneration and reform could be undertaken without jeopardising either Confucian principles or the Qing dynasty. This was the philosophy of Zeng Guofan (1811–71), a successful general and administrator who did all in his power to apply *Shi Yizhi*. Among his achievements were the construction of China's first steamship, sending Chinese students to universities in Europe and America, and the introduction of those vital ingredients of industrial progress, machine tools, which were imported from the United States.

The Chinese would eventually call this policy *zingiang*, which means 'self-strengthening'. Paradoxically, Lin Zexu, whose zeal had done so much to start the Opium War, was an early believer in self-strengthening: he had attempted to construct a paddle-steamer powered by men operating a capstan during the early phase of the war.[14] Other contemporary mandarins were aware that China had become a stagnant society in need of regeneration and innovation and were prepared to look beyond her borders for guidance and example.[15] There was also a need for precise knowledge of the wider world beyond which led to a proliferation of geographical texts.[16]

The notion that a balance between modernisation and old systems and values could be achieved appealed to intellectuals, open-minded bureaucrats and the landowning and merchant classes. The last were particularly attracted by the opportunities for investment and enterprise offered by free trade with the West and the adoption of Western technology. By learning how to imitate the Europeans, the Chinese could compete with them. This was the intention of the group of Chinese merchants who successfully challenged the Anglo-American monopoly of steamship transport in Chinese coastal waters and rivers. In 1872 they formed the China Merchants Steam Navigation Company, with headquarters in Hong Kong.[17] It soon became the country's largest shipping firm and today is a major global corporation with multiple interests.

On a personal level, the Chinese elite were intrigued by and welcomed the European novelties which began to flow into their country. One such was photography, which had arrived with the British army. During the 1842 Nanjing offensive, two British officers took daguerreotype images of local scenery which have since been lost. The camera, invented just three years before, was then the latest example of Western scientific ingenuity. In 1846 a photographic studio was opened in Hong Kong and a second appeared in Shanghai in 1857.[18] Many more followed in China's cities and towns in response to a demand for personal and family photographs and nearly all were run by Chinese. Reactionaries fulminated against 'a dark mysterious instrument' with the power 'to see into men's souls', but to no effect.[19]

British soldiers and sailors who had encountered the Chinese would have been unsurprised by these efforts at modernisation, for they had immediately recognised them as an intelligent, industrious and adaptable people. The scientific sailor Captain Hall of the *Nemesis* predicted that 'when once a spirit of change and improvement has taken hold of the Chinese, it is impossible to say where it will stop among so ingenious and indefatigable people'.[20] Lieutenant Cunynghame looked forward to the transformation of a 'wonderful nation' whose 'ant-like population' was capable of 'unceasing industry'. Like many others he was astonished by the custom of the binding of ladies' feet at birth, which he likened to the wearing of corsets by the 'tight ladies of London and Paris'.[21] Other observers cited this habit as an example of backwardness and barbarism.

Assumptions of superiority were also tempered by widespread admiration for Chinese art. This was natural for officers from aristocratic and gentry backgrounds with their tradition of connoisseurship which prized Chinese textiles and ceramics. From the eighteenth century onwards, imported Chinese silks, hangings, decorative pottery and tableware were the insignia of taste and, for those who could not afford the originals, there were plenty of British workshops which provided passable imitations. Soldiers and sailors in China were able to bring home the real thing, by either purchase or plunder.

Off-duty soldiers and sailors stole or bought curios as souvenirs or gifts for their families. Others explored captured cities and wandered around temples. The intricate metalwork of one temple bell prompted one sightseer to praise 'the advanced state' of China's ancient 'arts and inventions'. During the 1842 occupation of Nanjing, a party of soldiers climbed the early-fifteenth-century Porcelain Tower, admired what they saw, drank a toast to the queen and went on their way with pockets filled with keepsakes prised from the pagoda's decorations.[22] These tourists were lucky to enjoy one of the architectural wonders of China, for it was destroyed twelve years later during an unforeseen and catastrophic civil war.

# 4

## Heavenly Kingdom: Civil War and Foreign Invasion, 1847–1858

The founders of new religions have much to answer for. The self-deification of Hong Xiuquan was a tragedy for China which cost the lives of at least 20 million of his countrymen and women over roughly fifteen years. He was born into a family of farmers in about 1814 and was a member of the Hakka people, who had emigrated from central China to the hinterland of Guangzhou. Hong had ambitions to become a mandarin but failed the exams four times. Disheartened, he immersed himself in spiritual and metaphysical speculation and examined Christian texts supplied by an American Baptist missionary, who later disowned him. Hong's quest for truth ended dramatically in 1847, when he convinced himself, his kinfolk and rural neighbours that he was the son of God and, therefore, the younger brother of Jesus Christ.

Once a godhead, Hong used his authority to create and lead a mass millennialist movement that would fulfil the will of his heavenly father. His overriding goals were the conversion of China to his version of Christianity and the replacement of the heretical 'celestial' empire of the heathen and degenerate Qings with a truly divine polity. Like the old regime it would be an autocracy, with Hong exercising supreme authority of a state called 'Taiping', which meant 'heavenly kingdom of peace'.

Hong's creed shared much in common with those recurrent mil-lennialist movements of medieval and early modern Europe. All rested upon interpretations of contemporary events that indicated an imminent apocalypse. China in the 1840s and 1850s seemed to be lurching towards a chaos from which it would never recover. Seen from below, defeat by the British, the flooding of the Yellow River, endemic banditry and localised uprisings appeared to mark the beginning of the end of times. Hong promised to avert them and redeem China through his supernatural power. Millions, without hope and fearful for the future, believed him.

Within three years of declaring himself a god, Hong had gathered 20,000 followers – many were people who, in his words, had 'ambition but no cash' or were 'penniless and hungry'.[1] Millions of the desperate flocked to the new Messiah. They were promised land redistribution, a limited emancipation of women, and the abolition of the degrading pigtail and the official insistence that all Han Chinese men shave their upper foreheads. Hong's male followers were distinguished by their shagginess. There was, however, no social revolution within the Taiping state, which was hierarchical and authoritarian. As his star rose, Hong adopted the distinctive yellow robes of the Qing emperors and, like them, he used vermilion ink for his correspondence. All power flowed downwards through subordinate 'kings' who governed regions and army generals. Hong's policies were based upon divine revelations delivered when he was in a trance.

War was integral to Hong's vision of the new China. First, he and his followers had to overcome feeble efforts to suppress them, and then his armies had to defeat the larger forces that had been ordered to crush them. He had good generals, including a former charcoal burner, Yang Xiupin, who helped create a formidable and devoted army. It contained two women's regiments, presumably nimble Hakkas who had rejected the traditional binding of girls' feet. In January 1851, Taiping forces had the strength and confidence to advance north-eastwards and push back Qing armies. Within two years Hong had captured Nanjing, which became his capital. Conquered lands and cities provided new recruits and the wherewithal to pay and equip them in the form of silver *taels* looted from provincial treasuries. Stolen Qing taxes funded Western arms, including modern artillery, which were smuggled in. The advance of Taiping armies was marked by murders, rapes and robberies. The fall of Nanjing was followed by the massacre of thousands of Manchus, a race demonised as the hybrid spawn of the mating of a red and a white fox. Their emperor, Xianfeng (1850–61), a fragile and lethargic twenty-one-year-old who had succeeded in 1850, was vilified as a 'barbarian' and 'demon'.

By 1851, there were two sources of authority in China, both sanctioned by heaven, and each intent on extinguishing the other. The Qing emperor came from Manchu stock and owed his throne to invaders, while Hong came from the majority Han people. He drew his strength from the Han population, who were conscious that their sufferings were a consequence of Manchu rule; the recent psychological and physical consequences of Manchu rule strongly suggested that it had somehow forfeited the 'mandate of heaven'. From below and the perspective of the times, it seemed that things were set to get worse. Each contestant in this power struggle offered an absolutist government, upheld by religious dogma and undertaken by an elite of mandarins.

The swift triumphs of the Taiping offensives stunned Western observers. A new state had emerged from nowhere, creating an apparently unbeatable war machine, and the ancient regime was falling apart. The fall of Nanjing threatened to disrupt grain distribution across northern China and provided Hong with a springboard for an offensive against Beijing.

These unexpected events placed Britain in a quandary. If, as seemed likely, the Taiping revolt prevailed, there was a chance that China might soon become a Christian nation. Despite Hong's divine pretensions, unorthodox theology and brutality, he appeared to offer Christianity an opportunity as great as Constantine's conversion in the fourth century. Britain's all-powerful Christian lobbies had therefore followed Hong's career with a mixture of stunned amazement and joyful anticipation. George Smith, a former China missionary and Bishop of Victoria (Hong Kong), spoke for the hopeful in a sermon preached to the Church Missionary Society in the Evangelical stronghold Exeter Hall in London in May 1857.[2] He began with a recital of commonplace racial stereotypes: the Chinese people were 'unintelligible' and suffered under the 'turbulent violence' which characterised 'Oriental monarchies'. Suddenly, deliverance was at hand, for the bishop predicted that 'Manchoo-Tartar' could soon be replaced 'by a dynasty which in its own strange way professes to be a Christian dynasty'. There were drawbacks, and he deplored the massacres that had followed the fall of Nanjing. These were, however, outweighed by the blessings of the new regime: the Bible had replaced Confucian texts as the basis for civil service exams and the ascetic Hong had banned opium-smoking, alcohol and fornication.

'Orientals', the bishop concluded, now had to be 'viewed with the tolerant indulgence' that Christian Britons could summon up. Such pragmatic tolerance was vital since he had detected the hand of Providence behind recent events and a miracle appeared to be in the offing – the conversion of 400 million Chinese. Bishop Smith's cocktail of condescension and optimism summed up the reactions and hopes of Britain's churchgoers.

The men on the spot were less easily converted. The fervent Evangelical Sir John Bowring, who had been appointed governor of Hong Kong in 1853, dismissed Hong's theology as 'the oddest jumble of truth and falsehood' and a creed for a band of 'fanatical and bloodthirsty robbers'.[3]

The Taiping insurgency coincided with the first of two major crises for the British Empire: the Crimean War (1854–56) and the Indian Mutiny (1857–58). Each represented a challenge to imperial strategic and political interests in Asia and each required a concentration of military and naval resources. The war against Russia was fought to block encroachments on Turkey's Black Sea provinces and the Straits, both of which were interpreted as threats to British interests in the Near East and Mediterranean. The route to India had to be protected whatever the cost in blood and treasure.

Operations were confined to Europe, where Anglo-French forces besieged Sebastopol in the Crimea and undertook naval sorties in the Baltic. There was also a sideshow in the Far East, where a Royal Navy squadron based in Hong Kong attacked Russian outposts on the Pacific coast of Siberia. These reminded Russia of Britain's latent capacity to frustrate her expansion in the region. Meanwhile, on the European fronts, Russia suffered reverse after reverse, which exposed the obsolescence of her military machine and its decrepit administration. As with China, defeat turned out to be the catalyst for critical introspection and eventual reform. But St Petersburg's ambitions for conquests in Central Asia and beyond remained unchanged. Evidence of this in the form of intrigues in Persia prompted Britain to send an Anglo-Indian army there at the end of 1856 to convince the shah that Queen Victoria was more to be feared than Tsar Alexander II, at least for the time being.

At the same time as the Persian expedition there was an unexpected crisis in Guangzhou, the resolution of which required a further application of minatory force to convince the local Chinese authorities to adhere to the terms of the Nanjing Treaty. In common with other treaty ports, Guangzhou's economy was suffering from competition with Hong Kong and Shanghai. Resentment simmered and was reported by Harry Parkes, who served as consul in Guangzhou and Governor Bowring's interpreter. He found handbills circulated in the streets which vilified 'foreign devils', particularly the British. One compared 'the injuries, the deceits, the cruel deeds of the English residents' to 'the hairs of the head'. Naval officers were advised always to carry 'at least one double-barrelled pistol' in their pockets whenever they walked in the streets.[4]

Bowring and Parkes persuaded themselves that abuse of foreigners was being fomented by the local authorities and reflected overall Qing policy to frustrate the enforcement of the terms of the Nanjing Treaty. Their fears were confirmed in the summer of 1856, when Bowring attempted to present his credentials as Britain's official plenipotentiary to Emperor Xianfeng. He and the American consul in Guangzhou were rebuffed when they landed at Tianjin and were compelled to return to Hong Kong.

A further humiliation – or at least an incident that could be construed as a deliberate humiliation – proved the final straw for Bowring and gave him a welcome opportunity to teach China the futility of obstructing free trade. In September, the Guangzhou authorities intercepted the *Arrow*, a vessel suspected of piracy, hauled down the British flag and arrested its Irish captain and Chinese crew. A furious Parkes demanded the release of the prisoners for trial under British law in Hong Kong. Ye Mincheng, the provincial governor-general, handed over all but one of the suspects but insisted that the *Arrow*'s registration as a British ship had lapsed. His actions had therefore been legal. This was a moot point, but Bowring treated the incident as a stick with which to beat the Chinese and restore British prestige. 'Are we prepared to bite?' asked one naval officer. If not, then his country could expect further calculated affronts.[5]

Bowring was a self-taught polymath, a fervent Evangelical, a prolific pamphleteer and a champion of universal free trade – he once claimed that Jesus had been a free trader. He was obstinate and pugnacious and keen to bring the Chinese to heel. Bowring also suspected that Russia was covertly encouraging China to flout the Nanjing Treaty.[6]

Bowring's temperament and outlook reflected those of Palmerston, who was now prime minister. He shared Bowring's doubts about China's good faith and the need to make her submit to the terms of the Nanjing Treaty. Palmerston was able to control events with greater ease than his predecessors. New telegraph links from London via Paris and Marseilles to Alexandria nearly halved the time of communications with China. And fast steamers had cut the sailing time from Calcutta to Hong Kong to fifteen days.[7]

Confident of Palmerston's approval and egged on by Parkes, Bowring planned a *coup de main* against Guangzhou designed to remind China of British hard power and resolve. British warships opened the war with successful bombardment of the city's seaward forts, but the follow-up was postponed when in May 1857 reinforcements had to be diverted to Calcutta to suppress the recent and unexpected uprisings in northern and central India, known as the Indian Mutiny. Saving British India (and with it British pretensions as an Asian and global power) took strategic priority and operations against Guangzhou were placed on hold. Bowring had to wait until December before launching an amphibious assault on the city.

In the meantime, Bowring's actions had come under sharp criticism in Britain. They were fiercely debated in the Commons at the end of February 1857. Richard Cobden, a radical, pacifist and mill owner who treated his workers strictly, opened the attack on the ministry. He claimed that the Chinese government was sincerely trying to fulfil its treaty obligations. Britain was responding with a 'haughty and inflexible' policy of coercion. The Tory Lord Robert Cecil (the future prime minister the Marquess of Salisbury) drily noted that Britain calmly suffered rebuffs 'from a strong nation like America' but browbeat 'weak powers like China' and so repudiated the national virtues of 'honour, justice and truth'.[8]

Palmerston side-stepped the wider moral issue and appealed to the electorate. He dissolved Parliament in March and called a general election, the only one in British history in which the conduct of foreign policy was the main issue. For him the issue at stake was national prestige, as he explained in his manifesto to the voters of his own constituency, Tiverton. 'An insolent barbarian, wielding authority in Canton, had violated the British flag, broken the engagements of treaties, offered rewards for the heads of British subjects in that part of China and planned their destruction by murder, assassination and poisons.' A vote for Palmerston and the Whigs was a vote for the punishment of Governor Ye and the humbling of China, while a Tory vote was tacit approval of his misdeeds and Chinese duplicity.

On the first day of a four-week campaign, Palmerston's adversaries fired their broadside at a meeting in the Freemasons' Hall in

London. Cobden was present alongside the radical Henry Layard, the archaeologist who had excavated Nineveh and was a Liberal MP for Aylesbury. He too invoked national honour. The 'Opium War', fought eighteen years before, had been the 'most disgraceful in history', unlike the recently ended 'fair stand-up fight with Russia'. Once again, Britain was bullying 'a feeble nation', to the shame of her people.[9] The *Morning Post* railed against a 'barbarian Eastern power' and insisted that there was 'no way of reaching the heart of China but by the sword'. Two-thirds of the 700,000 voters agreed, including those of Maidstone, who had read in a newspaper that the Tory candidate as a close friend of Governor Ye. The Whigs and their Liberal partners gained 73 seats and the Tories lost 65. Palmerston's patriotic card had turned up trumps: he would remain prime minister until his death in 1865 and the war with China would continue. Bowring had got his way with the help of a British electorate still ebullient with John Bullish pride after the recent victory over Russia.

Vindicated by his fellow countrymen, Bowring had to wait until the last week in December 1857 to resume operations against Guangzhou. By then the Indian emergency was all but over bar mopping-up operations against scattered rebels. Sufficient troops were now available to besiege and storm the city. After a heavy naval bombardment, Guangzhou was attacked by 4,600 British troops and 1,000 French marines. These had been sent by Napoleon III to avenge the execution of a French Catholic missionary who had defied a Chinese ban on inland travel by foreigners. Parkes was exultant: 'I confidentially hope... that a satisfactory adjustment of all difficulties may be obtained with a slight effusion of blood.'[10] After Guangzhou had suffered a well-deserved chastisement, he looked forward to a contrite and humble emperor accepting a British embassy in Beijing. Bowring's bombardment of Guangzhou was the first stage in a sequence of campaigns that lasted until 1860 and became known as the Second China War. Its overriding objective was to convince the Chinese government that the earlier Treaty of Nanjing was binding, and that evasion or resistance to its terms were futile. Britain would punish any backsliding.

By the first week of January 1858, Guangzhou was in British hands after what one observer considered a 'resolute' resistance. Ye's palace had been deliberately targeted by the warships' cannon. He was captured by a party of sailors who stole his mandarin's robes and dressed up in them, sending one outfit to their commanding officer, Admiral Sir Michael Seymour.[11] Ye himself was arrested and deported to Calcutta, where he was photographed and where he died a few months later.

Looters traversed the city and made beelines for 'josses' (temples and shrines) where there were known to be storehouses of valuables. Vandalism went hand in hand with theft. According to one naval officer, plundering sailors knocked off the heads and limbs of religious statues. He crassly remarked that this vandalism must have weakened 'the Chinese faith in their Gods'.[12] Sporting officers were ordered not to venture too far into the nearby paddy fields.[13] The Chinese had been cowed, but violent resentment remained.

# 5

## Knuckle Down:
## More Wars, 1858–1864

In early 1858, Britain and India mobilised for what Palmerston hoped would be a final, overwhelming and decisive offensive against China. 'We want no conquest,' he later told the Commons, adding that victory would 'increase the prosperity of the Chinese'.[1] It would also enrich Britain, for the ambassador Lord Elgin had been instructed to demand the confirmation and extension of the commercial concessions and legal privileges of all foreigners within China. If necessary, he would negotiate directly with the emperor, or more realistically with his closest ministers, since Xianfeng was dying from dropsy.

France was a partner in this enterprise. Elgin was accompanied by Baron Jean-Baptiste-Louis Gros, an experienced diplomat who supplemented Britain's demands with French claims for the protection of all Catholic missions, their clergy and converts. Like Britain, France had lost patience with Chinese backsliding and prevarication: in February 1860 Napoleon III told the National Assembly that his soldiers were fighting in China 'to punish her for her perfidy'.[2] France was also aware of Beijing's support for the resistance to her forces in Indo-China.

This desire for retribution was also strong among British patriots, one of whom rejoiced at the prospect of demolishing the 'Great Wall of Mandarin Knavery'. Soldiers were of like mind. Captain Garnet Wolseley, a twenty-five-year-old ambitious and observant staff officer, regretted that the promotion of 'commerce' took precedence over 'revenge for past injuries' and 'the maintenance of national honour'.[3] The war was a step along the path of promotion and a chance to catch public attention by the publication of his campaign journal. His career blossomed and he ended up as commander-in-chief of the army, with a viscountcy and an equestrian statue in Horse Guards Parade. Wolseley was also celebrated as 'the model of a major-general' in Gilbert and Sullivan's *Pirates of Penzance*.

The war with China was fraught with political hazards. British voters had backed Palmerston's China policy in principle, but radical journalists and MPs continued to criticise the conflict on moral grounds and the rising costs of the campaign. The bill was, however, shared by the Indian treasury, which continued to rely on levies on exported opium.

MPs were anxious that the campaign would run out of control and that Britain would somehow find itself sucked into an extended and expensive campaign and with it the occupation of Chinese territory. Underlying this fear was a belief that China could easily become another India, where, for the past 100 or so years, headstrong officials and commanders had overridden the government at home and pressed ahead with wars of annexation on the grounds of local security. News of these concerns reached the front line and Wolseley observed in his campaign journal that there was domestic pressure for a quick war.[4]

By far the greatest problem faced by the Allies was how to deal with the Taiping state, which, like them, was waging a war against the Qings. Hong Xiuquan was keen to secure foreign help in his struggle, not least because it would facilitate the flow of Western arms for his forces. Some years before, he had asked for and received profiles of the powers then engaged in China. According to this report, the British were intelligent, instinctively 'proud' and the 'most powerful nation' thanks to their monarchy and stable institutions. The United States chose its rulers by putting names 'in large boxes' and its consuming passion was the accumulation of 'wealth'. Artistic ingenuity and mass attachment to 'mystical religion' characterised the French.[5]

Yet a common adversary did not make for common interests between Britain, France and Hong – rather the contrary, for the chaos created by China's civil war was damaging British trade and investment. Moreover, any partnership with Hong's Taiping kingdom was anathema to French Catholics, who regarded its faith as a heresy whose spread would undermine their own missions. London and Paris, therefore, chose to use their power to support the Qings, having first secured their submission. Once the emperor had accepted Allied terms, they would help the dynasty to restore its authority. A biddable China under Qing rule was the natural partner for British commerce and investment, for it represented political continuity and possessed an administrative machine which would restore and preserve public order, which was vital for commercial growth. Any pact with Hong was, therefore, out of the question, although he vainly offered one to Elgin in November 1858 and afterwards promised to adhere to the treaties agreed between Britain and the imperial government.[6]

British officers and officials who had contacts with Hong and his followers were unimpressed and sometimes contemptuous. A naval officer who accompanied Elgin to Nanjing was appalled by 'the disorderly rabble of opium-smoking, disreputable-looking men and youths' he found there.[7] There was also disgust at the brutal treatment of the rural peasantry by Hong's soldiers. Wolseley, who met Hong in Nanjing in 1860, likened him in his yellow silk robes to a creature from a 'monstrous Christmas pantomime'.[8] He was, however, disturbed by rumours circulating among the Chinese that, having beaten Qing armies in a number of battles, the Taipings would be more than a match for the Allies. The Taiping state and its war with the Qings were a tiresome distraction for the Allied generals and at times hindered their operations. Guangzhou was threatened, a blockade was established on the Yangtze and troops had to be diverted to Shanghai to resist a Taiping offensive in August 1860.

Overall Allied strategy in the Second Opium War was dictated by diplomatic objectives, as it had been in the previous war. An armada of more than 150 warships and transports would concentrate in Bohai Bay prior to an amphibious assault on the Dagu forts. Once these had been destroyed, Allied troops would advance inland to Tianjin, where, it was assumed, the emperor's envoys would make further concessions which would be embodied in a fresh treaty.

Extracting a new treaty required an army of 19,000, one-third French and two-thirds Anglo-Indian. In theory this force was more than capable of overcoming a Chinese army ten times as large and which, like its predecessors, was armed with matchlocks, bows and arrows and bladed weapons. The latest technology more than compensated for the disparity of numbers. The new British Armstrong breech-loading cannon fired exploding shells at a range of 3,000 yards and the Enfield rifle was accurate at 1,000. Unsurprisingly, Wolseley discovered that some Chinese characterised the British as a 'people famous for the construction of guns'.[9] As in the last war, superior firepower led to a gross imbalance of casualties. 'It is pitiable for such brave fellows to be engaged in hopeless conflict,' wrote one British officer, and Wolseley admired the pluckiness of Chinese advancing in the teeth of devastating cannon and rifle fire.[10]

A British soldier serving in China was more likely to die from local maladies than from the actions of his foes. 'Heat, work and sickness' had thinned the ranks during the last war, when at one stage 252 men of the 26th (Cameronian) Regiment had been laid up in hospital.[11] Heatstroke was common during the summer, when temperatures rose to the nineties and low hundreds. Miseries were intensified by the Cameronians' colonel, who insisted that his men always kept their collars of their red jackets tightly buttoned. Heat exhaustion, fevers and 'Chinese dysentery' were responsible for the deaths of 137 soldiers from the 59th (Nottinghamshire) Regiment stationed in Hong Kong during the 1850s.[12] High wastage rates from disease were another reason why politicians and generals wanted a short campaign.

Wolseley noticed that 'fatigue' and 'thirst' were the commonest discomforts of the second war. The latter was exacerbated by the soldiers' staple ration of salted meat, which was handed out in six-day portions and soon decayed in the heat. More palatable and nourishing were the grapes and 'good vegetables' sold by enterprising Chinese.[13] Wolseley also observed, perhaps enviously, that French soldiers enjoyed fresh pork from stolen Chinese pigs. Camp life varied, depending on situation and season. Soaked and hungry men on the march shivered without fires when the enemy was close. When he was not, camp fires were lit in the nocturnal cool and Wolseley slept snugly with his cloak as a blanket. He enjoyed evenings spent with 'jovial comrades, talking of home, love, war, and hunting'. Pipes of Virginia tobacco and tots of rum and water added to this sense of conviviality.[14] Off-duty officers in already cosmopolitan Shanghai organised shooting parties in the neighbouring countryside, but Wolseley was dismayed by the city's 'dismal-looking race course' and the absence of a gentleman's club. These shortcomings would soon be remedied.

The campaign opened well and vindicated Allied strategy. After a heavy naval bombardment, the Dagu forts fell to an amphibious assault in March 1858. British and French troops proceeded to Tianjin, where they were met by representatives of Emperor Xianfeng. They complied with Allied demands and conceded a treaty which confirmed the terms of the 1842 Nanjing agreement and extended earlier concessions to all foreigners in China. Tainan and Tamsui (both now in Taiwan),

Haikou, Shantou, Penglai and Nanjing were added to the list of Treaty ports. British, French and American subjects were granted freedom of movement throughout China, foreign merchantmen and warships were allowed free navigation on the Yangtze and foreign men-o'-war were given access to all Chinese ports. The emperor promised full toleration of Christians and outlawed the use of the word 'barbarian' and its scornful derivatives.

China also agreed to pay 6 million silver *taels* to the Allied governments to cover the costs of the war. Inland China was now open to foreign economic penetration and policing by foreign gunboats. All foreigners were exempt from Chinese laws and their interests were to be upheld by permanent foreign missions in Beijing. In time, China established embassies abroad and so became integrated in the international diplomatic system and accepted its customs and rules. Notions of uniqueness and the concept of the emperor's universal dominion finally passed into oblivion.

Reactionaries in Beijing were aghast at this surrender of real and abstract sovereignty and successfully urged Xianfeng to repudiate the Tianjin Treaty. Reinforcements were summoned up, including several thousand Mongol cavalry, and the imperial general Sengge Rinchen ordered the defences of the Dagu forts to be rebuilt.

The Allies responded with another attack on the Dagu forts in June 1859, which went awry thanks to the accuracy of the Chinese artillery. Several ships were sunk or severely damaged, among them the gunboat HMS *Plover*. Seamen from an American ship helped rescue the wounded and briefly manned the *Plover*'s guns. Josiah Tattnall, the commander of the United States East India Squadron, excused this breach of his country's neutrality with the comment 'Blood is thicker than water'. Washington concurred and his remark was later invoked as a sentimental justification for Anglo-American friendship and co-operation.

The second battle of the Dagu forts seemed to vindicate the decision to cancel the Tianjin Treaty, but it turned out to be a fluke victory. In July 1860 a third Allied armada hove to and shelled the forts, and the infantry stormed ashore to establish a bridgehead. Felice Beato, a photographer, joined them and produced stark images of the shattered defences and the scattered corpses of Chinese gunners. He also took pictures of the vast encampment of the 17,000 British, Indian and French soldiers who were soon marching towards Beijing. The opposition was swept aside by high-explosive shells and bullets, and British dragoons and Indian lancers proved themselves more than a match for Mongol horsemen. At least one British onlooker was pleased that his countrymen were masters of traditional as well as modern warfare.[15]

Patriots at home were stirred by the tale of John Moyse, an Irish private of the 3rd (East Kent) Regiment with a harum-scarum reputation. Taken prisoner, he refused to kowtow to the Chinese general San Kao Lin Chin and was immediately beheaded. Moyse's defiance was celebrated by Sir Francis Doyle's poem, 'A Private of the Buffs':

> He stands in Elgin's place
> Ambassador for Britain's crown
> And type of all her race.

Those who were moved by this poem would have applauded a *Punch* cartoon which showed a stern Lord Elgin, cannonball in hand, confronting the Chinese emperor with the caption 'Come, knuckle down! No cheating this time.'[16]

Early in September 1860, the hawks in Beijing panicked as the Allied armies approached the city. The upshot was a blunder for which China paid dearly. Chinese troops seized an advance party of British and French envoys and their escort of Indian lancers and imprisoned and tortured them. Half of the thirty-nine prisoners died as a result of their cruel usage. Nothing was gained by this brutality and Xianfeng and his courtiers fled Beijing to escape capture and the humiliation that was bound to follow. Allied forces occupied the city with little resistance.

The power vacuum in Beijing was filled by the emperor's twenty-seven-year-old half-brother Yixin, known to the British as Prince Gong. By the last week in September, defiance had proved disastrous, Chinese armies had been routed and were scattered and, as a pragmatist, he had no option but to revert to the policy of appeasement. At the end of September, the surviving hostages from the British and French envoys were returned.

Once the extent of the torments of the British and French envoys were known, Elgin and Gros decided that the emperor should be punished for flouting international conventions as to the treatment of diplomats and for the murders. Retaliation would be directed against Xianfeng rather than the Chinese people, and so orders were given for the destruction of his summer palace, a vast complex of gardens and galleries housing the imperial art collections. The artefacts were looted by Allied soldiers over three days and then the buildings were burned. British officers confiscated some of the plunder, which was subsequently auctioned. The alternative was collective vengeance against the people of Beijing, which would have involved Allied soldiers running amok, killing and robbing its citizens. Such terror had been employed by the French in Algeria and, recently, by the British during the suppression of the Indian Mutiny.

Wolseley got some ceramics of the 'old familiar blue willow-pattern', while other officers had their loot shipped home, where it was sold in London and Paris. The Empress Eugenie purchased many arte-facts, which were coyly described as 'property of an officer of Fane's Horse', while one London auctioneer advertised Chinese lots as taken by soldiers from a temple in 'Chunan'. One dealer recommended his recently acquired artworks to 'grocers wishing to decorate their shops with Chinese curiosities'.[17] So it was that treasures from the summer palace helped promote the sale of China tea to English housewives.

Britain was briefly the dominant power in China and the government policy was to support the Qing war effort against the Taipings. Its implementation required considerable political dexterity, for domestic opinion was hostile to direct involvement and local business interests were opposed to any action that might extend the war. The defence of the perimeter of Shanghai was an exception to this rule. Anglo-French units repelled a Taiping offensive in August 1860, and again in 1862 and 1863. A small detachment also helped evict the Taipings from the treaty port of Ningbo.

Britain's proxy war against the Taipings consisted of the provision of modern firearms imported through the treaty ports and a squadron of shallow-draught river gunboats hastily built in British yards. Russia also offered 10,000 troops, but Beijing was suspicious of her motive and refused.[18] British officers were seconded to train and, on some occasions, command Chinese troops. The most famous was Major Charles Gordon, an engineer who created and commanded the 'Ever Victorious Army', which included Taiping prisoners of war. Like Robert Clive and later T.E. Lawrence, 'Chinese' Gordon had an extraordinary knack of disciplining and inspiring foreign soldiers, which, for many of his countrymen, was proof that the British possessed the genetic qualities of a race predestined to rule. Gordon was also a fervent Evangelical and became a national hero when he commanded another native army (Egyptians this time) against the slave trade in Sudan. He died there in 1885 at the hands of Muslim jihadis after the fall of Khartoum.

The Chinese too had an excellent general, Zeng Guofan, the champion of the 'self-strengthening' movement. His counter-offensives broke the back of the Taiping movement which, by 1864, had all but collapsed. Hong died as his kingdom crumbled.

The final defeat of the Taipings was the first success of the new regime in Beijing. In August 1861 Xianfeng had died and he was succeeded by his five-year-old son, Donghzi. Just over two months later, a palace coup placed power in the hands of a council of regency dominated by the new emperor's uncle, Prince Yixin, and his mother Cixi, formerly chief concubine to Xianfeng. It was a victory for the hesitant progressives over the traditionalists whose blunders had led to the brief Allied occupation of Beijing. Unwittingly, they had further pushed China along the path of internal reform and regeneration.

Seen from abroad, the palace revolution was a promising development that justified the war and subsequent backing for the Qings. For many of their subjects, the new order in China represented the tightening of the grip of foreigners on their country. In one new treaty port, an indignant landowner protested that 'some of our government officials are so terrified of the *fan* [foreign ghosts] that they grant them all their wishes'. He offered fifty silver yuan each for the heads of foreigners and stirred up a local insurrection which was suppressed by Qing troops.[19] This incident was a token of the Qings' willingness to comply with the treaties.

Britain got everything that it wanted from the Second Opium War. For China, the result of the contest was a galvanic shock. Henceforward, the Qing Empire was open to unrestricted international trade and investment which, in turn, would create a new Western-style infrastructure and lay the foundations of an industrial revolution. China was integrated into the international diplomatic order with its own Foreign Ministry (the *Tsungli Yamen*) in Beijing, which was soon home to a growing number of foreign embassies. The legations were a permanent reminder that the emperor was in theory now one among equals. His authority was curtailed, for much of China's diplomatic activity revolved around matters involving foreigners and their legal rights. For the time being, the Qing dynasty was compelled to accept Britain as its protector and the guarantor of what remained of its empire's integrity. And this alliance would soon be needed, for within two decades other European powers would begin to encroach on China's outlying borders.

# 6

# Pure Magic:
# Machines and Money

From 1860 onwards China edged slowly into the modern world guided by foreigners, of whom the British were the most active. It was a journey which caused widespread unease and sometimes anger among the Chinese, although some were delighted. 'Pure magic' was how Song Xialian described his short journey on the newly opened Kaiping–Tianjin Railway in 1890.[1] He was part of the new China, a young clerk working in the offices of a gold-mining company, one of many fledgling enterprises that were part of the early phase of China's long industrial revolution.

The creation of the Kaiping–Tianjin Railway was a perfect example of how imported technology and finance, the mechanisms of nineteenth-century globalisation, were transforming China. Geological surveys revealed that the country had abundant reserves of energy in the form of coal; in 1931 they were estimated at 200,000 million tons and sufficient for at least 5,000 years of production at present levels. Annual output stood at 489,000 tons in 1896 and more than doubled in the next five years. China, therefore, possessed an abundant source of cheap energy, the prerequisite for an industrial revolution.

Western technology provided the machines and methods which exploited underground seams and transported the coal to where it was needed. In 1888 the directors of the Kaiping mine built a railway to take coal to Tianjin, from where it could be conveyed by water to Shanghai. There it helped replenish the bunkers which served the port's merchant shipping. The trains were hauled by engines manufactured by Robert Stephenson and Company of Newcastle and the Grant Locomotive Works of New Jersey and ran on rails made of Krupp steel. In 1898 the line was extended to become the Imperial North China Railway, which was funded by loans of £2.3 million raised by London finance houses. The company's managing director was Wu Tinfang, who had been educated in an American mission and then in the United States: his staff included Chinese and European engineers.

Passengers on the Imperial North China Railway completed their journeys by rickshaws. These relied on manpower (always plentiful in China) and had been invented in 1868 by John Globe, an American missionary in Japan. Within a decade there were 25,000 rickshaws in Shanghai and by the 1920s, the total for the whole country was 400,000; all were made in China.[2] During the 1890s adventurous Chinese could purchase penny-farthing bicycles imported from Japan, which were soon replaced by more stable models. In 1898 the dowager empress Cixi received a motor car, a present from the Benz Company. Court protocol prevented her from taking to the roads, for the vehicle needed a chauffeur who would have to sit in front her, which was unthinkable.[3] Yet traditional China was happy to embrace foreign novelties for personal diversion. Cixi liked having her photograph taken and possessed a phonograph with cylinders which played Chinese and Western music.

Rail travel, rickshaws, bicycles, gramophones and, in time, telephones and motor cars were the visible and, for consumers, desirable results of China's grudging acceptance of free trade. For a long time these novelties were confined to the coastal and riverine treaty ports and their immediate hinterlands. Beyond these hubs of modernity, rural and predominantly agrarian China had limited contact with what the industries of the West had to offer. Nonetheless, these products eventually penetrated rural markets and quickly became popular. Western technology in the form of kerosene stoves and lamps provided both urban and rural China with warmth, light and fuel for cooking. Imports of kerosene rose from 41 million gallons in 1878 to 156 million in 1905, of which more than a half came from the United States.[4] Foreign-made safety matches also poured into China: the total rose from 79,000 gross of boxes in 1867 to 156 million in 1905. Many were used to light cigarettes, another foreign novelty which quickly became popular with all classes.

Constructing China's new infrastructure created friction between foreign developers and the Chinese. Clashes often occurred whenever the former required land occupied by tombs and graveyards which were sacred sites, integral to ancestor worship and the metaphysical concept of *feng shui*. This emphasised a natural harmony created by an equilibrium of elemental forces, and upsetting this balance could bring misfortune. In 1904, the London and China Mining Company began building roads to a new mine in Anhui province which threatened the ancestral tombs of the local landowning Pan family. There was stiff opposition from local people of all classes, who feared a violation both of the memorials and of the *feng shui* associated with them. Violence was threatened and the case passed to the British embassy and the *Tsungli Yamen*. A compromise was hammered out by which the company abandoned the roads and the Chinese government paid £52,000 in compensation. There were other cases of sacrilege which did not end so happily, and the Qing authorities were compelled to use force to protect foreign companies and their employees.

China's nascent consumer revolution and economic growth owed everything to a British-dominated agency founded in 1854, the Chinese Maritime Customs Service (CMCS), and its presiding genius, Sir Robert Hart. His official title was 'inspector-general', but he fancied himself as 'inspector-general of everything', which was true. He was appointed in 1864 and stayed in office until 1911, during which time he played the dual roles of a strict accountant and a wise but generous godfather. His position was always ambivalent. On the one hand, he was a servant of the Qings and their guide and adviser in the unfamiliar worlds of industrial development and international finance. On the other, he was enforcing the policies of the Foreign Office, whose aims were to foster free trade, protect and encourage British commercial interests, and preserve China's political stability and territorial integrity. Early in his career Hart had a Chinese mistress who may have contributed to his accumulated local knowledge. Its sheer scale and scope were valued by the Foreign Office, which soon depended upon him for intelligence and advice. He had no difficulty in serving two masters, for he was convinced that Britain was the ideal partner for the Qings.

Hart expected loyalty and dedication from his staff of fifty-seven, of whom over half were British and the rest American, French and German. Hart preferred self-confident Irishmen like himself, who were gentlemen with a manly bearing, but he was wary of the alumni of the post-Arnoldian public schools whom he considered rigid and over-disciplined. He expected all his staff to become fluent in Chinese and promoted men according to their ability and performance.[5]

The CMCS had two tasks. The first was the collection of import tariffs, which gave the Qings a dependable income that grew as trade increased. The second was to do all in its power to lubricate China's growth as a trading and manufacturing nation. Hart was a pragmatist who was always conscious that his greatest obstacle was the under-current of resentment among Chinese of all ranks of modernisation imposed by outsiders. Soon after an outbreak of anti-foreigner riots in Tianjin in September 1870, he remarked that China's submission rested solely on the memories of what he bluntly called 'former whippings' at the hands of European troops. From mandarins to peasants, 'one and all think that China would be far better without us' and secretly hoped that they would 'expel the foreigner sooner or later, by hook or by crook'.[6] Ironically, the CMCS was contributing to this tension by buying up sacred burial grounds for resale to foreign contractors.

Undeterred by the persistent eddies of resistance, Hart persevered, particularly with the creation of an infrastructure that would facilitate seaborne and inland trade. Among the CMCS's domestic responsibilities was the funding, construction and maintenance of lightships, light-houses and beacons along coasts and rivers. In all over 1,700 of these aids to navigation were installed over eighty years.[7] The technology was British and French, and individual lightships and lighthouses were run by British engineers with a staff of local mechanics and labourers.

In spite of all the apprehension about foreign domination, there were always plenty of Chinese willing to participate in their country's transformation and profit from it. Their number grew in the last quarter of the nineteenth century as more and more Chinese became qualified to serve as executives, managers, accountants, clerks and technicians in both foreign and home-owned businesses. Training these men was an additional responsibility of the CMCS, which financed domestic colleges and education abroad.

Chinese economic progress was always dependent on foreign capital. Hart and his staff were empowered to negotiate foreign loans on behalf of the *Tsungli Yamen* to finance transport, communications, mining and industrial projects. The CMCS also acted as agents for the purchase of modern arms and warships from foreign manufacturers and shipyards to equip a modernised Chinese army and navy. A photograph taken in the 1870s shows two bemused mandarins in traditional dress staring at an imported Gatling machine gun. Thanks to the CMCS, China could now theoretically defend itself on equal terms with the West.

By the 1890s, China's efforts to secure capital were becoming entangled with international diplomacy. Hart was fearful that funds supplied by French, German and Russian banks would place China in a vulnerable position, for their governments expected political and territorial concessions as well as dividends. His anxieties were confirmed in 1895, when China attempted to negotiate loans on the Continental money markets to pay off the huge indemnity imposed by Japan after her victory in the Sino-Japanese War (1904–05), which was an unequal contest. Russian, German and French bankers stepped forward but, at the bidding of their governments, demanded that the CMCS was nationalised.[8] Hart recognised a ploy to dilute British influence, the Foreign Office agreed and a diplomatic wrangle followed. To Hart's relief, it was resolved early in 1896 when a consortium of the Hong Kong and Shanghai Banking Corporation agreed to a £16 million loan without political strings. By 1906 the CMCS was responsible for all Chinese debts to foreign lenders, which totalled £40 million.

## Fear of Demons:
## Missionaries and Their Enemies

In 1869, a British diplomat asked Prince Yixin how Anglo-Chinese relations could be improved. He answered: 'Take away your opium and your missionaries and you would be welcomed.' This was impossible. The first would have been an unthinkable rejection of the principles of free trade and the second would have outraged millions of Britons who fervently believed that their nation had a divinely ordained duty to spread Christianity across the world. In Victorian Sunday schools children sang:

> Ask you why Britain's fleets superior ride
> On the blue waves of each obedient tide?
> Ask you why Britain's wealth securely grows
> Where 'ere the wind careers or sunbeam glows?
> 'Tis that her rule of Empire is to SAVE.
> She gives the Bible, and she frees the slave!

Since the mid-eighteenth century, Britain had undergone a spiritual revolution. Its impetus had been the Evangelical revival preached by the Wesley brothers and its outcome was the creation of an enlarged, active congregation that embraced all classes. Britain's reconversion was a spur to a more ambitious enterprise: the conversion of the infidels of Asia, Africa and the islands of the Pacific. This supposedly sacred task was supported by sermons, prayers, tracts and popular magazines: the Baptist *Joyful News* had a weekly circulation of 55,000 in the 1880s.[1] Private donations funded the overseas missions. In 1878 the wealthy Anglican congregations of Tunbridge Wells and Brighton gave £1,000 each to the Church Missionary Society and worshippers in the village church at Hatherop in Gloucestershire contributed £9. The pennies of Sunday school pupils at the London parish of St Clement Danes raised £3.[2] (Multiply these figures by 66 to get their modern equivalent.)

Whether they gave sovereigns or pennies, donors believed that the redemption of heathendom had been ordained by that same Divine Providence which had also given Britain its prosperity. The British were a chosen people, a message proclaimed by the prolific Evangelical novelist and poetaster Mrs Sherwood in her *Juvenile Missionary Manual* of 1843:

> I thank the goodness and the grace
> Which on my birth has smiled
> And made me, in these Christian days
> A happy English child.

In churches and chapels, these children and their parents heard stories about the unhappy lives of children whose families languished in ignorance of Jesus and were in thrall to idolatry and its attendant enormities. Luridly described pagan excesses were a staple of popular missionary tracts. Congregations who sang Bishop Heber's missionary anthem 'From Greenland's Icy Mountains' were reminded that cruelty and licentiousness were rife in the pagan world, 'where only man is vile'.

Variations on themes of heathen ignorance and turpitude were printed in missionary literature alongside inspiring tales of missionary devotion and fortitude.[3] Often repeated, the theme of pagan savagery contributed to the growth of racial stereotypes and assumptions of racial superiority. In 1893 a working-class British sailor told a Shanghai consular court that he was one of 'the children of the dominant race' which entitled him 'to show the swabs of natives, all over the world, that we are still dominant'.[4] But not all missionaries thought like this, nor did all civilians and servicemen in China.

Missionary visions of global salvation and popular impressions of the so-called depravity of Asian and African people assumed a political significance during the last quarter of the nineteenth century. From roughly 1870 onwards, Britain, France, Germany, Italy and the United States were drawn into what was often called a 'scramble' for territories in Africa, Asia and Oceania. Newly annexed colonies were reservoirs of potential converts and so the missionary societies used their political influence to support the new imperialism. Their lobbying carried considerable weight in Britain, France, Germany and the United States, all of which were gradually moving towards universal suffrage.

There was a general, international consensus that China offered the most promising opportunity for mass conversion. Conditions were favourable, for the missionaries enjoyed the robust backing of their embassies, provincial consulates and, when all else failed, gunboats. The *Tsungli Yamen* co-operated by demoting local officials who had failed to protect missionaries from popular hostility.[5] Individual missions flaunted the power behind the pulpit. The first British mission in Fukien was within walking distance of the British consulate, and the German flag flew over the missions of the Catholic Society of the Divine Word.[6]

Optimistic missionaries, and most were, prophesied miracles. In 1898, an American zealot spoke for many when he foretold the imminent conversion of all of China. He predicted the 'shattering' of her ancient faiths and the culture they had created. 'The strongholds of superstition are falling to the ground', and 'supercilious pride and prejudice' would soon be uprooted and replaced by 'the sway of the meek and humble Jesus, the saviour of the world'.[7]

These daydreams were premature. Since 1898, there had been a flow of reports of an upsurge in popular violence towards missionaries, their property and converts across northern China. These outrages were dismissed as the fruits of ignorance and the wiles of those Chinese with a vested interest in the preservation of traditional faith and customs, in particular the 'literati', which was the missionary name for Confucian scholars. Missionaries of all nationalities and denominations became scapegoats for wider anti-foreigner grievances. They were the most conspicuous foreigners in China. By the turn of the century there were 20,000 Roman Catholic and 2,800 Protestant (over half of them women) missionaries scattered across China.[8] Missionaries settled outside the treaty ports, where most Europeans congregated and established their churches and schools in the countryside. So whenever a Chinese encountered a 'foreign devil', he or she was likely to be a missionary. All were of the same species, for the Chinese took no notice of sectarian differences. Aware of this, the British government advised caution. Missionaries were advised to stay within the limits of the treaty ports and not to 'ramble through the country'.[9] Errant Presbyterian missionaries in Taiwan had provoked riots which in turn had led to the despatch of gunboats, much to the annoyance of London.

Christian zeal bred a scathing contempt for China's religious traditions and popular culture, which were dismissed as perverse and idolatrous. In 1898, one missionary journal contemptuously dismissed the Chinese 'fear of demons' and temples that venerated the 'fairy fox, weasel, snake or rat'.[10] In China, this disdain was expressed by the missionaries' conspicuous isolation from communal activities, religious and secular. They exempted themselves from the voluntary levies which paid for village operas, refused to contribute to temple repair funds and would not supplement pagan prayers for rain.[11]

Missions also purchased and thereby profaned the sites of redundant temples. American missionaries dug up a graveyard in Fuzhou in 1887 and cut down adjacent fir trees, disturbing the *feng shui* of the site.[12] Intruders who were capable of such sacrilege were capable of worse outrages. There were frequent accusations, often conveyed by handbills, of missionaries harbouring criminals among their converts and the abduction of babies and children for forced baptism and rumoured ritual murders. The latter charges surfaced during the 1870 Tianjin anti-missionary riots and tumults.[13]

Relations with the Chinese were further embittered by missionaries who demanded that the legal privileges granted to all foreigners were extended to Christian converts.[14] They encouraged them to pursue civil cases, such as suing for debt before the consular courts where they were assured more favourable treatment. Methodist missionaries discovered this to be a valuable means of attracting converts.[15]

Meddling with lawsuits was one of the charges made against the clergy of the Catholic Society of the Divine Word in Zhang Jia village in Shandong province. Others included alleged sexual assaults. In November 1897, a gang of at least twenty attacked the mission and murdered two missionaries. The clandestine Big Sword secret society was blamed, but the one missionary who escaped attributed the attack to 'the hatred and malice of Satan'.[16] The incident provided a welcome excuse for Germany's violent intrusion into China the following year, which apparently confirmed popular fears that the missionaries were partners in the exploitation of their country.

The missions were at the forefront of importing European knowledge into China. Missionary presses published modern historical, geographical, political and scientific texts in translation. In some circles it was imagined that missions could convert the elite of the country and so accelerate China's modernisation. This was a vain hope, for, as missionaries discovered, conservative landlords and Confucian scholars were among their most implacable opponents.

As in Europe and America, the salvation of souls was inseparable from moral regeneration. Both were achieved in *Yin Jia Dang Do* (Leading the Family in the Right Way), a religious novel of 1882 written for potential converts. Its hero, Mr Li, is 'a very pleasant man from the middle class' who loses his wealth and position by haunting gambling dens and brothels. He wanders into a mission church, listens to a sermon on redemption and converts. Li's fortunes are restored and his wife and daughter join him in the local congregation. He forsakes debauchery and opium and his new faith opens his mind, for Li is keen that his daughter should seek an education.[17] The message is clear: conversion liberated the mind. The story of a real middle-class convert, Mr Chang, published at the same time, describes him as encouraging his son to learn English. He also breaks with his cultural and religious past by banning idols from his house.[18]

Very few Chinese followed Chang's path to conversion and a way of life akin to that of a respectable, middle-class English churchgoer. There were only about 55,000 converts in China by the 1890s, but their number was slowly growing. So too was the friction between them and their clergy and the Chinese who saw both as a threat to their faith and culture.

# I Always Mistrust a Russian:
# Power Struggles

The 1890s was a precarious decade for China during which her independence and territorial integrity were placed in jeopardy. It now
seemed likely that, as in contemporary Africa, the country would be
divided between the European powers and a new competitor in the
race for empire, Japan. Britain's position began to look shaky and, at
the end of 1897, nervous members of the British business community
in China urged the Foreign Office to pre-empt rivals by assuming a
protectorate over the entire Yangtze basin.[1]

For the past thirty years, Britain had successfully achieved its goal
of political and economic predominance in China thanks to naval
supremacy and indirect control of the Chinese customs service. The
'mandate of heaven' on which Qing authority had rested had effectively
been replaced by the mandate of Britain. This arrangement worked,
but was always fragile insofar as it rested on a faith in China's willingness to accept modernisation and the fact that other powers remained
content with a status quo that favoured Britain's.

This dispensation of influence was challenged by Britain's old rival
in Asia, Russia. Her efforts to expand into the Near East at the expense
of the Ottoman Empire in 1877 had been checkmated by British
diplomacy backed by the threat of war. British war plans included an
amphibious assault on Vladivostok by Anglo-Indian forces supported
by the Far Eastern Fleet based at Hong Kong.[2] Having been frustrated
in the Near East, Russia stepped up pressure in Central Asia, which
revived British fears of an invasion of India via Afghanistan, a theoretic
masterstroke that stirred the imaginations of generals in St Petersburg
and caused terror among their counterparts in London and Calcutta.
Whether the Russian war machine could manage the logistics of such
a massive operation was open to question.

Nevertheless, successive British governments took the risk of
Cossacks cantering down the Khyber Pass very seriously. A minor

Russian incursion across the Persian border triggered British mobilisation in 1885 and the mere hint of a threat to the Indian state of Chitral high in the Himalayas led to a large-scale expedition to occupy it in 1895. This operation was part of what became known as the 'Great Game', a sort of Asian Cold War of spying and shadow boxing between Britain and Russia waged wherever their interests clashed. Late Victorians saw Russia as a cunning and resourceful enemy, and the new popular journalism fed fear and loathing. It was depicted as a barbaric despotism in which progress was hampered by the lack of a respectable and politically active middle class. Russia was also a land of drunkards besotted with vodka, which, one journalist who had toured the country claimed, 'tasted like bilge water, vitriol, turpentine, copal varnish, fire and castor oil'.[3]

By 1890 Russian imperialism had entered a new phase with a fresh objective: the Chinese province of Manchuria. The Trans-Siberian Railway, begun in 1893, was intended to carry armies to Russia's frontier with Manchuria, reducing a journey that had hitherto taken several months to a fortnight. Soldiers would be followed by peasant settlers and Cossacks who would grow crops and mine minerals. Increased food production was needed because Russia was hard pressed to feed its growing population. Count Sergei Witte, who became minister of finance in 1892, dreamed of 'agricultural colonies' in China and Persia that would feed Russia's industrial workers.[4]

Russia's ambitions were matched by her growing military strength. The Russian industrial revolution was gathering momentum, with a strong emphasis on armaments, and the military budget rose from 156 to 426 million roubles between 1880 and 1900. In 1892 Russia made an alliance with Britain's other global rival, France. Seen from a Far Eastern perspective, French bases and coaling stations made it easier for Russian warships to steam from the Baltic to Chinese waters. In 1895 an eighteen-strong squadron of Russian men-o'-war over-wintered in Jiaozhou Bay on the Shandong peninsula. Their presence was a warning to the Royal Navy.

Ideology as well as land hunger drove Russian imperialism. The generals and proconsuls who twisted the arms of local khans and pushed Russia's frontiers eastwards believed themselves to be the advance guard of civilisation. Baron Romanovich Rosen, a diplomat with Far Eastern experience, spoke airily of 'Russia's cultural mission' to the empty spaces beyond the Steppes.[5] Interestingly, he remarked that

Russian culture was inferior to European but higher than Asian. Such humility was exceptional: rival imperial powers stressed the innate superiority of their missions to enlighten and uplift.

Rosen was one of a knot of like-minded and dedicated staff officers, academics and veterans of Asian campaigns who formed the Asiatic Department of the General Staff. It was the powerhouse behind Russia's imperial policy, amassing intelligence, planning offensives and persuading susceptible tsars that Russia's imperial destiny lay in the Far East. History appeared to be on Russia's side, for over the past 100 years her thrust eastwards had added 8.67 million square miles to the Romanov dominions.

Russia's piecemeal conquests had already led to friction with China. In the 1870s Russia had given covert encouragement to Muslim jihadist rebels in Xinjiang. The uprising was crushed after a considerable effort by the Qing army, and afterwards Beijing imported Chinese settlers into the province and introduced compulsory Confucian teaching in schools. Similar measures were introduced after a recrudescence of Muslim unrest in the early twenty-first century.

Russian military intelligence took a close interest in China's rearmament programmes. In 1880 the Asiatic Department officials were perturbed by reports that Chinese officials were hastily buying modern weaponry from German manufacturers. Spies were immediately despatched to discover details of Beijing's shopping list.[6] The purchases had been approved by Hart and funded by the CMCS as part of a policy to modernise China's armed forces. Assisting the modernisation of its army and navy was a way of reminding China that Britain was its guardian and would resist any Russian encroachments on her frontiers.

The schemes and dreams of the planners in St Petersburg at this time took slight account of the sudden and swift transformation of Japan. It had begun in 1868 with the Meiji ('brilliant rule') political revolution, which was the catalyst for the astonishing transition of a largely isolated, agrarian medieval state into a modern industrial nation and imperial power. Japan looked to the West and America for models and technical guidance and, thanks to a predominately aristocratic administration in which power flowed downwards, oversaw an economic revolution. Imagine the England of Richard II with the industries, infrastructure, army and navy of late-Victorian Britain.

The upshot of Japan's forced industrialisation was a rise in gross domestic product from 26.6 million yen in 1880 to 188 million in 1900. Textiles and metal wares were her chief exports and China her closest and principal market. Economic growth ran parallel with a rise in population from 32 million in 1868 to 53 million in 1913. This increase raised the question of how Japan could feed its people. The national staple was rice and the margin of survival was thin; in the past harvests had failed and there had been times of shortage. The Tenpō famine of the 1830s, for example, had cost over a million lives. Imported rice from Korea and China underpinned the survival of Westernised Japan.

A contemporary European theory supplied Japan with the inner drive needed to maintain the momentum of economic expansion and enter the international contest for empire. Japan's ruling class took to heart the notion that the Darwinian theory of survival of the fittest and most adaptable applied to nations as well as animals. Acceptance of this idea also gave Japan a moral justification for obtaining by direct or indirect force the markets, raw materials and food needed to build on her economic miracle.

Japan joined the international Darwinian power struggle in August 1894 by waging an acquisitive war against China. Her excuse was a festering dispute over political influence in China's subject state, Korea. Japan's strategic objectives were to replace China as the dominant power in Korea, the elimination of the Chinese navy, the acquisition of Taiwan and toeholds on mainland China, and to share economic and diplomatic equality there with the Western powers. For the moment, Britain had nothing to fear from Japan. It had revealed the military weakness of the Qings, but had not imperilled the political status quo in China and its territorial acquisitions had been minor. Japan was, however, a potential economic competitor in the Chinese market, but this was acceptable to a nation that still believed in free trade.

The war was an unequal contest. An army and navy which had been totally modernised outmatched forces that had not yet completed the transformation from old to new. Three out of every five Chinese soldiers carried spears, swords and bows and arrows.[7] They wore traditional uniforms while Japanese infantry were dressed in the tunics and kepis of Western troops. Many Japanese soldiers were conscripts, for Japan had followed the examples of Germany, France and Russia and introduced compulsory military service in 1878. Up to date in all things, the Japanese government embedded photographers within its forces who produced a vivid record of the war which was subsequently published.[8]

Chinese strategic planning was desultory, and inadequate command and logistic structures fell apart quickly.[9] The Imperial Japanese Navy (IJN), which had been trained by officers of the Royal Navy, had absorbed the Nelsonian spirit of audacity and aggression. Both were shown in engagements which established Japanese mastery of the North China Sea. The way was open for amphibious operations against the Korean and Chinese mainlands and the movement of reinforcements on all fronts. Japanese soldiers took the offensive in Korea, defeating and expelling Chinese armies. By October 1894 they had crossed the Yalu and were edging along the Liaodong peninsula into Manchuria. In April 1895 Port Arthur (Dalian) was captured. During the siege, the Chinese had displayed the mutilated corpses of Japanese soldiers and the Japanese responded with a massacre of civilians. Western journalists overlooked this outrage. Like the contemporary European imperial powers, the Japanese had assumed a sense of inborn racial superiority which qualified them to rule others less blessed. These included the 'liedeng dongwu' (lesser animals), that is, the Chinese.[10]

The speed and completeness of Japan's victory stunned the West. Japanese troops were within 500 miles of Beijing and the Qing Empire appeared to be entering its final days. Russia reacted quickly and aggressively: warships and transports carrying 10,000 men were ordered to Vladivostok in February 1895. Sir Robert Hart had expected such a move and vainly pleaded with the Foreign Office for naval reinforcements to prevent Japanese forces landing in north-eastern China and so provoking Russian intervention.[11] The Cabinet rejected this suggestion, and for the next few months Britain held her breath and waited on events. Meanwhile, conquest was followed by colonisation: 170,000 Japanese emigrated to Korea and a substantial number to Taiwan, where local resistance flickered on for some years.

Japan congratulated herself. Tokutomi Sohō, a conservative journalist, saw the war as Japan's debut as a global power: 'Now we have tested our strength we know ourselves and we are known by the world.' A cynical but perceptive view was taken by the art scholar Okakura Kakuzō, who remarked that now Japan had 'proved its capacity to match the West in killing and destruction, it was accepted as civilised'.[12]

As a 'civilised' power, Japan imposed on China terms as severe as those demanded from France by Germany at the end of the Franco-Prussian War in 1871. The Treaty of Shimonoseki of April 1895, which ended the Sino-Japanese War, required China to pay an indemnity of £50 million, to renounce its authority over Korea (where it was replaced by Japan) and to hand over Taiwan (renamed Formosa), the Pescadores, Port Arthur and the Liaodong peninsula. Henceforward, Japan would enjoy the same legal and economic privileges in China as the Western powers. The Japanese prime minister, Prince Itō Hirobumi, declared that 'China has at last awakened from her long sleep'.

The Liberal prime minister, Archibald Primrose, 5th Earl of Rosebery, was a Whig grandee married to Hannah Rothschild, the banking heiress. He was an aloof patrician, an imperialist and a sportsman whose less than two years as prime minister, from March 1894 to June 1895, were distinguished by his horses consecutively winning the Derby. His foreign secretary, John Wodehouse, the 3rd Earl of Kimberley, came from the same thoroughbred stable that provided late-Victorian Britain with ministers and diplomats.

As Liberals, Rosebery and Kimberley endeavoured to follow the party's traditional pacific policy of promoting international harmony, despite the shift in balance of power in China. True to their background, they were prejudiced against foreigners. Rosebery once remarked, 'I always mistrust a Russian' and Kimberley considered the French to be 'slippery' and the Germans 'nasty'. He was, however, conciliatory towards the Russians. Kimberley argued that 'it was perfectly natural that as a great Asiatic Power we should desire to be on cordial terms with Russia, the other great power'.[13] He despaired of China, which he thought was in 'continuous decay' and irredeemable since her 'governing classes' were 'rotten to the core'.[14] Kimberley's conclusions echoed those of other China hands who advised the Foreign Office. Sir Ernest Satow, who had served in the Tokyo embassy, where he acquired a Japanese mistress, compared China to 'India rubber' on which 'you can make an impression' which instantly vanishes when the pressure is removed'.[15]

Perceived Chinese recidivism was frustrating, but the alternative of Qing collapse and the creation of a political vacuum that would be filled by Russia was unthinkable. France too was nursing ambitions in China: in 1884–85 her advances in northern Indo-China had led to a brief naval war against China, opening up the opportunity to extend French influence northwards into Yunnan province. Germany was also showing an interest in Far Eastern acquisitions as part of the expansionist, imperial policy favoured by Kaiser Wilhelm II. United by rapacity and a dread of being left behind, these three powers decided that Japan had to be forced to disgorge the Liaodong peninsula and Port Arthur. With the great European powers united, Britain was hamstrung and could offer Japan no more than sympathy. In November, Japan sullenly agreed to withdraw her forces from the disputed areas, leaving them open to Russia.

The hard truth was that the Far Eastern balance of power had changed dramatically and Britain alone could no longer uphold the status quo in China. Henceforward, as Rosebery appreciated, her future standing would depend on the closet cultivation of Japan, a potential rival in the region, as a friend and counterweight to Russia. At the end of 1895 Japan had ordered six battleships and six cruisers, nearly all from British yards.[16]

By now a new government was in power. The previous August a general election swept the Tories into office with a large majority and 60 per cent of the popular vote. The new prime minister, Robert Gascoyne-Cecil, 3rd Marquess of Salisbury, presided over a Cabinet which favoured an aggressive and forward imperial policy. Britain would not fall behind in the race for colonies then under way in Africa and Asia. Bullishness masked inner uncertainties about strategic overstretch and diplomatic isolation.

Britain's new policy was applied to China, where the Japanese victory had been a spur for fresh demands for concessions for the British from the Chinese between 1896 and 1898. A contemporary French cartoon vividly portrayed the process and the participants. Queen Victoria, Kaiser Wilhelm, Tsar Nicholas II, a pretty Marianne wearing her red cap of Liberty (France) and a Japanese man in traditional robes sit around a table. They are brandishing large knives and are about to carve a huge flat cake labelled 'Chine'. Behind, an anguished mandarin raises his arms in horror.

The diners' appetites were only partly satisfied. In November 1897 the murder of German missionaries provided the Kaiser with what he called 'a splendid opportunity' to intervene in China and to show its rulers that Germany was a power to be reckoned with. A squadron of men-o'-war anchored in Jiaozhou Bay on the Shandong peninsula and soldiers followed, as they always did whenever a foreign power was angling for new concessions. The Opium Wars had set a baleful precedent and it worked again, for Beijing succumbed and ceded the port of Qingdao, which was immediately designated as a base for Germany's projected Far Eastern cruiser squadron. Investment followed the ironclads and the *Shandong Eisenbahn Gesellschaft* soon began work on a railway to link Qingdao with the provincial capital, Jinan.

Russia, falsely promising diplomatic backing for China, persuaded Beijing to give permission for an extension of the Trans-Siberian Railway to the Manchurian town of Harbin and for Russian forces to occupy that part of the Liaodong peninsula recently evacuated by Japan and Port Arthur. Operations were soon under way to transform it into a fortified base for a projected Russian Far Eastern squadron.

Both Germany and Russia were determined to challenge British naval supremacy in Chinese waters and secure future ports where armies could be disembarked unopposed. Britain's response was to strengthen its position. A ninety-nine-year lease on the fertile Kowloon peninsula guaranteed supplies of water and food for her main base, Hong Kong, and its growing population. A similar lease was agreed for Weihai on the shores of the Yellow Sea, which became a coaling station and forward base for the British Far Eastern Fleet. It was between eight and nine hours' sailing time from Qingdao and Port Arthur. The Japanese too extracted an asset of future strategic value: control over the Manchurian telegraph network.[17]

While Germany, Russia and Britain concentrated on strongholds that would maintain their warships in the event of a contested partition of China, France's diplomatic efforts were directed towards acquiring a preponderance of influence in the province of Yunnan with a view to its annexation if Qing power should dissolve. The fragmentation of China seemed imminent and was freely discussed in the capitals of Europe. Lord Salisbury was unhappy, not least because France, Russia and Germany were protectionist powers and, if they annexed Chinese provinces, were bound to introduce tariffs on British imports. For this reason he declared: 'We aim at no partition of territory, but only a partition of predominance.'[18]

Inside China, the view from below was pessimistic and angry. Some Chinese likened the predations of the 1890s to 'carving up the melon'. Yet its core was not soft. In the spring of 1898 parts of north-eastern

China were convulsed by localised demonstrations of defiant young men shouting 'Support the Qing' and 'Destroy the foreigners'.[19] Some of the protesters called themselves 'Fists United in Righteousness'. Foreigners amused by their antics called them 'Boxers'. They would not be amused for long.

# The Hearts and Minds of the People: The Boxer Uprising, 1898–1900

The Boxers were people cast adrift in a changing world and fearful about their future. Yet they did not look afraid when they posed for foreign photographers. Their images reveal sturdy young men in the everyday dress of peasants and artisans who stare at the cameras boldly even though many were facing execution. One grins at a device which symbolised what he had risked his life to destroy: the transformation of his country by outsiders and their technology.

Anxieties about the incomers and how they and their innovations threatened the lives of the masses had been simmering for the past fifty years. During the second half of 1898, these concerns exploded in a wave of bitter frustration that quickly spread across the densely populated villages of the northern Chinese plain.

Life in this region was always precarious, resting on the caprices of climate. Sparse summer rain, the flooding of the Yellow River and the collapse of irrigation systems tipped the balance between survival and famine. Economic forces added to the woes of the peasant farmers. Their cash crop of cotton was being squeezed out of the market by foreign imports and the mechanised mills in Shanghai. Insecure incomes were supplemented by theft and extortion, which the authorities called banditry and were unable to suppress. The ruled accused their masters of corruption and resented the taxes they could not afford.

Tight-knit communities had always managed to survive thanks to bonds of kinship, a fertile popular culture and devotion to familiar gods. In 1898 and 1899 these gods failed them: the Yellow River flooded, crops failed and food was short. Natural calamities coincided with events beyond the immediate horizon. China had recently been defeated by Japan and her government was making further concessions to foreigners. In Shandong, the future hotbed of Boxer agitation, Germany was staking its claims and missionaries were making their

presence felt in a provocative manner. These misfortunes coalesced in
a verse of a Boxer song:

> No rain comes from Heaven,
> The earth is parched and dry.
> And all because the churches
> Have bottled up the sky.[1]

Shandong was a perfect nursery for Boxer agitation. It was a turbulent
province where the peasantry, artisans and labourers drew moral
strength from local warrior traditions and the clandestine cults that
kept them alive. These attracted young men and fostered the martial
arts and virtues. Boxing, swordplay, physical agility, magic rituals and
the wearing of protective charms created invulnerable supermen who
were the natural guardians of the communities they had sprung from.
Breathtaking displays of fighting skills entertained villagers, for whom
the warriors became the living counterparts of heroic gods whose deeds
were kept alive by popular folk operas and fiction. Like their legendary
predecessors, these fighting men affected supernatural powers and were
ready to defend communities from oppression. These warriors also
hired themselves out as guards for landlords.

The most powerful and popular of the martial arts cults were the
Big Sword Society and the Fists United in Righteousness (Boxers). Their
displays of martial prowess and virtuosity attracted many young men.
One Boxer later remembered his youthful enthusiasm: 'I said playing
at Spirit Boxing is really good stuff, let's do it ... We did it for three or
four months, and so there were lots of us.' He had entered a celibate,
egalitarian brotherhood with strong bonds and high local prestige.[2]
Boxers were also staunch patriots bent on saving their country and
emperor. Their favourite rallying call was the slogan 'Fu-Qing mie
yang!' – 'Back the Qing, destroy the foreign!'

The Boxer movement was not revolutionary; rather its members
saw themselves as the defenders of tradition and allies of an emperor
beguiled by foreigners and their collaborators at court. By the spring
of 1899, Boxers were attacking missions and killing missionaries and
their converts. For example, in Shandong there were clashes between
German troops guarding missions, and Boxers. Official reactions
varied: some provincial governors were sympathetic to the insurgents
while others took a sterner line, fearful that their antics would provoke

foreign powers. Many local administrators faced a crisis of conscience. A Norwegian customs official reported that 'there is little sympathy among the officials for the Boxers, but that does not mean they do not hate the foreigners'.[3]

Beijing offered no clear policy on the Boxers, for the government was divided. The Japanese victory in 1895 had given a fresh impetus to reformers. They insisted that a fledgling industrial country could no longer afford to creep into the modern world guided by a government whose administrators were schooled in and never deviated from Confucian principles. The old way had left China vulnerable to foreign predation and she could only save herself by adopting the Japanese economic and military model. One leading reformer, General Zhang Zhidong, called for the closest co-operation with Japan and encouraged bright young men to study in Japanese colleges and army and naval cadet schools. There were 6,000 of these students by 1906.

The progressives gained a breakthrough in June 1898. Over the next three months, the twenty-seven-year-old Emperor Guangxu issued a sequence of edicts which were a blueprint for a modern industrial state. There were provisions for a national rail network, a Western education system in which Confucian textual studies were replaced by mathematics and science and, most radical of all, plans for a constitutional monarchy. In a display of humility which would have stunned his ancestors, the emperor asked the Japanese prime minister for advice and help in the 'process of reform' which had been so successful in his country. China would follow Japan.

Appalled traditionalists looked to the Dowager Empress Cixi for help. She obliged by organising a palace coup with the assistance of two conservative generals, Dong Fuxiang and Rongui, whose troops seized Guangxu and bundled him off to an island near Beijing, where he remained under house arrest. One prominent reformer was beheaded as a warning to others.

Throughout her life Cixi had dedicated herself to the preservation of the Qing dynasty and the Confucian ideals that underwrote its authority. Political power had come her way through a sequence of premature deaths. Born in 1835, the daughter of a boatman, her beauty won her the post of chief mistress of the Emperor Xianfeng, who died in 1861 aged thirty. Cixi served as regent for his short-lived son, Tongzhi, and her nephew Guangxu, who succeeded in 1875 aged four.

Having achieved power by accident she kept it through her natural sagacity and talent for court intrigue; her instincts were conservative. The unlooked-for and spreading Boxer insurgency was the first test of her political dexterity.

The tumults were not just a matter of internal security, for they also offered excuses for armed intervention by the foreign powers, particularly Russia and Germany. The former was already moving troops along the Trans-Siberian Railway into Manchuria. An advance guard was sent to Beijing. In May 1899, the ever watchful Sir Robert Hart warned London that the 'natural rowdyism' of the Boxers was running out of control and challenging the authority of the foreign powers.[4] Lord Salisbury was unmoved and assured Queen Victoria that the Boxers were 'a mere mob' and no threat to British interests.[5] Nevertheless, he thought it would be prudent for a concert of interested powers to suppress the lawlessness which was threatening Beijing by the winter of 1899–1900. The prime minister's precaution was shared, and by May 1900 Japan, Russia, France, Germany and the United States were reinforcing their naval presence in Chinese waters.

News of the flotilla anchored in Bohai Bay was welcomed by the Europeans in Beijing. For several months, Boxers had been pouring into the city from the countryside. Among them were the Red Lanterns Shining, an auxiliary women's corps who cooked and undertook chores for the warriors. Its leader was a former prostitute, 'Lotus' Huang, who allegedly possessed supernatural powers.[6] Inside the city, the Boxers destroyed shops selling imported goods and accosted and insulted foreigners, who now ventured on to the streets armed with revolvers.

Cixi, her ministers and generals prevaricated. Did they satisfy the foreign powers and pre-empt their intervention by suppressing the rebels, or did they give their blessing to patriots who would defend their country and its dynasty? Equivocation provoked a new crisis. The British minister Sir Claude MacDonald, a veteran of campaigns in Sudan and wearer of a formidable imperial moustache, treated the Boxers as a danger to Europeans in Beijing and an aberration. Like his government, MacDonald was convinced that China's future would be determined by the Chinese, who would become less and less reliant on outside help.[7] In the meantime, the immediate safety of foreigners in Beijing demanded the swift application of coercive measures. Nine hundred men, roughly half of them civilians, and three machine guns (one regularly jammed) were insufficient to defend the legations.

Reinforcements were essential and so, on 10 June, MacDonald wired for assistance from the naval units lying off the Dagu forts. Command of this flotilla had been assumed by the senior British officer Admiral Sir Edward Seymour, a veteran of the 1860 China campaign.

Like MacDonald, Seymour believed in the well-tested imperial formula that power had to be felt as well as seen. Seizing the initiative and delivering swift hammer blows always paid dividends in the face of insubordination or defiance. Seymour rigged up a well-armed, multinational relief force of just over 2,000, under a half of whom were British marines and sailors.

The Beijing relief force disembarked, occupied the Dagu forts and entrained at Tianjin on 17 June. Boxers sabotaged the line and launched ambushes, hurling themselves headlong into rifle and machine-gun fire. Warriors protected by chanted mantras and magical talismans and armed with staves and bladed weapons were shot down in droves. In one ambush, the piles of dead and dying made it impossible to sight the Maxim machine guns accurately. A Chinese servant warned a British officer that the corpses were 'make-believe Boxers' and that those whose faith was genuine would rise up and fight again.[8] They did not, of course, but the sabotage of railway tracks and extended and imperilled lines of communications compelled Seymour's force to withdraw in a fighting retreat. They struggled back to find that Tianjin had been penetrated by insurgents who were barely contained by the small European garrison. Beijing was now isolated, for the Boxers had cut the telegraph lines.

For the fifth time in nearly sixty years China had been invaded by foreign troops. Cixi's hand was forced and she plumped for an alliance with the Boxers. It was a measure of desperation, as she explained. 'Today China is extremely weak. We have only the people's hearts and minds to depend upon. If we cast them aside and lose the people's hearts, what can we use to sustain the country?' On 21 June, she declared war on Britain, Russia, Germany, France, Italy, Austria-Hungary, the United States and Japan. She outlined her reasons: 'The foreigners have been aggressive towards us, infringed upon our territorial integrity, trampled our people under their feet... They oppress our people and blaspheme our gods. The common people suffer greatly at their hands and each one of them is vengeful. Thus it is that the brave followers of the Boxers have been burning churches and killing Christians.'

Cixi and her advisers were living in cloud-cuckoo land. They imagined that an alliance of throne and people could defeat the armies of eight powers. Imperial generals, including the conservative Rongui, had no confidence in this policy, opted for neutrality and ordered substantial bodies of troops to stand aside from the conflict. This caution at the top deprived the insurgents of modern Krupp artillery, which could have breached the legations' defences and hindered the advance of Allied armies. Two of Cixi's senior advisers warned that the slaughter of the defenders was counter to international law and would provoke a massive retaliation; they were executed for their foresight. The great power equilibrium was restored in China after the Boxer episode and for the next decade the big players shifted their attention and ambitions to Morocco and the Balkans.

Cixi's quixotic gesture had turned a domestic crisis into a war. The eight challenged powers reinforced their naval units and began to ship thousands of soldiers to China. Restoring order to countries where it had broken down was the stock justification for intervention and occupation: the British had successfully used it in Egypt in 1882. Over 100 years later the same reasoning was used to vindicate international interventions in the Balkans, Afghanistan and Syria. European racial prestige was also at stake. Restoring order in China was 'a struggle of Asia against entire Europe' commented Prince Heinrich von Bismarck, the son of the statesman, and a former German foreign secretary.[9] Many in Europe and the United States would have agreed. Yet Asians played a large part in Europe's short war against China. Eight thousand of the 21,000-strong army that marched to relieve the legations were Japanese, and by the time punitive operations were over, Britain had 21,000 Indian troops deployed across northern China and began recruiting Chinese auxiliaries in Weihaiwei.

A few years before the Kaiser had predicted such a contest and had his fears dramatically realised in a picture which was copied and circulated in Europe. It showed allegorical figures representing the powers of Europe standing on high ground and 'Germania' (in Wagneresque armour) pointing towards a distant horizon. There is seated 'Asia' in the form of a Buddha-like figure behind which are dim masses of people. This grotesque image embodied the notion of the 'Yellow Peril': huge swarms of Chinese advancing towards world domination. An offshoot of the 'Yellow Peril' was the demonic figure of Fu Manchu of Sax Rohmer's pulp-fiction and horror movies. He first appeared in 1913 and for the next fifty years scared readers and filmgoers with his fiendish conspiracies. Fu was clever, resourceful and ruthless and, in the popular imagination, he provided a sinister Chinese stereotype which still persists among the paranoid.

Racial antipathies surfaced during and after the fighting, as they so often did in such punitive campaigns. During the occupation of the Dagu fortifications, Admiral James Bruce was appalled by the 'very slow and inhumanly brutal' Russians who shot 'every unoffending' Chinese they met and the bayoneting of the wounded Chinese soldiers by the Japanese.[10] The German contingent was ordered to follow their example.

The day before war had been declared, a former Chinese soldier had assassinated the German minister Clemens von Ketteler. The perpetrator had claimed that he was avenging the murder of a Chinese boy shot by the diplomat a few days before; von Ketteler had been a zealous hunter of Boxers on the streets of Beijing. The killer had also stolen his victim's gold watch, which he'd later tried to sell, a transaction that had led to his detection and beheading. On hearing the news of the assassination of his representative, the Kaiser promised 'revenge the world has never yet seen'.[11] He kept his word.

Just before they embarked for China, the Kaiser exhorted his soldiers to show no mercy. 'No quarter will be given! Prisoners will not be taken! ... Just as a thousand years ago the Huns under their King Attila made a name for themselves ... may the name German be affirmed by you in such a way in China that no Chinese will ever again dare to look askance at a German.' A journalist leaked this bloodthirsty outburst to the world's press. The German Foreign Office tried to make amends for diplomatic reasons and inserted a more emollient closing line which claimed that the campaign in China would 'open the way to civilisation once and for all'. Variations of this theme were composed by politicians and newspaper editors in Europe and the United States.

It took fifty-five days to relieve the legations, during which the press and the public agonised over dramatic reports of the perils that faced the Allied forces. Thanks to the telegraph links with China, events there were relayed to America and Europe within twenty-four hours. Rumour mingled with fact, including one that the legations had fallen and their defenders had been massacred; MacDonald's obituary appeared in *The Times*.

The relief column was commanded by Major-General Alfred Gaselee, a veteran of the small wars of pacification waged in India. Indian lancers led the Allied breakthrough into Beijing on 15 August. Cixi fled Beijing disguised as a peasant shortly before the Allies entered the city. The Allies' next objective was to restore order inside Beijing and then fan out across the adjacent areas to suppress and chastise the Boxers and their collaborators. What followed was systematic terror conducted by Allied troops and the Chinese authorities designed to shatter the Boxer movement: its ingredients were summary executions, looting, rape and random massacres. A detachment of Indian cavalry and German infantry ordered to pacify Liangxiang, fifteen miles west of Beijing, killed 150 Boxers and a further 800 Chinese.[12] Here and elsewhere, officials who had encouraged the Boxers were executed. Among them was Yu-Xian, a former governor of Shandong who had been transferred to Shanxi, where he had presided over the massacre of missionaries and their converts.

A macabre feature of these forays was the photographs taken of the beheadings of Boxers in the presence of onlookers from the Allied forces. Some of the pictures were reproduced as postcards which were sold in Shanghai for some years afterwards. (There was also a contemporary market for postcards of public executions by guillotine in France and lynchings in the southern states of America.) Looting was common by civilians and soldiers of all armies and was witnessed by George Lynch, an Irish war correspondent, who also watched auctions of plundered items in Beijing. Jade items were particularly prized.[13] There was Parliamentary denial that British troops were involved.

China paid a heavy price for her blunders: the Allies extracted £67.5 million in reparations to be paid in gold over thirty-nine years together with 4 per cent interest on the outstanding capital. Twenty-nine per cent went to Russia, 20 per cent to Germany, 16 per cent to France, 11 per cent to Britain and 7 per cent to the United States. In 1908 the American government decided its payments would be diverted into a scholarship fund for Chinese students in American universities. The Boxers had inadvertently been responsible for the further spread of those foreign influences which they abhorred.

How did the Chinese react to this painful and humiliating episode? Reformers regarded the Boxer Uprising as a futile backlash against the modern world by the misguided and ignorant who had interrupted their country's progress.[14] But during the 1920s, the Boxers were reborn as patriots seeking the liberation of China from foreigners whose oppressive influence seemed to be getting stronger. Forty years later their fortitude and resolution were invoked during Mao Zedong's Cultural Revolution, when propagandists singled out the Red Lanterns as an example of womanpower. In the 1980s Boxer resistance to Russian forces on the banks of the Amur River was recalled during a confrontation with the Soviet Union.[15] In this way, rebels who had died to preserve China's ancient regime were reinvented to suit the ideologies of its Nationalist and Communist successors.

# The Oncoming Awakening:
# War and Revolution, 1901–1912

The Boxer Uprising provided an excuse for Russia to encroach on Chinese territory. As always, the motive was land for settlement and raw materials for an industrial revolution that had been gathering pace for the past forty years. In St Petersburg, the giddier hawks believed that the Qings were on the eve of extinction, and that a single battalion could unseat them and proceed to scoop up Manchuria.[1] Realists prevailed and 100,000 soldiers were sent via the Trans-Siberian Railway to northern China, where some joined operations against the Boxers while others tightened Russia's grip on her Manchurian concessions. One detachment attempted to seize control of the British-owned Chinese Northern Railway.

Alarm bells rang in London and for a brief time there was talk of an Anglo-Russian war. The Kaiser took Britain's part on the assumption that a conflict in the Far East would have repercussions in Europe that might be to Germany's disadvantage. Russia temporised, but there was no guarantee that the notoriously fickle Wilhelm II would restrain his cousin Nicholas II in the future.

Russia's stepping down reduced tensions in China and greatly relieved Lord Salisbury and the Foreign Office. Both were already coming to terms with a new dispensation of world power which was not in Britain's favour. In 1900 the British Empire was no longer strong everywhere. Salisbury rallied his party and much of the country with the comforting phrase 'splendid isolation', but recent events had shown that an isolated Britain had been unable to safeguard her investments and commerce in China. The fervent imperialist colonial secretary Joseph Chamberlain likened his country to a 'weary Titan' and mournfully speculated about future eclipse. Britain's isolation was made worse by a comparative decline in the strength of the Royal Navy over the past twenty years. The French, Russian, American and German fleets were expanding, and Admiralty strategists calculated that the battleships of the first three outnumbered Britain's.[2] Russia was most to be feared: according to Lord Selborne, the First Lord of the Admiralty, she had become a constant 'menace' to British interests in China.[3]

The solution to this problem was to find a strong ally. None could be found among the Continental powers, and no reliance could be placed on the two Continental power blocs: the Franco-Russian alliance and the German-Austro-Hungarian. France had nearly gone to war in 1898 over British claims to Sudan and Egypt, and for a century Russia had been an aggressive rival in Asia and the Far East. Since their 1892 alliance, both powers were treated as potential challengers to British control of the Mediterranean and the Suez Canal, and groundless fears that Russian agents were active in Tibet in 1903 prompted an invasion of that country.

Japan provided an immediate answer to the problems of isolation and imperial lifelines. There were some objections from imperialists who thought in racist terms and were apprehensive about aligning with a non-white nation, even though Japan had all the economic and military credentials of an advanced European state. But checkmating Russia in Asia ultimately outweighed this consideration. In 1902, Japan and Britain signed an alliance which at a stroke ended Britain's isolation and underwrote the security of her Chinese interests. Britain and Japan agreed to support each other if one was attacked by two or more foreign powers. This clause deprived Russia of French aid if she went to war with Japan over Manchuria. In Tokyo, Japanese strategists began preparations for a land and sea offensive designed to expel the Russians from that province.

The British public welcomed an alliance. Journalists praised the Japanese as a race that seemed to possess all the virtues and values cherished by their new ally: they were plucky islanders with grit and determination. During the suppression of the Boxer Rebellion one reporter had praised the Japanese soldiers' 'magnificent fighting spirit' which matched the crack British regiments he had recently witnessed in action in South Africa.[4] The Japanese reciprocated. Nitobe Inazō, a Japanese intellectual and civil servant, sensed a mystic bond between his people and the British: 'There is a brotherhood between an Englishman and a Japanese samurai – a spiritual bond between them.' A Japanese samurai would have been welcomed at King Arthur's Camelot.

Bonds of chivalry and abstract national affinities were but a welcome addition to a hard-nosed agreement contrived to resolve shared political and strategic problems. Britain was now free to transfer warships from the Far East to European waters and Japan could press ahead with war plans to drive the Russians from Manchuria. Her prime tactical aims were the destruction of the Russian Far Eastern naval squadron, the total occupation of Korea and the capture of Port Arthur. Britain played a hidden but practical part in the Japanese war effort. There was secret collaboration between British and Japanese naval intelligence departments, which shared decrypted Russian telegraphic and wireless signals. The British took advantage of, and were impressed by, their ally's spy networks in China and Manchuria. And after war broke out, Royal Navy intelligence officers supplied details of Russia's plans to send her Baltic Fleet to the Far East.

The war began in February 1904 after a collapse in Russo-Japanese negotiations for the future sharing of influence in Manchuria and northern Korea. Expansionist zealots in St Petersburg pressed for war and were encouraged in their case by what turned out to be flawed estimates of Japan's capabilities. One report alleged that 'the Japanese army is far from perfect' and many Russians, including Nicholas II, dismissed the Japanese as 'monkeys'. Myths of racial superiority haunted the tsar and his subjects. His prejudices owed much to the suggestions of the Kaiser, who was obsessed by the threat that the 'Yellow Peril' posed to Western, Christian civilisation. It was, he told his cousin 'Nicky', his 'sacred duty' to remove this peril. Converting his kinsman was an easy task, for, as Wilhelm once remarked, he was 'only fit to live in a country house and grow turnips'. He added 'the only way to deal with him is to be the last to leave the room'.

Japan began the war with a pre-emptive attack on Russian warships at anchor in Port Arthur and kept the initiative with a sequence of daring actions which severely mauled the Russian Far Eastern squadron, which was bottled up the port. The surviving vessels were finally sunk by the fire of land artillery placed on high ground overlooking the harbour in October. Predominant at sea, Japan was free to deploy her land forces in Korea and Manchuria, where they encircled and besieged Port Arthur.

On paper, Russia had a huge advantage in numbers, with 1.1 million men in arms and a further 2.5 million reservists. These hordes provided the impetus behind what would later be called the 'Russian steamroller', an outwardly impressive machine whose inner mechanisms proved defective and whose drivers fumbled with the controls. Russia's Manchurian campaign depended on the 5,500-mile-long Trans-Siberian Railway, which struggled to reinforce, equip, feed and clothe an army of a quarter of a million men. Russian command was pedestrian and irresolute, as it would be at the outbreak of the First World War in 1914.

Japanese leadership was flexible and audacious in what quickly became a static contest of attrition for Port Arthur, which finally surrendered in January 1905. Both sides were on the verge of exhaustion and each was under external pressure to accept an armistice. Japan was running out of money and Russia was convulsed by popular uprisings. The British ambassador in St Petersburg noted that the agitation was fiercest in areas where reservists were being mobilised for a war that Russia was clearly losing. Soldiers returning from the front were prominent among the protesters.

A peace was brokered by President Theodore Roosevelt, for which he received one of the first Nobel Prizes. Japan kept Korea, nearly all the Liaodong peninsula and Port Arthur. In Britain, politicians, the press and the public celebrated: the alliance had paid dividends, for the Russian threat to China had been eliminated. Enthusiasm for Japan and her fighting men had reached fever pitch during the final stages of the war, when ships of Admiral Zinovy Rozhestvensky's Baltic Fleet opened fire on some British trawlers in the North Sea during the first stage of its voyage to the Far East. Ineptitude and panic had been to blame, for Russian officers had imagined that the fishing vessels were Japanese torpedo boats. The press clamoured for war and the Russian armada was humiliatingly shadowed by a Royal Navy squadron as it steamed southwards. Coaled and victualled in French colonial ports, Rozhestvensky's task force was then destroyed, with the loss of thirty warships, by Admiral Tōgō at the Battle of Tsushima in May 1905. Six of the Japanese battleships had been made in British yards and the British press hailed Tōgō as a second Nelson.

Britain's confidence in her victorious ally was premature and naive. Japan had defeated Russia as part of its long-term, highly ambitious aims for the political, economic and territorial penetration of China. The resulting peace treaty allowed for a permanent garrison of 10,000 in Manchuria, known as the Kwantung army. Field Marshal Prince

Yamagata Aritomo, architect of the Imperial Japanese Army (IJA), was of the view that China had nothing to fear from Japan and that it should share in a victory that would turn out to be a step forwards for all Asians. He argued that Russia's defeat was a sign that henceforward the peace of Asia depended on Japan, which shared 'a common race and culture' with the Chinese.[5] Russians too sensed a forthcoming racial struggle. Prince Alexei Kuropatkin, who had been Russian minister of war at the start of the war against Japan, was fearful of 'the encroaching danger from the awakening of the yellow races'.[6]

Kuropatkin was right insofar as Japanese imperialists recognised that the victory over Russia had been a blow to the prestige of the Europeans throughout Asia. This included Britain, with Japan secretly planning moves to reduce her power in China. By 1911, the IJA's staff officers were preparing for the occupation of the British sphere of influence in the Yangtze basin in the event of disorders there.[7] Britain's ally was already looking ahead to a contest for the control of China.

The Chinese had rejoiced in Japan's victory over Russia, which had proved at long last that European armies and navies were not invincible. At the same time, it had showed what an Asian people could achieve if they set their hearts and minds to the process of catching up with the West. Modernisation worked and within a generation had transformed Japan into the first modern, Asian superpower. This awareness and the hope it engendered led to an exodus of Chinese students to Japan. They included China's future leader Chiang Kai-shek, who spent three years in a military academy and a further two training with the IJA. He was one of a generation of young, educated and predominantly middle-class Chinese born in the 1870s and 1880s exasperated with the snail-paced and half-hearted Qing reforms. For these young men and women, nothing short of a revolution could transform China into a second Japan able to face the West on equal terms.

What form would the reborn China take? Those hungry for change found no shortage of models. Intellectual dissidents pored over the works of European philosophers, political theorisers and economists for guidance. Socialism was tempting because its tenets chimed with latent resentments against foreign capitalist exploitation. An early champion of women's rights declared that 'We Chinese women are all about to be sold and all will become slaves of England.'[8] And a poster displayed during disturbances in Chengdu in 1911 portrayed 'running dog' Qing officials kneeling to a foreigner and pleading with him 'to take all the nation's finance, railways, river, peoples and lands'.⁹

The evolutionary theories of Europe's Social Darwinists also found some favour. In essence, they suggested that, like animals, successful nations adapted to external forces, taking advantage of new conditions and ideas. The inflexible fell by the wayside while the innovative flourished and moved onwards and upwards. The recent remaking of Japan proved this principle, but how and by whom would a modernised China be governed? Democracy was attractive to some, although the cautious were uneasy about delivering power to what one sceptic called 'the vulgar and rustic' who formed the mass of the population.

China's frustrated progressives wanted a revolution, but they had neither a plan nor the unity to bring it about. Nor was there any agreement as to what form the new state would take and what policies it would adopt. There was, however, an umbrella organisation called the Revolutionary Alliance led by Dr Sun Yat-sen, a revered and much-travelled idealist who had spent his life promoting 'the cause of the people's revolution that would herald the elevation of China to a position of freedom and an equality among nations'. While the restlessness of soldiers and civilians was taking form and spreading, he was in Britain raising cash and support. He rushed back to China and arrived on Christmas Day 1911 to an enthusiastic reception, but he was too late to impose his will on a civilian insurrection and the mass mutiny of the Chinese army.

Meanwhile, another young activist, Liang Qichao, had seen American democracy at work and was impressed by it, but preferred a government that would give priority to national cohesion. China, he insisted, needed an Oliver Cromwell rather than a Jean-Jacques Rousseau.¹⁰ Liang also favoured a constitutional monarchy, while the majority of reformers preferred a republic. Mao Zedong, a farmer's son born in 1893, agreed with general theories of progressive evolution but was captivated by the idea of a Napoleonic figure, a dynamic man of action who would 'charge on horseback amid the clash of arms'. There was also a degree of relief in London, where there had been misgivings as to whether the Qing government had the will or authority to reform and rebuild China. Their replacement could only be a move forwards and none of the revolutionaries were demanding radical changes in China's relations with Britain or her economic system.

Liang and Mao were among the swarm of young theorisers who banded together in clandestine and subversive cells in towns and cities and argued about the nature of a post-revolutionary China. A few threw bombs and fomented minor uprisings and found themselves persecuted by the secret police. Trade unions, a Western novelty which were springing up in the industrial cities, extended the agitation to the urban working classes. Politically, China had caught up with the governments of Europe and America, which were also facing waves of radical protest.

Yet the strongest element in the revolutionary movement was China's New Army, paradoxically a recent creation of hasty Qing reforms. Its soldiers wore Western-style uniforms and were armed with the latest repeating rifles, machine guns and modern artillery, purchased from Germany. Army pay was good and it attracted literate recruits: a high proportion of officers had university degrees and had been exposed to revolutionary ideas,[11] and they commanded a force whose morale, discipline and professional ethos impressed Western observers. Officers and men joined radical groups whose names reflected their members' passions and objectives. In Wuhan, these cells included the 'Society for Increasing Knowledge' and the 'Progressive and Literary Society'.

The revolution came in the winter of 1911–12 and was an untidy and ultimately inconclusive affair. It began in October 1911 in Wuhan with a popular and spontaneous protest against a foreign-funded railway project, one of many embarked on by the Qing government as part of a crash modernisation programme. Rioters were joined by soldiers and the demonstrations soon triggered further urban riots and garrison mutinies. These spread northwards and westwards. The immediate aim of the insurgents was the overthrow of the Qings, and racial animosities soon surfaced in Nanjing where Manchu civilians were massacred. Despite resistance by some loyal units, the government and the dynasty it represented found themselves increasingly helpless.

Foreigners in China were alarmed, while their governments held their breath. Garrisons were reinforced and warships despatched to protect civilians, their property and investments. Winston Churchill, then First Lord of the Admiralty, reassured an anxious House of Commons that gunboat patrols had been stepped up. Such precautions were needless; for once, populist Chinese fury did not vent itself on the barbarians and their property.

As the Qing dynasty collapsed, it created a political vacuum. It was filled, revealingly, by a leading mutineer called General Yuan Shikai. He was a respected and well-liked commander of the Northern Beiyang Army who had been hurriedly appointed prime minister by the Qing court during the early stages of the uprising. Yuan quickly decided that the cause of five-year-old Emperor Puyi was lost and shifted his allegiance to his fellow officers and the rebels.

General Yuan had no plans for a democracy, something which many of the revolutionaries believed was impossible in a country where nearly all the population were illiterate peasant farmers, artisans and labourers. In 1912, when China's population was estimated at 440 million, her schools had only 2.9 million pupils of whom 141,000 were girls. Yuan instead proceeded to broker a deal by which the child emperor abdicated and then he installed himself as the first president of the Chinese Republic. In short, a canny and ambitious senior officer had hijacked the revolution to secure a coup d'état – Napoleon would have admired his audacity and timing.

In 2011, when the centenary of what had become known as the 'Xinhai' Revolution was being celebrated in Hong Kong, a local television station conducted a survey of local opinion as to its significance.[12] Just over half of the 15,000 participants believed that it marked the end of 'the feudal Qing dynasty' and just over a quarter thought that it had popularised 'the republican ideal'. Just under 10 per cent saw the revolution as the beginning of an extended period of political violence.

Each response contained an element of truth, yet no one mentioned the role of the Chinese army, whose collective disobedience had made the revolution possible and guaranteed its short-term success. Thanks to the killing power of modern weaponry, mass civilian uprisings had become an anachronism, as the suppression of the 1871 Paris Commune had dramatically shown. The intervention of the Chinese National Army had been decisive. Henceforward, armed force and violence would dominate political life in the country. The revolution was followed by the era of local warlords and the civil war between Nationalist and Communist armies in the 1920s and again between 1945 and 1949. And popular agitation against the Communist regime was thereafter suppressed by a loyal army, most notably the 1989 Tiananmen Square demonstration.

Equally significant was the fact that the Xinhai Revolution had left intact a prominent feature of China's ancient regime. The extensive economic, legal and policing powers exercised by Britain and the other powers remained, and they used the revolution as an excuse to extract further concessions, including an extension of their grip on Tibet. The Chinese who watched foreign warships drop anchor off Shanghai and who were manhandled by Sikh policemen commanded by British officers could have been forgiven for asking what had been changed by the revolution.

# Better Our Condition:
# The Fortunes of Hong Kong

News of the Xinhai Revolution sparked rejoicing in Hong Kong. The colony's governor, Sir Frederick Lugard, told the Colonial Office that the Chinese were 'demented with joy', the 'riff raff' had spontaneously taken to the streets to celebrate, and local barbers waived charges for cutting off the hated pigtails. Their British rulers were happy too, but more constrained. 'Speaking as one man to another,' the British consul-general in Guangzhou confided to a Chinese rebel general, 'you have done the right thing.'[1]

For the past seventy years, British rule had spared the people of Hong Kong from the chronic disorders which had punctuated the decline and fall of the Qings. Unlike the rest of China, the colony had managed the rite of passage into the modern world without trauma and with astonishing success. The island colony had also expanded: the Kowloon peninsula was annexed in 1860 and the New Territories were acquired on a ninety-nine-year lease in 1898. Both provided water and food for a growing population, which rose from just over 5,000 in 1841 to 821,000 in 1931.

The incomers were Chinese immigrants for whom Hong Kong was an El Dorado, where the enterprising and industrious were free to make their fortunes and exploit opportunities that were unavailable in the rest of China. The colonial government's laissez-faire policies, the introduction of British commercial law and official toleration of freedom of movement helped enormously. The colony also became a staging post for Chinese seeking work, mostly onerous, abroad. By the 1870s, Chinese labourers were being shipped to South America, the United States, Australia, Canada and South-East Asia. By sheer graft, and often in the face of racial prejudice, many got rich.

Consider Ah Toy, a tall, slim girl with the traditional bound feet who left Hong Kong in 1848 or 1849 'to better her condition' in that free-for-all for the ambitious, the California Gold Rush. Her looks and her fluency in English were her assets and prostitution her profession. Despite the efforts of the San Francisco Vigilance Committee, she flourished and, by 1852, was the madam of two brothels. Two years later she returned home to recruit more girls whom she purchased for $40 each.[2] Ah Toy's activities displeased some of her countrymen, but made her enough to settle in America with her husband.

Ng Wing's career was a more conventional Hong Kong success story. Born in Fujian, he arrived in the colony in 1877 and established himself as an agent for rice and sugar exports to Malaya and the Philippines, where he established offices. Capital from these enterprises provided the wherewithal for Ng to diversify into real estate, brewing and finance. He died in 1913 worth a quarter of a million Hong Kong dollars (£50,000).[3]

Chance and geography favoured Hong Kong's economic growth. The rapid, post-Gold Rush boom marked the beginnings of what became known as the Pacific rim economy. Hong Kong benefited as a source of imported labour, raw materials and food. The sea crossing from Hong Kong to San Francisco took between forty-five and fifty days, whereas goods from New York carried by the Cape Horn route took up to 115. This advantage lasted until the 1870s with the advent of the Trans-Pacific Railway. In the meantime, Hong Kong emerged as one of the hubs of a new economic system which extended across the Pacific and included the Philippines, the Dutch East Indies and Malaya. Always watchful for new sources of profit, Jardine Matheson secured a toehold in the kingdom of Hawaii in 1849.

Hong Kong's harbour provided a deep-water anchorage for 200 ships, civil and military. The coming and going of merchant vessels generated a source of local opportunities for making money. The owners of repair dockyards, chandlers, victuallers, marine-insurance brokers and coal merchants flourished. In 1913 Hong Kong imported 1.2 trillion tons of coal for sale to shipping companies. Sailors needed diversions, so taverns and brothels also proliferated. In the Victoria district the latter rose from thirty-two in 1850 to 126 in 1860.[4] Both sources of pleasure and disorder were a permanent headache for the authorities.

Hong Kong might have been the launching pad for figures like Ah Toy and Ng Wing, yet the majority of Hong Kong's upwardly mobile stuck to their old identities – only 11 per cent of the colony's Chinese adopted British nationality, and gratitude for British protection never extinguished emotional loyalty to China.[5] Attachments to soil, family and tradition always remained strong. Emigrants who flocked to America after the Gold Rush made complicated and expensive arrangements for their bodies to be returned by sea for burial in their native soil. The coffins passed through Hong Kong, where there was a locally funded graveyard for those who had no family to oversee their burial. It was called the Plum Blossom Estate.[6]

Chinese political patriotism remained deep-rooted and violently broke the surface during the short war between China and France in 1884. French forces depended on Hong Kong as a supply base for operations in northern Indo-China, which provoked strikes and violent demonstrations by Hong Kong dockyard workers who refused to unload French vessels. They fought battles with the colony's Sikh police and soldiers from the British garrison. 'A common national spirit' animated the rioters, according to the governor, George Brown, who cracked down on the disturbances.[7] There was, however, secret glee in the Foreign Office, where anything which hindered French efforts at empire-building anywhere was good news. Hong Kong's working class protested again in 1905 after the United States had passed racially inspired laws limiting Chinese immigration.

Regardless of their loyalty to China, Hong Kong's upwardly mobile Chinese submitted to British governance and laws rooted in the moral principles by which the Victorians justified their empire and its expansion. At their heart was a sense of reciprocity: in return for obedience and allegiance, the empire's subjects received protection from their enemies and each other, civil peace and even-handed laws. The Hong Kong Chinese witnessed the last of these in 1854 when two Europeans were publicly hanged for murdering a Chinese boy.[8] Then and later, the Chinese business community also benefited from the Royal Navy's relentless suppression of piracy.

Mostly fair, stable government provided opportunities for social and intellectual regeneration in the form of sharing the benefits of modern European civilisation. These included exposure to the ideas of the eighteenth-century Enlightenment and more recent developments in science, technology and philosophy. Hong Kong did well from what was offered. From 1842 onwards the colony's inhabitants had newspapers, gas in the 1860s, and electricity in the 1880s. In 1897 two cinemas were opened (in traditional tea gardens), and in 1906 the colony's first telephone service was introduced. A school of medicine was opened in 1887 which mutated into a university in 1911. Its syllabus was science-orientated, and it and schools received funds from the government and local businessmen.

Chinese students studying Chemistry by day and watching films in the evening represented the benevolent face of British imperialism. But progress required submission to a regime which never tolerated any challenge to its authority. This was made brutally clear in April 1899, when the poorly armed villagers of the recently acquired New Territories resisted the British forces which entered their territories. Chinese losses in a grossly unequal fight were estimated at between 350 and 400. There were no British casualties and it appears that no reports of this massacre appeared in the British press, which was fortunate for the local authorities and the government in London.[9]

As for the future of Hong Kong, there was never any suggestion that its inhabitants might achieve the democratic government that was being extended to the white populations of Australia, New Zealand and Canada. According to one Colonial Office official, such a move was unthinkable, for it would empower a lower class that was 'unruly, unbalanced and transient' and 'lacked morality'. Similar objections had been made to the enfranchisement of the working class in Britain, which only achieved universal franchise in 1928 when women over twenty-one got the vote.

Despite this, there was always a willingness on the part of colonial administrators to seek out and heed the opinions of the Chinese commercial elite. Across the empire, Britain made alliances of convenience with local figures whose status and wealth would be preserved and even enhanced by acquiescence and co-operation. Indian princes and African chiefs became accomplices and partners in imperial government. A similar arrangement was made in Hong Kong, where the government consulted a powerful association of Chinese businessmen called the *Tung Wah*. It was a charitable body guided by the Confucian principle that the rich had a moral obligation to help the poor, and so it funded schools and hospitals. The *Tung Wah* also lobbied the administration on behalf of the wider community. In 1883 it persuaded the government to withdraw a ban on rickshaw men parking their carriages in front of shops.[10]

Like every other Chinese city, Hong Kong was also host to a large number of voluntary Chinese brotherhoods, mutual-aid clubs, temple committees and trade-protection associations. These cared for their members' interests and at times defended their rights, as well as providing a social cement. The boycott of French shipping in 1884 had been organised by the dock workers' groups. Such bodies laid the foundations for Hong Kong's trade union movement, which emerged early in the next century. They also attracted political activists; in 1917 the embryonic Hong Kong Anarchist movement infiltrated the tea house clerks' and barbers' associations.[11] Hong Kong's paternalist administration never prevented political activism, association and debate, although then and later all were closely surveyed by the police. Imperial power flowed downwards, but it never stifled the expression and exchange of political ideas. This was true also of contemporary India, Egypt and some of the colonies where, by the first decade of the twenty-first century, there were vibrant nationalist and democratic movements and open criticism of the authorities. Neither was welcomed, but they were tolerated in an empire which publicly and often advertised its enlightenment and benevolence.

On the whole the British authorities attempted wherever possible to allow Chinese traditions to continue. This was never easy, given that colonial officials brought with them the Victorian values of their homeland. They were also all too conscious of the formidable political power of those domestic lobbies which demanded that the empire should be ruled in accord with British moral principles.

Collisions were unavoidable. One area where official and popular Chinese attitudes collided was animal welfare. In Britain, what we now call the 'animal rights' movement was a recent innovation and one which attracted huge public sympathy. This was why, in 1845, the Hong Kong government issued a law against cruelty to domestic pets and agricultural livestock. It was weakly enforced, with thirty-three prosecutions over the next forty years. In 1903 legal protection was extended to chickens, and in the same year the Hong Kong branch of the Royal Society for the Protection of Animals was founded. It campaigned against the eating of dogs, a habit which horrified the British. How could the Chinese justify eating dogs and also keeping them as pets? This culture war ended in 1949 when a rabies epidemic provided the government with an opportunity permanently to ban the sale of dog meat. There were protests, but dog meat vanished from Hong Kong menus and never returned.[12]

Actual and suspected people-trafficking generated another fiercer clash between the ethics of the rulers and customs of the ruled. The British people were united in their determination that 'Britons never, never shall be slaves' and that no one else in the world would be either. Britain's extended war against slavery in Africa and the Middle East was a source of national pride and a justification to some for empire. But what constituted slavery? In Hong Kong there were official misgivings about the workings of the legitimate business of the recruitment and shipping abroad of Chinese 'coolies' for physical labour. The 1855 Chinese Passengers Act regulated male emigrants but ignored the purchase of the daughters of poor families for foreign brothels. This appalled the *Tung Wah*, which assisted the government by hiring private detectives to investigate cases.

In the eyes of anti-slavery crusaders, the custom of selling small boys to childless, middle-class parents was tantamount to slave-trading. Sir John Smale, Hong Kong's chief justice in the 1870s, took this view, but the *Tung Wah* strongly disagreed, arguing that Confucius had insisted that the lack of a male heir was sinful.[13] Smale's misgivings were overridden by the government, which was willing to tolerate an ancient tradition.

There was also friction, this time between London and the Hong Kong government, over the official supervision of brothels. Spiralling rates of venereal diseases among the colony's garrison led to their regulation and frequent inspection by medical officers. This measure offended purity campaigners in Britain, who, in 1894, persuaded the Liberal government to ban this procedure on the grounds it was an official endorsement of prostitution. The fallen women were left in peace and within three years half the 1,000-strong garrison had contracted VD.[14]

Pragmatism, an entente with the local elite and the maintenance of customs that did not infringe the Victorian moral codes were the foundations of Hong Kong's colonial regime. In 1897, the year of Queen Victoria's Diamond Jubilee that saw celebrations across the empire, a Hong Kong businessman added to the chorus of gratitude. Hong Kong, he said, was a place of 'perfect protection' and 'equal justice and consideration' by its rulers.[15]

# Part Two

---

# World Wars and Civil Wars, 1912–1945

# 12

# No Hope for China, 1912–1927

As Mao Zedong famously observed, all political power comes from the 'barrel of a gun'. Events in post-revolutionary China amply confirmed his view. Generalissimo Yuan Shikai quickly dismissed his parliament and established a military dictatorship and, shortly before his death in 1915, he was scheming to declare himself emperor and found a new dynasty.

In the provinces other generals followed his example. Trusting the loyalty of their troops and arsenals of modern weapons, they made themselves little emperors. The world knew them as 'warlords'. Their power was absolute. They used terror to enforce their will, made alliances and waged wars against each other for territory and the revenues it yielded. Some extorted money from local banks. Between 1916 and 1927 the warlords dominated central and northern China.

There were roughly 1,000 warlords, most of whom were minnows, but there was a handful of sharks.[1] Both species were ambitious, pragmatic, inclined towards Confucian ideals and often eccentric. Feng Yuxiang was a soldier and sometime YMCA leader and known as the 'Christian General'. He encouraged Methodism among his soldiers, waged war against Buddhism, opium, alcohol and prostitution and briefly sought favours from the atheist Soviet Union. Zhang Zongchang, who held sway in Shandong, was nicknamed the 'Dogmeat General', which reflected his favourite food and an addiction to a gambling game of that name. He was a bull of a man, an opium smoker who succumbed to spasms of fury and crushed the skulls of prisoners with his sword, which he likened to 'smashing melons'. He boasted of having the largest penis in China and kept a harem of Chinese, Korean, Japanese, Russian and French concubines. In his previous life, Zhang had been a bandit.

For all their quirkiness, the warlords were politically astute. They took care that their forces did nothing to provoke foreigners and,

while often expressing nationalist sentiments, never attached themselves to an ideology. Between them the warlords commanded a million
soldiers who were deployed in over 100 intermittent and mostly minor
conflicts. The result was chaos, which worried the great powers, who
in 1923 briefly considered an embargo on arms imports. It would
have achieved little beyond antagonising the warlords, for the Soviet
Union was more than willing to supply weapons. In 1925 deals were
done with Feng Yuxiang, who received a tranche of arms that included
light tanks and aircraft.[2] In return he offered cash and future Russian
political influence in Manchuria.

During this time the government in Beijing remained, but its authority was diluted or ignored throughout much of the country, even
though it was treated as legitimate by the major powers. Amazingly,
this slide into chaos coincided with a period of soaring economic
growth, funded by overseas investment. Britain's share rose from
$607.5 million in 1914 to $1,189 million in 1931. Over a third of
this capital consisted of loans to the nominal Chinese government.

The fact that Russia, a traditionally hostile power, was exploiting
China's disintegration exposed the fundamental weakness of the new
republic. The Xinhai Revolution had not delivered democracy, reduced
the influence of foreign powers or raised China's status in the world.
The last of these was made brutally clear from her treatment by the
Allies after the First World War.

China had remained neutral until August 1917, when she joined
the Allies in the hope of regaining control of German concessions in
Shandong which had been occupied by Japanese and British forces at
the outbreak of the war three years before. Within a few months, Japan
was pressing for additional concessions in Manchuria.[3] A Japanese
squadron occupied the German Caroline Islands, an archipelago in
the Western Pacific, and established a naval base on Truk (Chuuk).
The Allies earmarked these for Japan together with the Shandong
concession. In return, Japan sent a squadron of destroyers to the
Mediterranean to help protect Allied convoys on their way to Egypt.

China had also helped the Allied war effort by allowing the
recruitment of Chinese labourers. In all, 140,000 volunteers enrolled
to assist the British and French armies on the Western Front and to
man factories in France during 1917 and 1918. Most were shipped to
Canada and carried by railway to Halifax, from where they embarked

for France. The British Chinese Labour Corps were deployed at ports, where they unloaded ships, and along the lines of communications, where they heaved and manhandled truckloads of foodstuffs and ammunition.

The official British account of the Chinese Labour Corps described them as 'men of perfect physique' tempered by 'stern discipline' and 'impartial handling'. They were commanded by Chinese-speaking British officers and NCOs, and the labourers were paid three francs a day, housed in camps, and forbidden to enter towns and villages where they might buy alcohol and visit brothels. There was intermittent friction over wages and conditions which erupted into strikes and violent demonstrations. Twice, in December 1917 and February 1918, troops opened fire on protesters, killing nineteen.[4] One cause of the trouble was German air raids on the Channel ports and inland depots in which Chinese had been killed and wounded. The survivors alleged that they had been promised they would never be exposed to enemy fire. Lieutenant Noah Williams, who had taught mining engineering at Shanxi University, witnessed another hazard: German snipers who picked off men digging trenches. Their comrades then attempted to retrieve the bodies for burial according to customary rites and in turn were killed by the sharpshooters.[5] In all, 3,000 died and many remained behind to clear up the detritus of war scattered across the French and Belgian countryside.

The losses and exertions of the Chinese labourers justified China's presence as one of the victorious Allies at the Versailles Peace Conference in January 1919. Their intention, in the words of the veteran Nationalist leader Sun Yat-sen, was 'the elevation of China to a position of freedom and equality among nations'.[6] Faith had been placed in the wartime promises of the American president, Woodrow Wilson, who had pledged support for ethnic nationalism in the old transnational empires. Self-determination was, however, rationed to Europeans. Poles, Czechs and Slovaks got independence, but Algerians and Arabs did not despite their contributions to the Allied war effort, and China's claim to Shandong was rejected. Moreover, Britain, France, Italy and the United States declined demands for an end to all the extra-territorial privileges granted since 1842. The British foreign secretary, Lord Curzon, observed: 'The great helpless, hopeless and inert mass of China' was 'utterly deficient in cohesion or strength' and 'engaged in perpetual conflict between the North and the South, [and is] destitute of military capacity, or ardour'.[7] He also suspected that at heart the Chinese were innately hostile towards all Western ideas.

Curzon echoed the prevailing overview of the Foreign Office, which paid lip service to Chinese sensibilities but remained convinced that full sovereignty had to be postponed until China had achieved internal stability and a government that had the power to give full protection to foreigners and their property. That time was still far off. Sir Robert Hart, the former head of the Maritime Customs Service (MCS), believed it would take a further fifty years for China to establish a dependable, honest and effective government. The British business community in China and their allies in London agreed. At present there was 'no hope for China', concluded a senior British official in Shanghai in 1918.[8] Nevertheless, British capital offered a life raft. In 1923, the Shanghai British Chamber of Commerce declared:

> But for the effort on behalf of the Hong Kong and Shanghai Bank, China would surely fall in to a deeper mine and her resources would remain unexploited for a duration and its people would remain unchanged century after century and China would lag further behind modern civilisation.

Versailles had made it clear that China was still deemed unfit to join the community of civilised nations. Its educated classes were furious. On 4 May 1919 there were student demonstrations in Beijing. They congregated in Tiananmen Square under placards which read 'Give back Tsingtao' and 'China belongs to the Chinese'. A Japanese diplomat was assaulted and Japanese products were boycotted. The protests spread to other cities and attracted the middle classes and industrial workers. The overall mood was one of impotent despair. Intellectuals convinced themselves that full nationhood could never be achieved so long as Confucian habits of mind persisted. They believed that a profound cultural revolution in which China unequivocally embraced Western science and philosophy was imperative.

The British government had approved China's treatment at Versailles, partly motivated by a strong wish to salvage as much as possible of the old world order which had been shaken by four years of total war. Restoring equilibrium required a common front against two indirect by-products of the war: Russian Communism and the spread of often violent nationalist agitation in British and French colonies in the Middle East, Asia and Africa. During 1919 and 1920 there were uprisings against the British in Ireland, Egypt, Iraq and, most disturbing of all, India, and against France in recently acquired Syria. All were subdued by force, ferociously applied. China had also been infected by the nationalist fervour, and when it surfaced it too was treated severely.

This wave of uprisings was blamed on Communist subversion directed by Lenin from Moscow following the 1917 revolution. An agency, Comintern, had been created to foment world revolution among the industrial working classes and the oppressed rural subjects of the old empires despite their lack of a coherent class consciousness. This prerequisite for proletarian revolution already existed in Europe. During 1919 and 1920 there were Communist uprisings in Berlin, Munich and Hungary, and Britain suffered a spate of strikes and violent disorders among demobilised soldiers. Tanks appeared on the streets of Glasgow after striking workers proclaimed a local 'soviet'. The disturbances flickered out, but the paranoia remained and became deeply entrenched. In the meantime, capitalism fought back: during 1919 and 1920, British, French, American, Canadian and Japanese forces fought a series of campaigns on the fringes of Russia in support of counter-revolutionary generals. All failed.

Retaliation took the form of the Soviet Politburo's adoption of a policy of supplying arms to countries then in conflict with the British Empire. At the same time, Moscow waged war against those provinces in Central Asia which had used the revolution and subsequent civil war to secure independence. Re-establishing the empire of the tsars was followed by a revival of the Great Game in which Moscow endeavoured to stir up trouble for Britain in Asia. Turkey, Persia, Afghanistan and China received supplies of modern weaponry; in one of the more bizarre paradoxes of modern history, weapons taken from anti-Soviet insurgents in the Caucasus found their way into the hands of Chinese nationalists.

Organised, popular Chinese nationalism was languishing. It had coalesced around the Guomindang (GMD) (Kuomintang), a coalition led by Sun Yat-sen, who projected himself as true political heir of the Xinhai Revolution and its liberal aspirations. He promised full independence, democracy and policies designed to promote the welfare of the masses. The odds against its success were high, for the GMD's power base was in southern China under the protection of a friendly warlord. Efforts to build an army were hampered by a British ban on the import of arms.

Isolated and frustrated in a China where political power now rested on force of arms, Sun decided that the GMD would never succeed until it acquired a modern, well-armed and disciplined army. In what was a measure of desperation, Sun approached the Russian ambassador, Adolf Joffe, in September 1922 and asked for weapons for a new National Revolutionary Army (NRA) that would overcome the warlords, reunite China and take power by force. Once again, power would come from the barrels of guns.

The Russians agreed and extracted concessions: an interest in the Chinese Eastern Railway and an enlarged garrison in Outer Mongolia.[9] The following year, Moscow twisted the arms of the nascent Chinese Communist Party (CCP), which had joined the GMD coalition. This shotgun marriage required doctrinal gymnastics, for the GMD's support was strongest among China's capitalist middle class. Nonetheless, Marxist-Leninist dogma could be made to accommodate the notion that making pacts with class enemies could open the way for the revolution of the working classes. Moreover, by beefing up the GMD Russia was striking a sideways blow against her prime antagonist, the British Empire. Some, including Stalin, wondered whether co-operation with the GMD might produce a friendly nationalist government which would join Russia in a common front against Russia's old rival, Japan.

Chiang Kai-shek, Sun's military adviser, shared the Soviet antipathy to Britain, which he saw as China's most shrewd, cunning, ruthless and dangerous enemy. In September 1923 he visited Moscow to negotiate the arms deal and settle arrangements for the import of a team of Red Army officers to train the new army. Between 1924 and 1926 the NRA received 24 aircraft, more than 200 artillery pieces, 295 machine guns and 70,000 rifles.[10]

Red Army veterans taught Chinese officers the arts of modern war at a new military academy at Huangpu on Whampoa island close to Guangzhou. Instructors were commanded by a resourceful and energetic Comintern agent, Mikhail Borodin, who combined the roles of ambassador and chief military adviser. His last posting had been in Glasgow, where he had been imprisoned for six months as an illegal immigrant. He spoke no Chinese but was fluent in English, which he spoke with a Midwestern American accent.

Borodin intended the Huangpu academy to be a nursery for a cadre of future revolutionaries: graduates included Zhou Enlai, the future first premier of the People's Republic of China, and Ho Chi Minh, the future Communist leader of Vietnam. These Communists were, however, exceptional, for most of Huangpu's intake were sons of the mandarin class, landowners and wealthy peasants. Between 1924 and 1926, 3,000 young officers passed through the academy to become the backbone of the NRA. Its first commander-in-chief was Chiang Kai-shek, who had assumed the leadership of the GMD after Sun's death in March 1925.

The first casualties of the Huangpu cadets were suffered in May 1925 in a one-sided engagement between rioters in Guangdong and British and French warships and troops. The disturbances were part of an eruption of localised protests in response to an incident in Shanghai which symbolised the continuing impotence of China and the callous arrogance of foreign powers. A lockout of workers in a Japanese-owned cotton mill led to the shooting dead of a protester by a Japanese employee. Unrest continued, and at the end of the month Sikh police commanded by a British inspector opened fire on demonstrators, killing eleven. Britain then pulled the strings on the Shanghai Municipal Authority, which upheld the inspector's decision.

A month later in Guangzhou, 100,000 demonstrators confronted British and French forces backed by warships on the approach to the Shaji Bridge. At least fifty were killed, including twenty-three cadets from the Huangpu Military Academy, and 170 were badly wounded. Chiang Kai-shek was consumed by rage, writing in his diary that the '*ying fang* [cunning barbarians] need[ed] to be destroyed'.

Hong Kong trade unionists called a general strike which lasted until February 1926. Demonstrators shouted: 'We are Chinese, we have suffered enough at the hands of the foreign devils.'[11] Communist agitators were active in the colony at that time, which might explain rumours circulating among the strikers that Soviet warships were blockading the port ready to support them. Songs were written for young protesters: one included the lines 'We are the children of workers and peasants / We will be masters of the new world.'[12] The authorities were firm but calm and there was no resort to condign measures.

There was, however, anger in Britain. In June the Shanghai shooting was debated in the Commons. For Labour MPs, the killing of workers revealed the brutal, snarling face of capitalism. One called on the government to form 'battalions of shareholders to go and do their own dirty work'. Others vilified the exploitation of Chinese workers, who included children. One Tory detected the secret and malevolent hand of 'Moscow' behind the troubles, while his colleagues emphasised the murderous intentions of the Chinese rioters. The exchanges ended with the prime minister, Stanley Baldwin, repeating the old mantra that Britain's paramount interest in China was the improvement and prosperity of the Chinese people.[13]

The Labour Party's contribution to the debates was a reminder that over the past twenty years they had replaced the Liberals as the party of the Left. It was broadly sympathetic to what it considered to be the benevolent aims of imperialism, but also had an idealistic attachment to colonial independence movements. Labour also believed in the international brotherhood of the proletariat and backed their struggles against capitalism throughout the world.

Capitalism was still safe in China and was becoming safer. In 1926 the NRA commanded by Chiang Kai-shek began a series of offensives which secured the paramountcy of the GMD in the central and eastern regions. A new government was formed, based in Nanjing. As Chiang's forces closed on Shanghai in April 1927, the foreign community trembled, fearing an imminent Red uprising. Their alarm was premature. Chiang, who considered the CCP to be a front for the infiltration of China, abandoned his Communist allies and ordered the massacre of as many Communists as could be caught. The killings and the dispersal of those who escaped was a hard knock for the Soviet Union. The prospect of a Red China faded for the time being, mass democracy was postponed and, despite the anti-foreign slogans, European, Japanese and American investments remained protected. So did the privileges of all foreigners.

Britain had watched nervously as the NRA's fortunes had risen. At the end of 1926, the foreign secretary, Austen Chamberlain, announced that Britain now recognised the strength and legitimacy of Chinese nationalism just as it had that of Egypt two years before. Pragmatism and the safety of British assets demanded an accommodation with the new regime and Chamberlain urged the other major powers to do likewise. This made sense despite the geographical limits to the new government's authority, which diminished the further one travelled from the new capital, Nanjing, and was barely detectable in some areas. Warlords remained in outlying regions and had to be treated as partners by Chiang.

Britain raised two cheers for the new regime. Chiang and the GMD government offered a degree of stability that was welcomed by Stanley Baldwin's Conservative Party, which was in office for most of the 1920s. Yet, while demands for self-government and independence had a moral validity, their premature acceptance was full of hazards. These included a loss of international prestige and the creation of power vacuums which might be exploited by the Soviet Union. When Emperor Hirohito's brother Prince Chichibu visited London in 1925, King George V urged his government to promote a 'friendly conjunction with Japan' to overcome 'the rather serious difficulties with which, thanks to the Bolshevists, we are confronted in China'.[14]

The Foreign Office pursued a policy of public statements supporting China in its painful struggle for progress and stability. Small gestures were made and included the remission of outstanding payments of the Boxer indemnity, greater Chinese participation in the still-all-powerful CMCS and promises to revise the old treaty concessions. Consuls in the treaty ports (there were now over seventy) were instructed to persuade British subjects to show greater civility towards the Chinese and avoid potentially provocative incidents, particularly when motoring on Chinese rural roads.[15]

# 13

# A Feeling of Power:
# The Coming of War, 1927–1937

The Second World War began on 7 July 1937 at Lugouqiao in northern China. Shots were exchanged between Chinese troops and soldiers from the local Japanese garrison installed there after the Boxer Rebellion to protect their country's interests. This skirmish, close to the Marco Polo Bridge and just over twelve miles from Beijing, quickly escalated into a full-scale war.

Chiang Kai-shek treated the incident as a provocation too far. Three days after the firefight he wrote in his diary: 'The Japanese have attacked at Lugouqiao, but their goals don't stop there.'[1] For the past few years the Japanese had become increasingly and violently assertive in Manchuria. Chiang interpreted the latest incident as the prelude to a full-scale invasion of northern China and ordered mobilisation. The Japanese followed suit and justified themselves with claims that they were protecting their countrymen in China. At the end of the month Japanese bombers launched air raids on Beijing and Tianjin. Japanese troops were already being reinforced for an assault on Shanghai and the Chinese prepared to defend the city. Japan's conquest of China was under way and would become part of a global war within two years.

Japan's war on China was a gamble, but the odds favoured the war party in Tokyo. Recent events on the far side of the world encouraged Japan, for they reduced the risks of intervention by other powers. The post-Versailles system of collective security, designed to preserve peace and enforced by the League of Nations, had crumbled. In 1934 Germany had reoccupied the Saar and, in 1936, the Rhineland. In the same year Mussolini invaded Abyssinia. Aggressive imperialism was back in fashion and Britain, France and the United States were disinclined to play the global policemen. Each was distracted by the domestic economic fallout from a global recession, and post-war disarmament policies had left them short of the necessary muscle to rein in the dictators or Japan.

When Britain suggested joint intervention in China, France and America refused. The British government had sympathised with China and for the past decade had been disturbed by Japan's forward policy, but lacked the naval and military wherewithal to act alone. As the crisis unfolded, Ivan Maisky, the Russian ambassador in London, asked the foreign secretary, Anthony Eden, what he intended to do. 'I don't know' was the answer. Two days later, a conversation with Neville Chamberlain revealed a prime minister preoccupied with reducing tensions on the Continent. China would be left to its own devices.

The truth was that Britain was now reduced to the role of spectator in the Far Eastern power game. She had been nudged aside by two new, stronger players, Japan and the United States, and an old one, Russia. In 1934 a Japanese naval officer remarked that 'the British Empire is already an old man', a view widely shared by his colleagues. Once again, Britain faced the problems of global overstretch and this time she was also confronted with domestic economic problems and predatory dictators in Europe.

Japan was a beneficiary of Britain's decline. Despite its victory over Russia in 1905, Japan had never been accepted as an equal world power by its European counterparts and the US. During the Versailles negotiations, the Japanese delegation had pressed for a racial equality clause in the League of Nations charter that insisted on the parity of all races. This was vetoed by Britain, France, Italy and the United States. The racial assumptions behind this snub permeated the Foreign Office: according to a secret policy memo of October 1921, Japan was 'the only non-white first-class Power, yet the white races will never be able to admit her equality'.[2] Two Royal Navy officers serving the Far East offered blunt explanations of why they thought this was so. One observed that the Japanese had 'peculiarly small brains' and another ranked them among 'the inferior yellow races'.[3] Prevailing Western racial attitudes simultaneously humiliated and marginalised Japan.

Asians under European rule saw things differently. Young nationalists had celebrated the Japanese victory over Russia as a symbolic triumph, full of promise for the future. The Japanese were hailed as a heroic people who had broken the spell of white superiority that had been created by a century of unequal wars. In spite of their desire for equality with the West, the Japanese had acquired friends among their neighbours in the East. Fugitive Indian nationalist agitators were welcomed in Tokyo and British attempts to extradite them were rebuffed.

Not only was Japan obstructive in matters of imperial security, her agents were engaging in covert anti-British intrigues in China. Details of these emerged during 1916 and 1917 through intercepted and deciphered telegrams from the Japanese consul in Yunnan. He was also making contacts with Burmese nationalists across the border.[4] At the same time, the Imperial General Staff in London concluded that long-term Japanese geopolitical strategy would concentrate on waging a naval war to acquire control over Malaya, the Dutch East Indies and the Philippines.[5] This prediction was endorsed by Admiral Lord Jellicoe after a brief tour of the region.

An ally was now treated as a potential and dangerous rival in the Far East, where it enjoyed a preponderance of sea power. Britain's colonies were threatened, and so was its primacy in China. As in 1902, Britain was forced to concede that she could not be strong everywhere and in the Far East her survival and prestige depended on an ally. In May 1921, the Cabinet debated the alternatives. The prime minister, Lloyd George, and Churchill favoured keeping the Japanese alliance, but they succumbed to pressure from a nervous Admiralty and War Office.[6] The response was to abandon the Japanese alliance and turn to the United States as a future regional partner.

Co-operation with America was attractive. Britain's wartime banker, armourer and ally was a liberal power with worldwide trading and investment interests and, therefore, a stake in preserving international order and stability. Moreover, the United States had long shared a common policy towards China which the Americans called the 'Open Door' – that is, free trade and equal rights for all countries who wished to do business there. In the past century, the United States had been a sleeping partner in Britain's efforts to prise open that door. Americans enjoyed all the privileges extracted from China and her gunboats patrolled her rivers to see that they were enforced.

Replacing an alliance with a loose understanding with America was a leap in the dark that would have painful consequences for Britain and China. Underpinning the new relationship was the presumption that common moral and political values and a shared interest in China's independence and economic progress would persuade Americans to restrain Japan. What was forgotten was that the United States was a hard-nosed commercial competitor in China. Furthermore, British statesmen had overlooked America's ambivalent attitude towards empires and her own imperial impulses in the Pacific and Far East.

A former colony, proud of its successful struggle to escape British rule, America had an ancestral distrust of empires. Yet her people possessed a home-grown and highly popular imperial spirit which was named 'Manifest Destiny'. It took root in the American mind in the early 1800s and remained embedded until the next century. Manifest Destiny embodied the moral right and duty of Americans to occupy the vast spaces to the west of old Atlantic colonies as far as the Pacific. This was a service to God and an economic and demographic necessity as more and more immigrants poured in from Europe. So, from the 1820s onwards, the frontier advanced westwards. It proceeded inexorably across prairies and mountains and brutally swept aside resistance from Mexicans and indigenous Americans, taking land from each.

By 1849 the frontier had reached California, where the discovery of gold gave a fresh impetus to Manifest Destiny. This time its momentum led not to a promised land but to a promised ocean, the Pacific, and, over the horizon, China. Speculators, entrepreneurs (including opium dealers), moneymen and missionaries hurried to stake their claims. The Stars and Stripes followed, for Washington had a duty to protect Americans abroad. The oceanic frontier soon had its string of outposts: by the 1850s the United States had secured a virtual protectorate over Hawaii and in 1898 formally annexed the island. 'We need Hawaii just as much and a good deal more than we did California,' announced President McKinley. 'It is Manifest Destiny.' So too was the 1867 purchase of Alaska from Russia for $7.2 million in gold. The money helped pay off debts from the Crimean War and fund Russia's railway programme.

Maritime Manifest Destiny reached its climax in 1898 when it mutated into flagrant imperialism in the European style. America went to war with Spain and her seaborne forces captured her Caribbean colonies and the Philippines, an archipelago of 7,000 islands and 7 million people. Its capital, Manila, was just over 800 miles from Hong Kong.

The United States was now an Asian power. Many Americans, mostly Republicans, were jubilant. 'The taste of Empire is in the mouth of the people,' proclaimed the *Washington Post*, and the United States could now enjoy parity among the great powers. Duty beckoned, as

Albert Beveridge reminded his fellow senators: 'We cannot retreat from any soil where Providence has unfurled our banner, it is ours to save that soil for liberty and Civilisation.'[7]

An ardent imperialist, Beveridge set off for China to learn about how to treat America's new subjects. His visit coincided with the Boxer Uprising and a British colonel told him: 'You must do nothing but fight them. When we are in a row with Orientals, that is what we do. They do not understand anything else.'[8] This advice was superfluous, since for a year the Americans had been doing just that in a ruthless campaign against those Filipinos who wanted independence. The revolt dragged on until 1902 and cost the lives of 20,000 insurgents and ten times that number of civilians who died from starvation and sickness. The American governor of the Philippines and future president William Howard Taft promised that his country would 'teach these people individual liberty which will lift them up to a point of civilisation' which will make them 'call the name of the United States blessed'.[9] Kipling wrote a poem on the tasks that lay ahead; its title was 'The White Man's Burden'.

American missionaries were already shouldering that 'burden' in China. Between 1900 and 1930 their number rose from 1,000 to 3,000. All regarded conversion as integral to the rebirth of China as a modern, democratic state. This task required a strong empathy with its people. In 1906 a champion of the American missionaries praised them for living closely alongside the Chinese: 'Even in many mud-walled villages and rural hamlets missionary families are now to be found quietly and permanently established in homes, in close touch and intimate association with the natives.'[10] While other foreigners were 'cursed' by the Chinese, none had 'anything but pleasant words to speak regarding the missionary enterprise as conducted by Americans'. Such paragons were encouraged by the Xinhai Revolution, which the *New York Times* hailed as a triumph for 'the new spirit of nationalism and patriotism' abroad in China and its fledgling democracy. Readers no doubt remembered that the United States had had such a revolution.

Cynics have remarked that Americans flattered themselves into believing that within each Chinese person there was an American struggling to get out and that they needed all the encouragement they could get.[11] China's old order, with its oppression and suffering, was revealed to Americans by the best-selling novels of Pearl Buck, the daughter of missionaries and a teacher at Nanjing University. Her *The Good Earth*

(1931) told the story of Wang Lung, a poor peasant farmer/rickshaw driver, and his family who strive to survive in an adverse world. His children are forced to beg, but their parents' fortune changes thanks to looting during an outbreak of civil chaos. The plunder is turned to cash; he acquires land, an ox and sends his son to a school. Wang Lung also buys a concubine, a reminder of the old, bad China. Yet Buck's narrative of perseverance and eventual reward contained echoes of the American rags-to-riches dream.

The American immigrant's vision of a fortune made in a foreign land had also inspired tens of thousands of Chinese to settle in America. They were not welcome and, during the 1870s, became the target for a populist racist campaign which led to exclusion laws which were extended to Hawaii and the Philippines in 1902. This ban was included in the 1924 Immigration Act which also halted Japanese immigration, a further racial insult that was bitterly resented in Tokyo.

There were similar reactions to Asian immigration in Australia which, between 1800 and 1875, became home to 70,000 Chinese. Efforts to curtail Chinese immigration to Australia grew during the 1880s and were opposed by the Foreign Office because they were bound to sour relations between Britain and the Chinese government. Whitehall could not, however, overrule the wishes of Australian voters. In 1901 the dominion government passed an Immigration Act that barred Chinese and laid the basis for the 'White Australia' policy. Canada too attempted to enforce a similar ban on Chinese immigrants by levying a tax of $50 a head, which quickly rose to $500 in 1903. More than forty years of white man's laws to keep out Chinese and Japanese intensified ethnic animosities.

Treated as a lesser race, the Japanese were also relegated to an inferior maritime status by the 1922 Washington Naval Treaty. This attempt at arms limitation permitted Britain and the United States five battleships each to three for the Japanese. These proportions were maintained by the 1930 London Naval Treaty, which permitted Britain and America ten cruisers each to the Japanese six. In October 1934, Japan repudiated both treaties, as did Italy two years later. Freed of Anglo-American restraints, Japan began a massive shipbuilding pro-gramme, including two 72,000-ton battleships and several aircraft carriers. Sir Robert Craigie, Britain's ambassador in Tokyo, concluded that the new fleet would give Japan 'a feeling of power' which might drive her to embark 'on adventures in the South Pacific'.[12]

It did, but for the time being Japanese aggression was directed against China. Its mainspring was an internal economic crisis, a by-product of the global recession of 1929–31. Japan was hard hit by the widespread adoption of protective tariffs. America, hitherto the recipient of 40 per cent of Japanese exports, imposed import duties in 1930 as did China soon after. The immediate reaction to shrinking overseas markets was the consolidation of Japanese control over Manchuria and its raw materials and industrial capacity. It was renamed Manchukuo and, in 1934, was given a figurehead emperor, Puyi. He had been the last Qing emperor and, aged six, had been deposed by the Xinhai Revolution. Few foreign powers recognised his puppet regime. Not that this troubled Japan, which had left the League of Nations and was now serving notice of its indifference towards collective security. It was, however, conscious of the need for like-minded friends and in 1936 joined Nazi Germany and Fascist Italy in the Anti-Comintern Pact against Russia.

Japan's alignment with the dictators suggests a kindred spirit. Certainly, the Japanese had been impressed by the successes of Hitler and Mussolini, and their friendship might prove valuable in the event of a Russian challenge in Manchuria. Stalin had been urging the CCP to join Chiang Kai-shek in a common front against Japan and had a quarter of a million troops deployed on the Manchurian border.[13]

Opposing Communism was part of a wider creed which gained currency in the 1930s and which focused Japanese minds on future wars of conquest. It imitated Nazism and Fascism by insisting on submission to an authoritarian and omnipotent state. Contemporary newsreels projected images of military parades, displays of mass synchronised gymnastics and uniformed schoolboys marching. Flags were also much in evidence.

Behind the public shows was an ideology whose ingredients were a mystic religion, a sense of ethnic superiority and a willingness to submit to the collective wisdom of generals and admirals. These men willed war in the sense that they convinced the people that it was the true and noble ambition for a chosen race. Total obedience to a divine emperor and the ancient chivalric cult of the samurai blended with modern realpolitik to create a national spirit that would overcome the materialist West and create a new Asia that would look to Japan as its ruler and guide. Consciences were numbed, for, like their counterparts in Europe, the new supermen of the East regarded terror as a legitimate instrument of policy. In 1932, for example, the Kwantung Army occupying Manchuria massacred 3,000 Chinese in Pingdingshan for allegedly hiding resistance fighters.[14]

The officer corps of the Kwantung Army embodied the ethos of Japan's war party, which inexorably gained control of the levers of political power in the early 1930s. Men in uniforms dominated, although soldiers and sailors disagreed as to a grand strategy. Generals favoured waging a war of annexation in China while admirals were intoxicated by a mass seaborne advance southwards which would overwhelm Malaya, the Dutch East Indies, the Philippines and extend westwards into Indo-China and Burma.

Japan's dreams of imperial conquest were the nightmares of British and American statesmen and strategists. Britain's regional resources were incapable of either deterring or blocking Japanese aggression in China. In 1930 the chiefs of staff feared that Britain's military position in the Far East was 'about as bad as it could be'. Hong Kong was judged highly vulnerable to Japanese seaborne assault and air raids launched from bases in Formosa. In the event of the Japanese occupying southern China, the colony would face a landward attack. Local defences were regularly updated, including an airfield and extended fieldworks known as the 'Gin Drinkers Line'.

Between 1936 and 1940, £3.9 million was spent by the British government on preparations for a siege. There were also unrealistic hopes that France and China might spring to Britain's help and assist in the defence of Hong Kong.[15] The colony's capture would obviously blight British prestige and the Foreign Office was pessimistic about its survival. Nonetheless, it was hoped that Japan had enough on its hands defeating China while keeping sufficient troops in reserve to counter the threat posed by the large Soviet army on the frontier of Manchuria.[16]

Britain's Far Eastern interests and colonies now rested on the Singapore strategy. This had evolved in response to the correct assumption that at some future date Japan was bound to launch its large-scale southward thrust to take Malaya, Indo-China, the Dutch East Indies and the Philippines. This seaborne advance would be blocked by the island fortress of Singapore, whose defences were completed in 1938.

Singapore would be able to hold out for up to five months, in which time an armada would steam through the Mediterranean, traverse the Suez Canal and proceed across the Indian Ocean to relieve it. During or soon after this voyage the fleet would engage and defeat the IJN. But this strategy to save Singapore depended on a benevolently neutral Italy allowing passage through the Mediterranean, which after 1935 was increasingly unlikely.

The United States had devised a similar strategy in 1911 known as 'Plan Orange'. In the event of a Japanese attack on the Philippines, a fleet based in Pearl Harbor would shatter the enemy in a single, decisive battle. Such an engagement would have pleased Admiral Tōgō, the hero of Tsushima, who in 1925 admitted that he hated Americans and would welcome 'another Tsushima' in which he would 'annihilate' the American navy as he had done the Russian.[17] Like Britain, America would fight Japan only if and when its possessions were directly endangered. In the meantime, China was left to fight alone.

# 14

## Japan Is Now Bullying Us: Appeasement in China, 1937–1939

When Neville Chamberlain became prime minister in May 1937 the British Empire was showing symptoms of its future liquidation. The will to govern and act as a global superpower was still strong in London. Yet, as the Sino-Japanese War would brutally demonstrate, resolve without power was not enough to sustain old supremacies.

The empire was in Chamberlain's blood. His father Joseph had been a pugnacious and acquisitive colonial secretary forty years before; Neville had spent his early manhood struggling and failing to run a sisal plantation in the Bahamas; and the Conservative Party he led was dedicated to imperial integrity and security. Chamberlain and his Cabinet faced the same problem that had troubled his father's generation: how to be strong everywhere. Then, the solution vis-à-vis Asia had been an alliance with Japan, but since 1922 Japan had been a hostile rival.

Between 1937 and 1939 the Japanese armies overran nearly half a million square miles of eastern and coastal China and killed 800,000 Chinese soldiers. Wherever the Japanese raised their flag, measures were taken to impede Britain's trade and diminish her prestige. This was just the beginning, for Japan's military cabal was already laying plans for a grand sea, land and air offensive against British, French, Dutch and American possessions in the Far East and Pacific.

Covert operations were under way to create fifth columns in the countries earmarked for conquest. Intelligence reports flowed into Whitehall with evidence of widespread Japanese subversion in Malaya, Burma and the Dutch East Indies. Japanese cruise tourists taking snapshots of the defences of Aden suggested that Tokyo was considering a challenge to Britain in the Indian Ocean, where the Royal Navy had ruled the waves since the Napoleonic Wars. In November 1938 Tokyo proclaimed the arrival of a 'new order' in Asia, which would embrace China and exclude Britain.

In normal times Britain might have responded to Japan without much difficulty. In 1898, when the elder Chamberlain had held sway in the Colonial Office, Britain had seen off a French challenge in Sudan by talking tough and mobilising the fleet. Such belligerent measures were no longer possible, for Britain had become entangled in the fissile power politics of Europe and was contriving ways in which to frustrate Mussolini's attempts to challenge her historic dominance of the Mediterranean. The Duce's daydreams had dire implications for Britain's Singapore strategy, which relied on a massive armada steaming through the Mediterranean and the Suez Canal.

The Japanese knew about the Singapore plan. One of the more disturbing intelligence reports which reached the Admiralty early in 1938 was an account of a conversation between a 'tipsy' IJN officer and an officer of the Australian naval reserve. The Japanese declared that his country had to fight England, would move swiftly, strike hard, take Singapore and destroy the relief force.[1]

Whether or not this decisive battle would occur depended on events in Europe. This had been acknowledged as early as 1935 by the chief of the Imperial General Staff, the splendidly named Field Marshal Sir Archibald Montgomery-Massingberd. Writing on the future defence of Hong Kong, he warned that 'The situation in Europe might not permit Britain to despatch large bodies of reinforcements to Asia.' This truth overshadowed British foreign and imperial policy for the next five years and goes a long way to explaining Chamberlain's position during the Munich Crisis in September 1938. His famous or, according to one's prejudices, infamous reference to 'a quarrel in a faraway country between people of whom we know nothing' may be an oblique reference to the dangers Britain faced in countries that the British people knew well and to which they were emotionally attached – Hong Kong, Malaya and Australia.

At Munich, the prime minister had gained a respite in which Britain could both secure time in which to rearm *and* somehow retrieve her former power and influence in the Far East and China. Allowing Hitler to occupy the Sudetenland in return for a promise of no further annexations did not, however, satisfy the Führer's land hunger, for he snatched what was left of Czechoslovakia in March 1939. Chamberlain's failed bargain did, on the other hand, enable Britain to settle two outstanding and vexatious imperial problems. Operations against Arab insurgents in Palestine (secretly urged on by

Mussolini) were successfully terminated, as was a major uprising on the North-West Frontier. Together these campaigns had tied down 110,000 British and Indian troops.

Munich also briefly removed another irksome imperial distraction. It was warmly welcomed in Australia, where local politicians were becoming jittery about the possibility of a Japanese seaborne invasion. Canberra's demands for naval reinforcements ceased. So too did London's fears that Australian troops might not appear, as they had in 1914, to defend the Suez Canal.

The demand for imperial forces became increasingly urgent after March 1939 when Britain and France agreed to defend Poland, Hitler's next target. As for the Far East, the outlook was increasingly bleak. A Foreign Office memo to the Admiralty predicted the imminent collapse of British power in the face of Japan's 'new order in East Asia'. 'Either in combination with Germany and Italy, or even alone' Japan was now 'a formidable threat to British interests throughout the Eastern hemisphere'.[2] Yet Japan was in no hurry. The generals and admirals in Tokyo were closely observing the events in Europe which would ultimately dictate when, if at all, the great Pacific and South-East Asia gambit would begin. The key factors in Japan's calculations were the course of the likely war between Britain and Germany and the stance taken by the Soviet Union.

While Britain endeavoured to rein in Hitler, China was losing a war. She lacked allies, although both Britain and Russia were willing to offer Chiang Kai-shek weapons and funds. Each had strong but selfish reasons to prevent China from becoming a Japanese colony. As ever, Britain was safeguarding her economic interests. In 1936 British investments in China were worth over £1,200 million, one-eighth of which were government loans. Shanghai and the rest of China's treaty ports were home to 13,000 British subjects, mostly engaged in commerce, although more and more Chinese were being employed in the higher echelons of business.

Local investment in British businesses was also rising: 90 per cent of the shares in Jardine Matheson's offshoot the Ewo Cotton and Spinning Company were Chinese.[3] The numbers of Chinese employed by the CMCS also increased, which prompted complaints that 'the flabbiness of the Chinese mind' rendered them unreliable.[4] Crude racial stereotypes persisted well into the period when Britain's relations with China were slowly shifting from domination towards a mutually enriching partnership.

Overturning Britain's economic position in China and eroding her prestige were central to Japan's strategy. Tariffs were placed on British imports, which fell from £4.1 million in the first half of 1937 to £1.9 million in the second half of 1938.[5] Japanese commanders repeatedly flouted the conventions of the treaty ports, rode roughshod over the rights hitherto enjoyed by foreigners and hindered British commerce. In the international quarter of Shanghai Chinese hands were prevented from working in British factories.

These incidents provoked outrage in the press and the Commons.[6] Official responses took the form of requests for apologies which were usually ignored by Tokyo. In December 1937, newspaper reports of injuries to British commercial interests in Guangzhou and the bombing of civilian targets were raised in the Commons and dismissed by that instinctive temporiser R.A. Butler, the under-secretary at the Foreign Office. He repeated the Japanese claim that the targets were railway facilities and added that he was waiting for further information.[7] The more forceful foreign secretary, Anthony Eden, regretted that Britain could no longer 'effectively assert white-race authority in the Far East'.[8]

The instruments of this authority were attacked in December 1938, when Japanese artillery and aircraft bombed and strafed the gunboats HMS *Bee* and *Ladybird* when they came to the help of the USS *Panay* which was escorting oil tankers bound for Nanjing.* An embarrassed Japan paid $2 million in compensation; Britain was fobbed off with another apology.

No one in Whitehall believed in a Chinese victory. The best that could be hoped for was that Chiang Kai-shek's armies would grind down the Japanese in a war of attrition on a vast battlefield while guerrilla bands played havoc with their extended lines of communication. For this to happen, Britain had to offer assistance in the form of credit that would allow the Chinese to buy arms and equipment. This was what Chiang wanted and, in November 1938, he warned Britain that the war was eroding her position and prestige in China by not providing the credit. He promised that his country would repay its war debts once the Japanese had been defeated.[9]

---

* British gunboats on the China station were named after insects: the crew of HMS *Cockchafer* were the victims of much lower-deck ribaldry.

Aid to China and what form it might take was discussed by the Cabinet during the early summer of 1938, but no decision was reached by ministers distracted by the Czech crisis. After Munich, attention returned to Chinese affairs. Logistics came first. Since the Japanese blocked all sea lanes to China, the land route northwards from Burma was the only feasible way of supplying the Nationalist army. In November Britain agreed to construct a railway branch line from Rangoon via the junction at Lashio to Kunming. The track and rolling stock were to be made in the United States. This railway would supplement the Burma Road, which had been started in 1937 and had just opened to traffic. It ran for over 700 miles across forested mountains and also terminated at Kunming.

After much debate and an unsuccessful attempt to secure funds from the United States, the Cabinet decided in March 1939 to underwrite £5 million in loans to China from British banks. This staved off the collapse of the Chinese currency and included £500,000 for the purchase of trucks to carry war material along the Burma Road.[10] Britain had taken the plunge: it had given China a fragile lifeline which might stave off total defeat.

For the past two years Britain had been secretly providing Chiang's forces with intelligence gathered from signals intercepted and decoded by the listening station in Hong Kong. Permission was granted for Chinese military intelligence to set up their own interception unit in Hong Kong. China's secret service was also allowed to operate inside Hong Kong, but Chiang's spooks were soon expelled for abusing their remit by pursuing his political enemies, some of whom were kidnapped and murdered.[11]

British public and press opinion favoured China. The Japanese were regarded as aggressors whose moral code was that might was right, and the militarist regime in Tokyo was compared with its counterparts in Berlin and Rome. Cinema audiences watched footage which showed air raids, the ruins of bombed cities, sword-brandishing Japanese officers and 'panic-stricken refugees' with their carts and baggage pouring into besieged Shanghai. One commentary reminded British cinemagoers that British subjects in the city risked a stray bullet if they dared to walk the streets.[12]

The collective inhumanity and skewed morality of all ranks of the Japanese army were revealed by American and British journalists and European onlookers who witnessed the atrocities committed after the fall of Nanjing in December 1937. Japanese soldiers ran amok, slaughtering Chinese POWs and civilians and raping women and young girls. No one counted the dead or the violated: Chinese estimates ran to over 200,000. Despite Japanese censorship of outward telegrams, details of the mass murders and rapes reached the rest of the world. *The Times* published some in mid-December and Harold Timperley, a *Manchester Guardian* correspondent who was on the spot, filed copy and produced a book (*Japanese Terror in China*) in November 1938.

In 1946 the Allied War Crimes Commission trial showed that the responsibility for the Nanjing massacres and mass rapes lay with the commander of the Central Army Area, General Iwane Matsui, a fervent nationalist. He was found guilty and hanged alongside sixteen other officers, including a lieutenant who boasted that he had killed 100 Chinese with his sword. The convicted men were said to have sung hymns to Emperor Hirohito before their execution.

Post-war Japan has been host to massacre deniers and nationalist historians who have reduced the death toll by two-thirds or more.[13] Number-counting revisionism changes nothing: the driving force behind the atrocities was Japanese imperialism. What happened in Nanjing revealed Japan's true nature to the people of Britain, just as the outrages of the *Kristallnacht* a year later exposed the true nature of Nazism.

Stalin shared Britain's alarm at Japan's invasion of China, but he sniffed advantages in a war between a historic rival and a country where Russia had long sought territory and influence. Stalin, who had once described himself as a sort of tsar, was keen to play the old Far Eastern Great Game.

In the 1930s Russia became involved in the volatile politics of Xinjiang on China's far-western frontier. Its governor, the virtually independent and ambitious warlord Shicai Sheng, looked to Moscow for support and patronage. He repeatedly announced his conversion to Communism, welcomed Soviet technicians and advisers, and badgered Moscow with requests for a loan. He might have been one of Lenin's 'useful fools', but he did present an opportunity for Russia to obtain indirect control over a frontier region that had attracted Tsar Alexander II's empire builders sixty years before. In 1938 Shicai went to Moscow, where he was privileged to meet Stalin and Molotov. Their conversations embraced the future of Xinjiang, its racial profile, potential resources and whether it was home to any Trotskyites. Shicai again expressed his wish to join the Communist Party and also touched on Soviet assistance in holding down Xinjiang's restless Muslim population.[14]

The upshot was an influx of Soviet military, political and economic advisers in Xinjiang, which now seemed to be well on the path to becoming a Soviet protectorate. This episode has not been forgotten by Chinese leadership today, which treats Xinjiang's Muslims as a disloyal fifth column.

Stalin's crab-like penetration of Xinjiang contrasted with his direct and forceful policy against Japan. Her victory would imperil Russia's standing and possessions in the Far East and frustrate any plan to secure Manchuria, now a Japanese satellite. There were also well-justified fears that the hardliners in Tokyo might extend the war in China as part of an ideological campaign to extinguish Communism throughout Asia. Moscow had much to lose if Japan prevailed in China.

Russian moral support for Chiang's army was immediately forth-coming with pressure on Mao's Communists, who were ordered to create a united, apolitical front against Japan. Russia soon became Chiang's arsenal, supplying fighters, tanks and field artillery, and 2,000 Russian pilots offered their service to the Nationalist air force.[15] In July 1938, when Chinese resistance was flagging, Stalin ordered an advance southwards from Vladivostok to force Japan to divert troops from southern China. At the Battle of Zhangufen, 20,000 Soviet troops trounced 2,000 Japanese, who hurriedly sent troops northwards to counter this unexpected threat.

In July 1939 a headstrong knot of Japanese officers of the Kwantung Army launched a pre-emptive and unauthorised offensive against Soviet forces in Mongolia. They dreamed of overthrowing Communism in Asia, but were either unaware of or indifferent to Soviet strength. Stalin had an army of 250,000 stationed along the Mongolian frontier, well backed by tanks and artillery and supported by between 700 and 1,000 fighters and bombers. Brilliantly commanded by General Georgi Zhukov, this force thrashed the Japanese at the Battle of Khalkhin Gol, in which 20,000 Japanese were killed and 41,000 wounded and cap-tured. Japan sought and got a peace; an outright victory in China was proving elusive and a war with Russia might render it unobtainable.

Zhukov had exploded the myth of Japanese invincibility, and Stalin continued to maintain a quarter of a million men on Russia's Far

Eastern frontier as a deterrent against further Japanese offensives. None occurred, and Stalin was free to concentrate on how to neutralise Germany, his enemy in the West.

Realpolitik might have led Britain and Russia to co-operate in saving China, but recent history ruled out any such accord. For Stalin, the British Empire represented a determined, stubborn, devious and resourceful adversary of Communism everywhere. For their part, the Conservative governments which were in power for most of the interwar years treated Russia as a brutal pariah state in pursuit of worldwide mischief. Moreover, the current balance of world power meant that any Anglo-Russian entente would nudge Tokyo towards Germany and Italy.

In June 1939, a series of provocative incidents in the foreign concessions in Shanghai and Tianjin (where the British authorities had been accused of helping Chinese terrorists) forced London to consider a robust response. Insults to British subjects stirred up newspaper demands for retaliation, but simmering tensions in Europe ruled out any serious sabre-rattling. If a naval force was ordered from the Mediterranean to the Far East, then Italy and Germany would quickly take advantage. Britain temporised and the *China Express* called the affair 'another Munich agreement'.[16] It was an instructive affirmation of the new status quo in China. Impotent gloom pervaded the Foreign Office. Oliver Harvey, secretary to Lord Halifax, the foreign secretary, noted in his diary that 'Japan is now bullying us. If we are weak again with Japan, we shall have Hitler and Mussolini beating us up.'

There were, however, flickers of hope in Whitehall. From 1937 onwards, Britain had reluctantly looked to the United States for a solution to the problem of China. America was perceived to be the only possible ally, for it possessed the economic and naval muscle to rein in Japan, rescue China and restore local British political and economic influence. This assumption lay behind a proposal made by Chamberlain at the end of 1937 for an Anglo-American display of naval force that would assemble at Singapore. President Roosevelt rejected this grand-scale gunboat diplomacy. His refusal confirmed feelings within the Foreign Office that the United States was perverse and unreliable. 'It is always safest to count on nothing from the Americans but words,' was Chamberlain's conclusion.[17]

Americans saw the world differently from the British. In March 1939 Senator Arthur Capper from Kansas told the Senate that he had received 700 letters from the 'small towns' of America. His correspondents loathed the 'ruthless barbarity' of the Japanese and the Nazis, but recoiled from war waged against either. Nor was there then or later much political enthusiasm for risking American lives to prop up the British Empire, from which the United States had broken free in 1783. Furthermore, a war against Japan would damage the American economy, still recovering from a recession and, in 1938–39, possibly facing another. Exports to Japan in 1937–38 totalled $150 million. American aviation fuel powered the bombers that had blitzed Chinese cities and towns and American scrap iron found its way into Japanese munitions factories.[18] As the heroically taciturn President Calvin Coolidge had observed a decade before: 'The Business of America is Business.'

Senator Capper would have been proud to have called himself an 'isolationist' who was expressing the deeply held views of millions of his countrymen and women. Isolationism was a complex phenomenon. It had nothing to do with pacifism. Americans were perfectly happy for marines to storm ashore in Haiti, Guatemala and Honduras to protect Wall Street's investments and corporate assets from local left-leaning revolutionaries. Few Americans objected to their gunboats shelling Chinese towns in response to threats to American lives and property.

Isolationism was about staying aloof from Europe and not repeating intervention in any war whose origins lay in the chicaneries and bellicose rivalries of the European powers. America had done so in 1917 and had lost blood and money for no gain. Worse still, the First World War had not chastened the rulers of Europe who, by the mid-1930s, were returning to the bad old ways. Faced with this recidivism, a majority of Americans would have applauded the novelist John Dos Passos who insisted that 'Rejection of Europe is what America is all about.'

However, those who agreed with Dos Passos were never wholly indifferent to what was happening in Europe and China. This would have been very hard in the face of newsreels and press reports from Germany, Italy and the war zones of Abyssinia, Spain and China. Americans were deeply shocked by what they saw and read. A Gallup poll of 1939 revealed that 95 per cent of them detested the mendacity and brutality of the Third Reich. Yet moral repulsion did not dissolve isolationist sentiments, for it was widely felt that Britain's navy and the French army could somehow stop Hitler if it came to a European war.[19]

Americans were also horrified by Japan's campaign in China. *Time* magazine, owned by Henry Luce, the son of a China missionary, printed vivid and partisan accounts of China's struggle against the 'violent Jingoes of the Japanese Army' and the 'fanatical clique' in Tokyo. Readers were made to feel that this was their war fought in their cities and countryside. Hankou was 'the Chicago of China' and Shanghai 'the New York City of China', and its defence in 1937 made it 'the Chinese Alamo'.[20] To such emotional appeals were added the warnings of hard-nosed naval officials in Washington disturbed by the growing strength of the IJN.

Practical assistance to China had been effectively ruled out by Congress's two Neutrality Acts in 1935 and 1936 which outlawed the exports of arms and ammunition to countries engaged in a war. The raw materials of war such as oil were excluded. The hands of Roosevelt and his advisers were, therefore, tied when it came to policy decisions on China: moral support and sympathy were freely available, but bombers and tanks were not.

President Roosevelt was a humane man who wanted his country to thrive in a stable world in which free trade was universal. He fruitlessly attempted to sponsor peace conferences in which goodwill would somehow eliminate international tensions. This was why the British government, which thought in terms of realpolitik, dismissed him as a woolly-minded idealist. Roosevelt also tended to postpone tough decisions. This became more and more difficult between 1937 and 1939, when the world was daily growing more volatile and dangerous. Nevertheless, a large number of Americans still grasped the isolationist comfort blanket even though it was wearing thin and frayed at the edges.

The Sino-Japanese War was low on Roosevelt's list of foreign policy priorities. Washington was well aware of Tokyo's plans for a great southward offensive whose targets included the Philippines, but was uncertain as to whether Japan would ever find the will or resources for such an enterprise. The president laid down new warships, including aircraft carriers, but did nothing to impede or provoke Japan. Under Roosevelt's guidance, America would wait, watch and avoid any action that might force the hand of the generals and admirals in Tokyo. This policy was a hostage to political fortune; early in 1941 the House

Un-American Activities Committee accused Roosevelt's administration of being 'lax, tolerant and soft towards the Japanese'.

The increasingly volatile state of Europe was a different matter, and one which urgently demanded the president's attention. From March 1939, Britain and France were pledged to fight a war if Hitler invaded Poland and there was every likelihood that Italy would join in on the Führer's side. The outcome of this conflict was far from clear, but the possibility of an Axis victory brought with it a direct strategic threat to the United States. The German and Italian navies would be supplemented by ships taken from Britain and France, which together could outgun America's Atlantic Fleet. Her eastern seaboard could only be guaranteed by transferring ships from the Pacific, which would be a spur to further Japanese aggression. The United States already had a compelling reason to back the Allies if and when war broke out.

Like the United States, Japan was also closely watching developments in Europe and making strategic calculations based on the result of a war between the Allies and the Axis. The defeat of the former would facilitate the occupation of British and French colonies in the Far East. Tokyo also speculated on a victorious Germany turning on her ideological foe, the Soviet Union. At a stroke, this would remove the Russian threat to Manchuria and cut Russian assistance to China. Stalin, faced with the possibility of a war on two fronts against formidable adversaries, plumped for a non-aggression pact with Germany which was hurriedly negotiated at the end of August 1939. Less than a week later, the Germans invaded Poland and found themselves at war with Britain and France. For the next nine months, battles fought in Europe would dictate events in China and the Far East.

# 15

## We Cannot Risk Another War: The Road to Pearl Harbor

The year 1940 was a bad one for China. Her armies were bogged down in an unwinnable war against a better-led and -armed adversary. By now, nearly 90 per cent of China's economic capacity was in Japan's hands, along with her major ports and industrial cities.[1] Japanese warplanes dominated China's skies, and air raids on Chongqing, Chiang Kai-shek's capital, increased in number and ferocity. In one attack a squadron of the new and devastating Mitsubishi Zeros shot down twenty-seven Soviet-built fighters.

Yet the pace of the Japanese advance was slackening, and its technical superiority did not compensate for stalemate on the ground and distended lines of communication. Tokyo tentatively turned towards a political solution of a kind that would soon be adopted by Germany in occupied Europe: the imposition of puppet regimes manned by closely supervised locals. In March Japan sponsored a quisling administration based in the former capital, Nanjing, and headed by a turncoat Nationalist politician, Wang Jingwei.

In July 1940, the Nationalist army's logistics were hamstrung when Britain closed the Burma Road. This desperate measure was adopted because, like China, Britain was in a precarious position. A German invasion army was mustering across the English Channel and the RAF was struggling to secure the superiority in the air that would be vital in preventing a landing on the south coast. The Battle of Britain meant little to Chiang Kai-shek, for whom cutting off supplies from Burma was a further example of British perfidy. 'Our name is mud in China' reported Sir Stafford Cripps, the vegetarian, chain-smoking Labour MP who visited Chongqing as part of a global fact-finding mission.

Events in Europe provided unsought advantages for Japan. Between April and June, Hitler's war machine successively overwhelmed and occupied Norway, Denmark, the Netherlands, Luxembourg, Belgium and

France. This string of victories persuaded Tokyo to join the winning side, and in September Japan joined the Axis but prudently offered its partners no pledges as to exactly when it would begin hostilities against Britain. This decision was dependent on the outcome of Hitler's widely expected invasion of Russia.

In the meantime, Japan reaped the fruits of Hitler's conquests. During July and August, Tokyo shifted troops from southern China across the border into French Indo-China, which was now under the thumb of Marshal Pétain's pro-Nazi regime based at Vichy. Garrisons were installed and eight airfields levelled in what quickly became a de facto Japanese colony and a forward base for future operations against Malaya.

The fall of the Netherlands offered a potential opportunity for Japan which, in May, sent a mission to Batavia (now Jakarta), the capital of the Dutch East Indies, with a request for higher quotas of oil. In 1938, the colony's oilfields had exported 6 million tons oil, of which 38 per cent went to Japan.[2] However, local authorities refused, with the backing of the London-based Dutch government in exile. No further pressure was exerted and Japan was compelled to continue relying upon the United States, which provided 53 per cent of her needs. Henceforward, Japan's ruling military and naval cabal was increasingly bedevilled by the problem of securing a dependable source of fuel for the warships and aircraft that would undertake offensives in South-East Asia and the Pacific.

For Britain, 1940 was a year of apprehension and heroic defiance. Its events have been transformed into a national epic with a blend of patriotism and drama akin to that of Shakespeare's *Henry V*, with Winston Churchill in the role of the king. Suffice it to say that under his inspiration and direction, Britain was able to rescue much of its stranded army from Dunkirk, secure mastery of her airspace, avert a seaborne invasion and achieve a wartime level of productivity that soon outstripped Germany's. Thanks to Churchill's foresight and perseverance, Britain moved closer towards the United States, which was persuaded that it was in her interest to become the country's banker and armourer.

Britain was never 'alone' in 1940 as some romantics still imagine. It was supported by the white dominions, India and the colonies. Canadian infantrymen stood alongside the Home Guard to defend her coastline and Australian, New Zealand, Indian and later African soldiers fought in the Middle and Far Eastern campaigns. As Hitler recognised, the British Empire was still a force to be reckoned with. Nonetheless, he imagined that once Russia had been defeated Britain would throw in the towel.

Defending the empire lay at the heart of Churchill's strategy once the invasion threat had diminished. From late June it was under direct land, air and sea assault by Mussolini who, in the wake of Hitler's victories, declared war on Britain. His aim was to replace her as the dominant power in the Mediterranean, the Middle East and East Africa. Fascist Italy was a more pressing and greater threat than expansionist Japan, for its prime target was Egypt and with it the Suez Canal. The last was the hub of imperial communications whose loss would cut the strategic and commercial lifeline that connected Britain with India, the Far East and the Pacific. For the next three years securing the Suez Canal and restoring naval paramountcy in the Mediterranean were two of Britain's prime strategic goals. The third was defeating the U-boats whose operations imperilled the supply of American war material shipped across the Atlantic.

Stiffening Chinese resistance was low on Britain's list of strategic priorities, even though China was now an unofficial ally, insofar as its armies were tying down Japanese forces that might otherwise be deployed in invading Britain's Far Eastern and Pacific empire. Once Enigma decrypts had revealed Hitler's postponement of the invasion of Great Britain, the Foreign Office decided to reopen the Burma Road. In mid-September, the foreign secretary, Lord Halifax, put China's case to the Cabinet and urged his listeners 'to stand up to the Japanese as firmly as would be consistent with being able to back down at the last moment'. This reversion to pre-war policy worried Churchill and he warned that 'we cannot afford another war'. There seemed little chance of this since the British ambassador in Tokyo reported that the Japanese 'wouldn't risk war in light of a victory in the Battle of Britain' and the possibility of America coming to Britain's aid.[3] Churchill and the Cabinet agreed and in October traffic began to move along the Burma Road.

Official British opinion of Japan was a melange of foreboding as to her ambitions and contempt as to her capacity to fulfil them. Sir Alexander Cadogan, the permanent under-secretary at the Foreign Office, dismissed the Japanese as 'dwarf slaves' who would never dare challenge America's navy. His colleague R.A. Butler imagined that Japan's aggressive spirit would evaporate at the slightest display of British resolve and suggested that sending a battlecruiser and an aircraft carrier to Ceylon would deter Tokyo from further aggression. Senior military and naval staff officers agreed, and Churchill viewed the Japanese as 'the wops' (Italians) of the Far East.[4] Racism permeated the Whitehall mind.

Misconceived notions of genetic superiority could not hide the truth that Britain was no longer capable of both defending its historic power in the Middle East and protecting Hong Kong, Malaya and Australia from Japanese aggression. Only the United States could do this, and Churchill pleaded with Roosevelt to convince Tokyo that the Pacific would remain an American lake and Europe's Far Eastern colonies were inviolate. Or, as the prime minister pungently expressed it, 'keep that Japanese dog quiet in the Pacific'.

Throughout 1940 and early 1941, Japan was concerned with the future activity of another beast, the Russian bear. Stalin still kept huge forces on the frontier with Manchuria which had just proved themselves more than a match for the Japanese garrison. By early 1941, he was preoccupied by the frightening prospect of wars on two distant fronts, one in Europe against Germany and the other in the Far East against Hitler's ally, Japan. Tokyo faced a similar quandary: how to defend Manchuria and wage a large-scale war against Britain and China (very likely with American assistance) in South-East Asia and the Pacific.

Stalin resolved Japan's dilemma. He and the Japanese foreign minister, Yōsuke Matsuoka, agreed a Russo-Japanese non-aggression pact in the Kremlin in April 1941. This largely forgotten accord would have an enormous impact on the course of the war in Europe and Asia. Its signing was celebrated with a drinking bout. Stalin, briefly forgetting Russia's aid to Chiang Kai-shek, expressed his support for Japan in China. This carouse included many toasts; before one Stalin told his guest: 'You are an Asiatic. So am I', and proposed the toast 'We are all Asiatics. Let's drink to the Asiatics.'[5] The way to Pearl Harbor was now theoretically open, but the Japanese high command preferred caution and waited to see how the Germans fared in Russia. Their invasion began on 22 June and, like the previous year's Blitzkrieg, astonished the world by its speed, ruthlessness and success.

*

The United States could never have allowed Britain and her empire to fall into German, Italian and Japanese hands. Such a catastrophe would have shattered a global economic equilibrium which, on the whole, favoured America. Protectionist powers would have seized raw materials and closed markets for American industry and investment. Furthermore, an Axis victory would have meant a new global dispensation of military power to America's severe disadvantage. This was the theme of Roosevelt's 'Fireside Chat' to the American people broadcast at the end of December 1940. 'The Axis powers will control the continents of Europe, Asia, Africa, Australia and the high seas – and they will be in a position to bring enormous military and naval resources against this hemisphere.' America could never have risked a policy of strict neutrality, although the president did hope that he could steer a course that would postpone entry into the war for as long as possible. In the meantime, and through the mechanisms of Lend-Lease, the United States undertook to fund and arm Britain and then Russia.

Benevolent neutrality was also extended to China, but on a minute scale, even after Pearl Harbor. During 1941 and 1942, China received $126 million in Lend-Lease, a mere 1.5 per cent of the total, in return for tying down 600,000 Japanese troops.[6] A permanent American military mission of advisers with a war chest of $45 million was also sent to Chongqing in February 1941, a physical reminder that America had replaced embattled Britain as the patron and paymaster of Nationalist China.

Beefing up Chiang Kai-shek made sense in Washington, where policy-makers were already contemplating a post-war world in which the United States would replace Britain as the global superpower. It was time for the American eagle to stretch its wings, sharpen its talons and soar over the world. Recent events had indicated that its predecessor, the British lion, had become a weary and arthritic beast with a muted roar.

A handful in Washington discreetly believed that there was no place in an American-dominated world for Europe's old empires. Roosevelt was sympathetic, although he was careful not to push his views too far with Churchill. This process was already under way in China, with Chiang Kai-shek now an America protégé. American policy was also aimed at Japanese imperialism, with the aim of stopping it from engrossing the British and French territorial empires in South-East Asia and the Pacific. Diplomatic assurances had been given to the Australian government that America would defend them from a Japanese invasion.

In October 1941, the new Labour prime minister of Australia, John Curtin, declared that 'Australians look to America, freed from any pangs as to our traditional links with the United Kingdom'. Churchill the realist acquiesced and in the same month told the Cabinet that 'We ought to regard the United States as having taken charge in the Far East. It is for them to take the lead in this area and we should support them.'[7]

To preserve China, America had first to curtail and reverse the expansion of Japan's empire. The theory was that if Japan was treated as a supplicant state, it would acknowledge American superiority and knuckle under. This policy and the assumptions behind it were summed up by Henry L. Stimson, soon to be Roosevelt's secretary of war: 'Japan has historically shown that when the United States indicates by clear language and bold actions that she intends to carry out a clear and affirmative policy in the Far East, Japan will yield to that policy, even though it conflicts with her own Asiatic policy and conceived interests.'[8] These condescending words might well have been uttered by a British statesman with reference to China 100 years before.

Stimson's remedy was applied between July 1940 until late November 1941. Japan was confronted with demands to withdraw from China and jettison plans for any southward advance. An adamantine policy was enforced by economic measures designed to deprive Japan of the means to wage war. Thus her virtual occupation of Indo-China in July 1940 provoked a ban on imports of American aviation fuel and scrap iron and steel. In December iron ore and pig iron were added to the list. The final push was made in July 1940, when Roosevelt cut off all supplies of oil, depriving Japan of more than 90 per cent of her supply. In the meantime, America's rearmament and conscription programmes were accelerated in readiness for a war which the president believed was now unavoidable.

Curbing Japan's capacity to fight a war did not weaken her will to wage one. Her rulers were aware that her industrial capacity was far smaller than America's and that an arms race was out of the question. Japan was feeling the strain of wartime expenditure which, by 1938, already consumed 70 per cent of the national budget. The July oil embargo meant that it was now imperative for Japan to seize the Dutch East Indies. Submission was unthinkable for the proud and self-confident admirals and generals who shaped Japan's war strategy, which left audacity as the only alternative. In October 1941, the Cabinet of

General Tojo ('the Razor') Hideki, an unbending imperialist and the new prime minister, prepared detailed plans for a rapid sequence of aerial and amphibious offensives that would simultaneously neuter the US navy and overwhelm Hong Kong, Malaya, the Dutch East Indies, the Philippines and the island colonies of the Western Pacific. This whirlwind of pre-emptive strikes would create a new Japanese empire within a few months, and all the oil its war machine needed. A paralysed and demoralised America would be forced to accept a fait accompli. The French, Dutch and British lacked the means to strike back, and the last of these would be distracted by an invasion of Burma launched from a biddable Thailand. In short, Japan would accomplish in Asia what Germany had accomplished in Europe in 1940 and was repeating in Russia.

In late November 1941, a Japanese battle fleet steamed away from its anchorage in the Kuril Islands for its secret voyage towards Pearl Harbor, the base of the US navy's Pacific Fleet. Six aircraft carriers formed the cutting edge of a force whose task was to sink American carriers and battleships and destroy docks, repair yards and fuel depots.* On the morning of 7 December, the battle cry 'Tora! Tora! Tora!' (Tiger! Tiger! Tiger!) launched the air attack which achieved complete surprise. It lasted for a little over an hour, but the results were disappointing: one battleship, the USS *Arizona*, was sunk by a fluke (a bomb hit its magazine), while the remaining eight were either beached or damaged. All were subsequently repaired. The prime targets, the US navy's four carriers, were at sea undertaking exercises. Naval facilities and oil storage tanks remained largely untouched. The balance of sea power in the Pacific had been jolted, but not decisively tilted.

What Roosevelt called a 'dastardly' attack provided an impeccable reason to declare war on Japan and secure massive and wholehearted public support. There was a bonus for the Allied forces when Hitler stuck to his alliance by declaring war on the United States. With hindsight, this seemed quixotic, but it did not appear so at the close of 1941, when German forces occupied swathes of Russia and Britain was barely holding her own in the Middle East. The Axis seemed to be winning the war and Hitler knew next to nothing about the United

* The carrier names were an odd mixture of sentimentality and ferocity: *Kaga* ('Increased Happiness'), *Shokaku* ('Soaring Crane') and *Hiryu* ('Flying Dragon').

States. He rated their officers as 'businessmen in uniform' and believed that America's industrial capacity was 'terribly overestimated'.[9]

News of Pearl Harbor exhilarated Chiang Kai-shek. On the last day of December he broadcast to the Chinese people with a message of hope: 'The confidence of our people in the eventual defeat of Japan is rendered all the more secure.' The current Japanese advances in Malaya were 'a draught of poison to quench thirst' and he reminded listeners that China now fought alongside America, Britain, Russia and Australia.[10] Churchill shared his relief and optimism: according to his war memoirs, after hearing of Pearl Harbor he went to bed certain of victory and 'slept the sleep of the saved and thankful'.

# 16

## What the Hell Is the Matter?: The World Turned Upside Down, 1942–1943

On 9 February 1942 Roosevelt briefed General Joseph ('Vinegar Joe') Stilwell on his duties as chief of staff to Chiang Kai-shek's army. His most urgent task was to 'Tell Chiang that Hitler is the number one enemy.'[1] This was Allied policy, recently agreed with Churchill during their recent meetings in Washington. The war against the Axis in North Africa and then Europe was the Allies' top priority and would remain so until the German surrender in May 1945. In terms of material and manpower, the fronts in China, the Far East and the Pacific were secondary. By way of consolation, the president told Stilwell to assure Chiang that China would regain all her lost territory once Japan had been beaten.

For the next three and a half years China was treated as a junior partner. Chiang resented this subordination and occasionally protested, but his position was weak, for his government and war effort depended on American cash and weaponry. China never enjoyed equality with Britain, Russia and the United States, whose representatives met regularly to hammer out grand strategy and, latterly, the post-war dispensation of world power. Chiang did not appear alongside Churchill, Roosevelt and Stalin at Tehran (November–December 1943), Yalta (February 1945) and Potsdam (July–August 1945). Only once, in November 1943, did Chiang meet Churchill and Roosevelt in Cairo, where their agenda was confined to Asian matters. The generalissimo's request that he join Churchill and Roosevelt at Tehran was refused.[2]

Despite her marginal status, China was expected to pull her weight in the Allied war effort. Making sure she did and ensuring that American funds and equipment were used effectively and according to Washington's wishes were Stilwell's duties. His qualification was his experience as the United States' military attaché to China between 1935 and 1939. His diaries were a chronicle of frustration and exasperation, which revealed his temperamental unfitness for a job that needed tact and patience. He was profane in his speech, overbearing and quarrelsome. He soon took a dislike to Chiang, whom he nicknamed 'the peanut', and he also quickly developed an equal loathing for his British allies, or the 'Limeys' as he called them.

On 18 February 1942, Stilwell's simmering rage boiled over: 'What the hell is the matter?' he wrote in his diary, which was a question being asked at every level of command in Washington, London and across the Far East and the Pacific. Malaya was lost to the Japanese, and with it Singapore, which had just capitulated. Hong Kong had been captured on Christmas Day 1941 and the British colonies of Borneo and Sarawak were overrun in January 1942. The Dutch East Indies (and their oil) were taken in April, and the Japanese completed their conquest of the Philippines by the end of the month. By then, Papua and New Guinea were being invaded and Australians feared that they would be next, although their country was not one of Japan's strategic objectives.[3] Elsewhere in the Western Pacific, the Japanese also secured a scattering of British and American islands. Thailand, having thrown in its lot with Japan, provided a base for a Japanese invasion of Burma which gathered unstoppable momentum during March.

In just under four months, the Japanese equivalent of the Blitzkrieg had shattered Allied armies, navies and air forces. A combination of superiority at sea, in the air and on land and co-ordinated amphibious landings had neutralised American power and amassed an empire that covered 3.3 million square miles and was populated by 463 million subjects, who made up a fifth of the world's population. Japan had engrossed the Far Eastern colonies of France, Britain and the Netherlands, extinguished European power inside China and appeared poised to invade Australia and India. A medical officer stationed on the North-West Frontier remembered a brief time in which preparations were in hand to prepare defences against the Germans advancing from the Caucasus and the Japanese advancing westwards across northern India.[4]

In Berlin, optimism soared. Grand Admiral Erich Raeder prophesied the beginning of the end. 'When Germany and Japan touch hands in the Indian Ocean, the final victory is not far away.'[5] Hitler was less happy, for he viewed Japanese victories in Asia as 'a defeat for the white race'.[6]

*

There was agreement among the stunned Allies that the Japanese had destroyed the old dispensation of power in the Far East and Pacific. The aftershock generated recriminations and speculation. What had gone wrong, who was to blame and why had the old imperial system proved so brittle? Introspection led to speculation about the future of Europe's empires and whether there was any place for them in a post-war world. Roosevelt and many who advised him had already concluded that the empires did not deserve to survive. Churchill disagreed forcibly and twice publicly affirmed that he would never permit the 'liquidation' of the British Empire.

Japan's victories gave Chiang Kai-shek a welcome opportunity for *Schadenfreude*. As the rout began, he told General Sir Archibald Wavell, the commander-in-chief of British, Dutch and Australian forces, that fighting the Japanese was 'not like colonial wars' and 'for this kind of job you British are incompetent'.[7] Britain's misfortunes, he believed, could be exploited to China's advantage. The old imperial order in the Far East was in its death throes and its Japanese replacement would prove transitory. Supported by America, a revived China would fill the vacuum and emerge from the war as a major Asian power. A century of impotence and submission would be reversed and China would assume her rightful place in the world.

Britain's eclipse offered an opportunity to remove all the legal and political shackles of foreign domination within China and give her true independence. In practical terms, the old treaties had been nullified by the Japanese occupation, but in theory they were still binding. British subjects and companies could still seek justice in twenty-six consular courts. Old obligations and inequalities continued to rankle with the Chinese. This resentment was aired by Chiang's American-educated wife Song Mei-ling in the *New York Times* in April 1942. 'By pointing a gun' at China, she argued, the West had piled 'humiliation after humiliation' upon the Chinese.[8] Perpetuating such iniquities had no place in a war being waged for liberty and justice. Among them was the British occupation of Hong Kong, which her husband was raising with the Americans.[9]

By taking a determined stand against imperialism in China, Chiang was bidding for the support of all Asian nationalists. Japan was already courting them with the slogan 'Asia for the Asiatics', which was the mask for a new empire that called itself 'The Pan-Asian Co-prosperity Sphere'. Like the Nazis in Europe, Japan set up quisling regimes in its conquered lands and was happy to partition territory in the old imperial style. Thailand's compliance was rewarded with a slice of Burma and the Malayan sultanates of Kedah and Kelantan. Again following the Nazis, the day-to-day government of Japan's empire was a devil's brew of military rule and extreme brutality.

A chastened Britain reacted to events in the Far East with despair and an urge to uncover individual and collective scapegoats. *The Times* judged the surrender of Singapore as the worst calamity suffered by the British Empire since General Cornwallis's surrender at Yorktown in 1781, which had confirmed the loss of the American colonies. A furious and disconsolate Churchill told the Cabinet that Singapore's capture signalled 'the loss of the white man's prestige'.[10]

Much to the prime minister's displeasure, the Commons held a post-mortem. Culpability was widely scattered and a strong emphasis was placed on negligence and lassitude at the top. One fault that was identified was the failure of the Malayan administration to mobilise Malaya's Chinese community, who were naturally hostile to Japan. Unfavourable comparisons were made with the Philippines, where the inhabitants had rallied to their American rulers and fought bravely against the invaders. In the Commons and beyond there was a strong feeling that the white commercial and administrative community had lacked a sense of touch in their handling of the Malay and Chinese population. Racial aloofness and condescension were commonplace, which may be why, a few years before, Noël Coward had described Malaya as a 'first-rate country for second-rate people'.

Similar criticisms were directed at Hong Kong's elite by an officer of the Middlesex Regiment which was part of the local garrison:

> Regrettable as it may sound, there was perhaps no British Colony which had been inviting disaster for quite so long as Hong Kong. This was due to poor Class and corrupt Government Administration, many old and atrophied Civil Servants, almost total lack of control by the Police, graft, loose living, drink and pleasure loving in every respect, the civilian population both white and coloured had for many years indulged in wishful thinking and had persuaded themselves in a complacent manner that no Japanese would ever come and take Hong Kong.[11]

Nevertheless, the heavily outnumbered garrison put up a gallant defence of Hong Kong. It comprised British, Indian and Canadian troops, the last reinforcements who had just completed their basic training. Towards the end of an eighteen-day battle fought without hope of relief, morale deteriorated.[12] To add to the sense of hopelessness and isolation, Japanese loudspeakers repeatedly played a record of 'Home Sweet Home' to men on the front line.[13] After the surrender, Japanese troops carried out the mass rapes and murders which were now regular occurrences wherever they advanced.

Singapore surrendered on 15 February 1942, and with it the rest of Malaya. As in Hong Kong, the local civil and military authorities were victims of what one observer called 'a dangerously complacent attitude'.[14] One ingredient was an overweening contempt for the enemy. 'Eastern races [are] less able to withstand the strain of war,' concluded General Henry Gordon Bennett *after* Singapore had fallen.[15] He commanded local Australian forces and was among the first to flee the besieged fortress where his men were in a state of mutiny.[16]

Morale had wilted soon after the Japanese had come ashore and advanced swiftly inland and southwards, brushing aside a disorganised resistance. Japan's air force had dominated the skies and her warships had commanded the seas. On 10 December 1941, flights of bombers based in southern Indo-China had sunk the capital ships HMS *Prince of Wales* and *Repulse*, which had been rushed to Singapore to forestall the landings.

The statistics of the Malayan campaign say it all. A 30,000-strong Japanese army had taken prisoner 55,000 British, Indian and Australian troops during the campaign and a further 80,000 had laid down their arms under the surrender terms. These included 15,000 Australians, a quarter of the dominion's army. Thirty thousand dismayed Indian prisoners defected to the Japanese to form the Indian National Army, a force that was earmarked for the liberation of India.

Bungling and slipshod command were also features of the British defence of Burma, which became a retreat through an unkind landscape of mountains and tropical rainforests plagued by mosquitoes. Anglo-Indian forces were reinforced by 70,000 Chinese, paid by the British, who were hurried south from Yunnan to protect supply lines in northern Burma. Stilwell commanded one battalion and found that its officers were 'a bunch of crap'. This experience may have added to his later conviction that the Chinese fighting man had a 'distaste for offensive combat'. The casualties suggested otherwise: in all, the Chinese lost 25,000 defending a British colony and more died falling back to Yunnan. Rangoon fell in March 1942 after a campaign which the British commander General Sir Harold Alexander called 'a complete military defeat'. The Japanese followed up with an advance northwards towards Assam and the Indian frontier. Operations were suspended by the onset of the April–May monsoon.

The loss of Burma was complemented by humiliation at sea. In March and April, a formidable squadron commanded by Admiral Nagumo steamed at will in the Indian Ocean. Carrier-based aircraft attacked Colombo and the naval base at Trincomalee in Ceylon and sank one British aircraft carrier and two cruisers. The remaining British warships in the Indian Ocean withdrew to Kalandini on the East African coast. Defeats were also inflicted in scratch British, American and Dutch squadrons in the waters around the Dutch East Indies.

Australia's response to the fall of Singapore was a heady cocktail of panic and recriminations against Britain. An official wireless broadcast warned that 'We in Australia might expect to be occupied for a considerable time before we are rescued.'[17] A frantic government ordered the 7th Australian Division, then in transit to Egypt, to return home, which angered Churchill. The bombing of Darwin on 19 February 1942 and subsequent air raids added to a sense of foreboding which only disappeared after the arrival of 60,000 American troops. There was a popular feeling that Australia had been left in the lurch by Britain, and there were vinegary exchanges between Churchill and H.V. Evatt, the minister for external affairs. Emotional ties with Britain were restored, while from that point onwards Australians turned to America for security. In 1962 an Australian contingent joined US forces in Vietnam.

Like Australia, India was wobbling. For the past twenty years it had been edging slowly towards self-government at a pace which disappointed nationalists and worried British officials, who still operated the levers of ultimate power. Political tensions increased as the war progressed and, seen from Delhi, were an impediment to India's war effort. The predominant and largely Hindu Congress Party was split between its spiritual guru Mahatma Gandhi, who advocated non-resistance to a Japanese invasion, and its political leader Jawaharlal Nehru, a pragmatist who favoured the Allied cause. Both saw the war as an opportunity to speed up progress towards total independence.

The British thought Chiang could heal this rift and so strengthen India's war effort. He was an Asian nationalist, a friend of Nehru and had spent five years fighting against Japanese imperialism. He was, therefore, invited to India in February 1942 as a mediator.

Chiang and his wife Song Mei-ling were welcomed in Delhi by the viceroy, the Marquess of Linlithgow, with a phrase from Confucius that it was 'delightful to have men of kindred spirit come to one from afar'. The generalissimo answered with another *bon mot* of the philosopher: 'To have a look at things is a hundred times more satisfactory than hearsay.' Driven in a Rolls-Royce, Chiang inspected Indian troops and toured munition factories. He failed to persuade Gandhi to abandon his pacifism and the British refused to hasten Indian independence. Chiang's support for the Indian nationalist movement irritated his hosts, but they did, however, award him an honorary knighthood of the Bath.

Chiang's fruitless excursion to India highlighted divisions among the Allies as to their war aims in the Far East. In August, the generalissimo and his wife continued to urge the British government to grant immediate independence to India and attempted to enlist Roosevelt. Churchill too approached Roosevelt on this subject and asked him to tell Chiang 'to mind his own business'.[18]

Chiang's pretensions as a champion of Asian nationalist movements led to a further extended confrontation with Britain over the future of Hong Kong. Chiang wanted the colony back and looked to his patron Roosevelt for assistance. In August 1941 Roosevelt had persuaded Churchill to agree to sign the Atlantic Charter, which was a death warrant for Europe's colonies, for it promised that after the war, 'all peoples' would enjoy the right 'to choose the form of government under which they live'.

Churchill agreed on the grounds that Britain would be unwise to quarrel with the country that was underwriting the costs of Britain's war effort and supplying her with fuel, aircraft and tanks. In principle, he agreed with the Atlantic Charter so far as it applied to Britain's informal empire in China. On 18 July 1940, he had told the Commons that his government would support 'a free and independent future for China' and was willing to renegotiate the old treaties that had given Britain its extra-territorial rights. Britain was also prepared to make new trade agreements based upon 'reciprocity and quality'.[19] This policy expressed what Foreign Office pragmatists had been proposing before Japan's invasion of China and was warmly endorsed by Roosevelt.

Negotiations on the old one-sided treaties dragged on until October 1943 with much quibbling by Britain's diplomats. Under the new 'equal' accord China secured full diplomatic and legal parity with the British and the old system of special privileges was dissolved. Roosevelt was well pleased: China was now moving along the path to full nationhood. However, discussions on future Anglo-Chinese trade foundered and remained unresolved at the end of the war.

While the old bonds which had constrained China were being loosened, the course of the war had changed decisively in favour of the Allies. In the Pacific, the Battles of the Coral Sea and Midway tilted the balance of sea power against Japan. The way was open for a gruelling campaign, known as 'island-hopping', which pushed back the southern frontier of the Japanese Empire. In the West, the Allies won a sequence of pivotal victories. The Battles of Stalingrad (August 1942–February 1943), El Alamein (October–November 1942) and the invasion and surrender of Italy in September 1943 meant that the Axis would not win the war.

It was against this background and the optimism it engendered that Churchill, Roosevelt and their staffs met at Cairo at the end of November 1943. The conference was concerned with strategic planning and included future operations in the Chinese theatre. Discussions also extended to the post-war political settlement of the Far East. Roosevelt reassured Chiang that China would recover territory lost to the Japanese and the two considered possible joint American and Chinese administrations in Korea and Indo-China. Manchuria proved a stumbling block. Chiang pressed for Tannu Tuva and Outer Mongolia, both in Russian hands, and full control of Manchuria. Roosevelt prevaricated and reminded the generalissimo that plans for its future would have to heed Russian interests. A State Department official noted that this was 'a subject that will cause trouble'.[20] Another source of trouble was Chiang's disparaging remarks about the performance of the Indian army, which were repudiated by Admiral Louis Mountbatten, the recently appointed Supreme Allied Commander of South-East Asia Command.[21]

British representatives at the conference were unimpressed by Chiang. Field Marshal Alanbrooke likened him to 'a cross between a pine marten and a ferret'. As a politician, he was 'a shrewd but small man' who was adept in 'leading the Americans down the garden path'. By contrast, his wife was an exotic and alluring figure. Madame Chiang chain-smoked cigarettes through a long black holder and appeared on one formal occasion in a long black velvet dress embroidered with yellow chrysanthemums and a slit which reached to 'her hip bone'. This caused 'a rustle' among delegates and drew stallion 'neighs' from some over-excited junior officers.[22]

Churchill dined with Chiang and his wife, who acted as an interpreter. Churchill inclined to her personal charms but stuck to his views on her country and its people. His doctor, Lord Moran, noted his feelings after the meeting. 'He is sceptical of China as a great power and grudges all the time that Roosevelt has given to her affairs. To the President, China means four hundred million people who are going to count in the world of tomorrow, but Winston thinks only of the colour of their skin: it is when he talks of China that you remember he is a Victorian.'[23]

Chiang recognised Churchill's misgivings about China and its future. The prime minister did not want a rejuvenated and strong China, equal in standing with Britain. Yet, he confessed a perverse admiration for his adversary: 'Britain has a power that extends to the furthest parts of the world ... Asia and Africa, even the untameable Muslim peoples obey their [sic] orders. You can't help admiring their magic powers.'[24] Yet, like China, this titan was in deep thrall to the United States and had no choice but to bow to her will.

# Territorial Ambitions:
# Victory and Rewards, 1944–1945

By the beginning of 1944 it was clear that the Allies would prevail on all fronts and win the war. Russia, Britain and the United States were laying plans that would lead to the invasion of Germany. Once it had surrendered, the whole weight of Allied power would be thrown against Japan. In the meantime, the Japanese were being slowly evicted from their recent conquests in the Pacific and Far East. In November 1944 the recapture of the Mariana Islands provided a base for the American aerial bombardment of mainland Japan, which would gather momentum and weight until the end of the war. Anglo-Indian and Chinese forces counter-attacked in Burma in March 1944 and, within a year, Mandalay and Rangoon were reattached to the British Empire.

China's war effort, however, was floundering. By the summer of 1944, exasperated American officials were considering the hitherto unthinkable and made a secret approach to Mao Zedong and the CCP for an alliance to stiffen the faltering Nationalists. Chiang was horrified and, revealingly, saw Britain as a partner in his betrayal. Once again, he portrayed China as the victim of the 'old imperialism' which he had fought in the 1920s when he had demanded the 'destruction' of the '*ying fang*'. For Chiang, Britain was still a formidable and duplicitous opponent, even though her prestige was in tatters. In private, Chiang railed against the 'cowardice and defeatism' that infected British forces from the top downwards.

The British government reciprocated Chiang's hostility, and from 1942 onwards British intelligence kept a close eye on people and events in Chongqing.[1] In particular, the British treated Chiang's support for Indian nationalism as a danger to imperial interests. Clement Attlee, the deputy prime minister and leader of the Labour Party, shared Churchill's lack of faith in Roosevelt's vision of a post-war China as a global superpower and dismissed the presidential plans for China as 'a piece of folly'.[2] Britain was reluctant to extend credit to the

Nationalist government and deeply suspicious of Madame Chiang's lobbying in Washington.[3] She and her husband were convinced that Britain wanted a weak and malleable China despite recent concessions on extra-territorial rights. Both were also keen to enlist American backing for the return of Hong Kong once Japan had been defeated.

Roosevelt was supportive on the matter of delivering Hong Kong to Chiang. It would strengthen America's position in post-war China and add to his political kudos. His Nationalist credentials would also be enhanced within China, where the reoccupation of Hong Kong would symbolise the final end of foreign domination. Churchill, on the other hand, was unmoved by what he regarded as an irritating and unjustifiable demand by the ruler of an inferior country. He responded with demands for the retention of Hong Kong along with the rest of British, French and Dutch possessions in the Far East. In an interview held in London in April 1945, Churchill told Patrick Hurley (one of Roosevelt's many globe-trotting roving envoys) that 'he would never yield an inch of territory that was under the British flag'.[4]

Roosevelt dreamed of a revitalised, independent, capitalist China, possibly a democracy, and certainly a political ally of America. She would also absorb American values. That champion of the Chinese people Pearl Buck reasserted her belief that 'If the American way of life was to prevail in the world, it had to prevail in Asia.'[5] Whether or not China was Americanised, Roosevelt promoted her international status. In the spring of 1945 he secured China's equality with the United States, the Soviet Union, Britain and France as a permanent member of the United Nations Security Council. Its task was to settle all international conflicts.

Post-war potential rather than wartime performance qualified China for this prestigious position. In April 1944, the Japanese had launched the Ichigo Offensive in southern China and, within eight months, had overrun 772,000 square miles of territory, much of it prime farm land. In a sequence of hard-fought battles, the Japanese had inflicted half a million casualties and themselves lost 100,000. The Japanese still had plenty of fight left in them at that stage, a harsh truth confirmed by operations in the Pacific.

China's reverses during the Ichigo Offensive confirmed the scepticism of Chiang's American and British critics. Her armies were disorganised, poorly led and unable to feed themselves. Nationalist soldiers lived off the land and plundered their countrymen and women who often fought back to protect their crops and livestock. Famine, exacerbated by the loss of fertile provinces, was a constant of daily life for the peasant masses. The growing numbers of Americans (there were 60,000 by May 1945) attached to the Nationalist forces contributed to shortages by demanding their domestic diet. Plough oxen were slaughtered to satisfy American appetites, which also required 1,000 chickens a day. Chronic inflation added to the sufferings of the people. Between 1941 and 1945 it soared at a rate of 10 per cent a month. Food prices spiralled: a kilogram of rice cost two yuan in 1940 and forty in 1942.

China's defeats and economic collapse left her allies fearful. For the last two years of the war the Allied leadership and its legions of strategic and political advisers wrangled over what could be done to remedy the multiple deficiencies of the Chinese government and high command. Many, more in London than Washington, thought that both were beyond redemption. American staff officers attached to Chiang's HQ in Chongqing doubted whether China possessed the qualities of a world leader. General John Magruder, director of the American Office of Strategic Services, the forerunner of the CIA, blamed China's setbacks on racist beliefs about the Chinese psyche. 'They frequently shut their eyes to hard and unpleasant actualities,' he wrote at the end of 1942.[6]

Optimists hoped that American pressure might inject some sense of reality into the Chongqing regime, but time was running out. In 1944 a Pentagon analyst concluded that when 'the Chinese army was adequately trained and equipped it would be too late to be of any assistance in the fight against Japan'.[7] Such pessimistic analyses flowed back to Washington and forced Roosevelt to admit that 'We can do little to prepare China to conduct a proper defence.' A further factor in the Chinese war effort was endemic corruption at the top which siphoned off American money and spawned many rumours of irregularities. Among them were Madame Chiang's spending sprees at New York couturiers and having her finery carried home to Chongqing in American transport aircraft.

Anglo-American bickering about China's place in the world spilled over into a wider dispute about the future of empires in Roosevelt's projected new world order. His fellow Americans viewed them with deep misgivings, with a 1945 opinion poll revealing that 55 per cent believed that British colonial rule was oppressive.[8] This belief extended to American servicemen who cynically rendered SEAC (South-East Asia Command) as 'Save Europe's Asian Colonies'. An alternative existed in the form of a world in which former colonies would become capitalist democracies which traded freely with America and were guided by her government. These new nations would be bound to the United States by benevolent cultural and economic imperialism. Yet these high-minded visions of a new global order coexisted with older, perhaps deeper feelings of racial superiority. At a Chongqing dinner party, Major-General Lyle H. Milton called China 'a twelfth-rate power' and called for some 'sing-song girls'.[9]

There was always a distinct racist dimension to the war in China and the Far East. At its beginning, it was imagined that genetic eyesight deficiencies made it impossible for the Japanese to fly aircraft and that those which attacked Malaya were flown by imported German pilots. Japanese officers depicted in cartoons tended to wear glasses. Allied propagandists soon exploited imagined inbred flaws in the Japanese moral character. A film commissioned by the American navy in the 'Know Your Enemy' series portrayed the Japanese as a naive people 'brainwashed' by 'fake religion' and intoxicated by 'fanatic samurai' traditions to the point where they had been purged of 'all human feelings'. They were also imperialists who were training officers to rule the conquered people of Asia. A recruiting poster reminded Americans of the cruelties inflicted on prisoners of war taken in the Philippines and urged fighting men to 'Stay on the job until every murdering Jap is wiped out.' Unsurprisingly, in the light of Japanese atrocities, there were plenty of similar exhortations to exterminate a barbaric and inhuman adversary.

An elementary guide to prevent GIs from mistaking a Chinese from a Japanese infantryman pointed out that the latter had buck teeth, while the former had 'evenly set choppers'. At a distance, the Japanese 'looks as if his legs are joined directly to the chest'. To judge by the accompanying illustrations, he was a simian brute. By contrast, an American poster showed a photograph of a smiling Chinese soldier with the caption: 'This man is your Friend. He fights for FREEDOM.' This image was one of a series that portrayed British, Russian and Australian soldiers who, it was claimed, were also fighting for the same cause.

But what, if anything, did this mean for a conscripted Chinese infantryman or his supreme commander, Chiang Kai-shek? Both wanted the liberation of China from Japanese occupation and Chiang had secured the virtual nullification of the treaties imposed on his country by foreign powers. Yet, in August 1945, he was prepared to offer America a naval base at Port Arthur.[10]

If Chiang got his way, Hong Kong would become an integral part of China. Since the end of 1941, it had been a major Japanese logistical base and its modern hospitals were filled with Japanese servicemen recovering from disease and wounds. It was also home to camps for prisoners of war and interned civilians.

One of the former, Staff Sergeant James O'Toole of the Royal Army Ordnance Corps, wrote in his prison diary that the Japanese commandant was 'very decent and does all he can to make life comfortable'. The Chinese wives of fellow prisoners were allowed to supply cigarettes, which were very much desired, and food; inmates were given anti-cholera injections; and home mail and Red Cross parcels appeared at irregular intervals. One consignment was delivered on the emperor's birthday.[11] O'Toole survived a spartan existence, unlike many of his comrades, and on the last day of 1942 admitted that 'I was either tough or lucky'. He survived the war in conditions that were rare in Japanese prisoner-of-war camps.

These mercies apart, frequently applied and vigorous terror was integral to Japanese imperial administration in Hong Kong, as it was everywhere else. In accordance with the British government's policy on war crimes, an intelligence unit was set up in Chongqing in May 1944 which monitored reports of atrocities in Hong Kong. When the city was reoccupied in August 1945, more than 200 Japanese soldiers and secret police officers were detained, charged and tried. Twenty-one were sentenced to death. Two cases may speak for many others. Sergeant-Major Yamada Kiichiro of the *Kempei* (Military Secret Police) was charged with the maltreatment of Chinese civilians, three of whom died from their torture in custody. A dozen Chinese workers and farmers testified against him and he was hanged. Sergeant Matsuda Kenichi was indicted for torturing to death Li Kam Moon, a baker who was a friend of a resistance fighter. He got eight years.[12] Courts martial of Japanese war criminals continued until 1949; a substantial number were officers and NCOs and their victims were predominately Chinese civilians.

Chinese resistance in Hong Kong during the war was assisted and guided by a small British intelligence unit known as the British Army Aid Group (BAAG), which was set up in August 1942 and organised by an Australian surgeon, Colonel Lindsay Ride ('The Smiling Tiger'), an escapee from a Japanese prison camp. He and his team worked with local partisans to help fugitive prisoners of war and created networks of spies inside Hong Kong, including Chinese dockyard workers. They provided intelligence on weather conditions and targets for American Liberator bombers flying from Kunming. From the summer of 1942, these aircraft undertook raids on Hong Kong's naval and shipping facilities.

Cloak-and-dagger operations in and around Hong Kong had awkward political implications. Colonel Ride's close relations with Chinese guerrilla groups in the hinterland involved co-operation with CCP units. This worried the British military attaché in Chongqing, who feared that it would antagonise the Nationalists.[13] A further and potentially more vexatious problem was who would liberate Hong Kong once Japan had surrendered. Early in 1945, the British government's Hong Kong planning unit sketched out possible scenarios: the worst were Nationalist troops or a local warlord seizing the city.

A British *coup de main* was suggested, although there were fears that this would antagonise the Americans. Nevertheless, the Indian government mission in Chongqing proposed the creation of a 30,000-strong Chinese partisan army in neighbouring Guangdong and Guangxi, which would converge on Hong Kong and recapture the city in Britain's name. This plot was vetoed by General Albert Wedemeyer, who had replaced Stilwell as Chiang's chief of staff in 1944. He was a fervent anti-Communist and sympathetic to Chiang's ambitions for himself and China. He was against a British takeover of Hong Kong and set about to frustrate it by secretly planning a land-based Sino-American assault to take the city immediately after Japan's surrender. Thirty-nine Chinese divisions with American backing were earmarked for a southward advance that would first secure Guangzhou and then Hong Kong. This plan was revealed by American officers to the British chiefs of staff during the Potsdam Conference in July 1945.[14]

Wedemeyer's gambit had ignored a new, fundamental shift in American foreign policy. Roosevelt had died in April 1945 and a new, chill wind was blowing through Washington. It swept away the president's dreams of America as the fairy godmother of a reformed, liberal world order. Events in Europe, where the Soviet Union was entrenching its power in countries overrun by the Red Army, were the catalyst for a profound change in American policies. The new president, Harry Truman, was forced to think in terms of realpolitik and a possible global balance of power that might prove unfavourable to the United States. A month before Roosevelt's death Averell Harriman, the US ambassador in Moscow, foretold an apocalyptic future. 'Unless we wish to accept the 20th century barbarian invasion of Europe, with repercussions extending further and further in the East as well, we must find ways to arrest the Soviet domineering policy... If we don't face these issues squarely now, history will record the period of the next generation as the Soviet age.'[15]

Harriman correctly assumed that the United States would shortly become engaged in what would later be called the Cold War. This was an awkward reality in the Far East, where the United States' power over Chiang made it a seemingly easy task to bring China on side. Yet there were two formidable impediments: Mao Zedong's Communist Party and the Yalta agreement, by which Stalin had promised to invade Manchuria in return for political and economic concessions. Lavishly armed with American weaponry and powered by American fuel, the Red Army and its air force launched its attack on Manchuria on 9 August. Within a week, the Chinese ambassador in Moscow cobbled together an agreement with Stalin (the Sino-Soviet Treaty of Friendship and Alliance) which granted China some limited concessions in the province.[16] After forty years, Stalin had effectively reversed the result of the Sino-Japanese War.

Prior to Russia's invasion of Manchuria, Japan was still unbeaten, and resistance on Okinawa and Iwo Jima demonstrated a determination to fight on despite hopeless odds. Her nemesis was unexpected and devastating. On 6 August an atomic bomb destroyed Hiroshima and three days later a second obliterated Nagasaki. Despite the attempts by diehards to continue the struggle, Emperor Hirohito agreed to an unconditional surrender on 10 August which was formally signed five days later on board the battleship USS *Missouri* in Tokyo Bay.

Once it was clear that Japan was willing to capitulate, Britain immediately moved to pre-empt the Chiang/Wedemeyer coup against Hong Kong. Attlee's Cabinet prepared a daring counter-thrust that would involve an amphibious landing to occupy the colony before the arrival of the Chinese. A telegram was sent to Truman asking whether he had any objections to British forces retaking the city once the Japanese surrendered.[17] On 17 August he replied that he had none, so long as his decision would not concern Hong Kong's 'future status'. This was tacit approval for the restoration of imperial government. In the next few weeks Washington permitted the British retrieval of Borneo, Sarawak and Malaya and the later deployment of Anglo-Indian forces to restore Dutch power in the East Indies and French in Indo-China. In both operations British commanders pitted Japanese prisoners of war against local nationalist partisans.

The United States navy even co-operated in the recapture of Hong Kong. Senior officers of the Pacific Fleet gave permission for British warships to detach themselves and steam to Hong Kong and offered minesweepers to clear their way into the harbour.[18] Meanwhile, BAAG operatives in Hong Kong had been alerted to the imminent arrival of the task force. Senior Japanese officers had accepted their emperor's surrender and there was no resistance from the 40,000-strong garrison. On 23 August, Attlee announced that Hong Kong would shortly be reoccupied by British forces.[19] On the 29th the aircraft carrier HMS *Vengeance* and the cruisers HMS *Swiftsure* and HMS *Euryalus* sailed into Hong Kong harbour accompanied by a flotilla of destroyers. The following day, Japanese generals signed a surrender agreement and handed over their samurai swords to British officers. Sailors and a battalion of Royal Marine commandos rounded up Japanese prisoners. Pathé cameramen recorded these events for British audiences.

Chiang and Wedemeyer had been thwarted, and the latter virtually abandoned by Washington. Their troops had advanced at a leisurely pace and were ordered to halt on 18 August. Chiang deceitfully declared that he had never had any 'territorial ambitions' for Hong Kong or, revealingly, Indo-China.[20] Peace had been restored to Hong Kong, but not to the rest of China. Japanese forces withdrew to their homeland (ferried in American planes and ships), but the Communists remained and were gaining strength. Yet again China's future would be decided by force.

# Part Three

---

# Cold War and Peace, 1946–2022

# The Fall of China:
# New Realities, 1946–1950

When British forces liberated Hong Kong in August 1945, the armies of Chiang Kai-shek and Mao Zedong were squaring up for a civil war that would decide the future of China. America backed the Nationalists and Russia the Communists, while Britain was a bystander racked by fears that Hong Kong and her commercial assets would be lost in the conflict. It was impossible to quarantine the colony from the conflict since it was host to activists from both sides. They were among the ground troops in a far wider contest that became known as the Cold War. It would soon encompass the whole world and would end in 1989 with the political and economic implosion of the Soviet Union and its Eastern European client states.

Britain had no choice but to engage in the Cold War as America's partner. This commitment was an extension of the wartime alliance and the fact that Britain's fractured economy was being revitalised by American loans. Moreover, and this weighed heavily with Attlee's Labour government, the British Empire was directly threatened by the Russian and later Chinese declarations of war against imperialism across the globe. Britain would meet this challenge head on. At the same time as Hong Kong was reoccupied, Anglo-Indian troops were driving Ho Chi Minh's Communist Viet Minh out of Hanoi.

A similar resolve marked British policy in Hong Kong. Officially, Chiang Kai-shek's followers were treated as irritating troublemakers but no threat to internal stability, while the numerous Communists were regarded as firebrands intent on subverting the colonial government. The response was a blend of rigorous coercion with what Sir Alexander Grantham (governor from 1947 to 1957) called 'benevolent autocracy'. He believed that the Chinese, who made up 95 per cent of the population, would never identify or assimilate with the empire and their hearts and minds would always be with China. Nevertheless, sensitive British rule would make its Chinese subjects 'satisfied and well content to devote their time to making money in one way or another'.[1] It would, he concluded, be wise to exempt Hong Kong from the Labour government's plans for constitutional government in the colonies and their future independence. Whitehall caved in on the grounds that the Communist presence ruled out the implementation of this policy in Hong Kong. It would not therefore proceed on the political road that was being taken by India and Ceylon (which became independent in 1947 and 1948 respectively) and would soon be followed by colonies in Africa and the Caribbean.

The velvet glove of paternal rule was balanced by the iron gauntlet of coercion, which fell heavily on Communist individuals and groups. The policy was officially called 'watchful toleration' and was applied by expanded intelligence agencies and a police force equipped with new ordinances imposed during 1947 and 1948. Trade unions had to register with the government and Communist-run schools were closed, as were cultural societies sympathetic to Communism. All teachers were vetted by the authorities and Communist agitators were deported. The police were permitted to 'take steps and use force (including the use of firearms) as may be necessary for securing compliance with any order'.[2] These measures were approved by the Labour government, for whom the menace of Communism outweighed libertarian principles. From 1946 onwards Hong Kong was run as a tight ship.

America also responded robustly to the Communist threat in China. Her goal was summed up by President Truman in January 1946: 'We should rehabilitate China and create a strong government there.'[3] 'Strong government' required national unity and, during the last phase of the war against Japan, American diplomats vainly attempted to stitch together a pact between Mao and Chiang Kai-shek. These included personal meetings between the rival leaders and a mission by Roosevelt's representative Patrick Hurley to Mao, whom he addressed as 'Moose Dung'.[4]

Ideology was an impassable barrier to any collusion. For Mao, Chiang was a 'Fascist ringleader' and an 'autocratic traitor' who enslaved the Chinese people to the interests of landlords and the 'big bourgeoisie'.[5] Their days and those of the capitalist system which sustained them were numbered. Mao's revolution would also purge China of foreigners who had grown rich from capitalism and corrupted her people.

Two symbolic acts marked the fall of Shanghai to the People's Liberation Army (PLA) in April 1949. The city's racecourse, created by 'British imperialist gold diggers', was paved over to become the 'People's Square'.[6] This act of grand-scale political theatre was complemented by a blow against moral corruption: the suppression of Shanghai's celebrated brothels. Some of their owners were executed and all prostitutes were rounded up, imprisoned and forced to undergo vigorous re-education.[7]

Severing China from its tainted past was a key part of the CCP's revolution of the masses. This process would impose equality and construct a reborn nation where wealth would be redistributed and a tightly centralised state would direct all agricultural and industrial production. After the revolution all power would be the monopoly of the CCP and would flow downwards. Chiang's Nationalists had no such blueprint for a new China.

Mao not only had the slogans to seduce and inspire a people battered by war and famine, he had the military sinew to defeat the Nationalists. Arms, including 700,000 rifles, 9,000 machine guns and 860 warplanes taken by the Russians from the Japanese in Manchuria, were delivered to the PLA.[8] By the beginning of 1946, Mao had superior firepower in the hands of soldiers who believed that they were risking their lives for a better country. They were also blessed with superior commanders, most notably Marshal Lin Biao.

America backed Chiang with economic aid – $1.5 billion in all – together with military advisers, who were often ignored. General George C. Marshall, whose master plan of financial support was shoring up post-war Western Europe, visited China in late 1946 to assess the military and political situation. He judged it hopeless, a view shared by other men on the spot. The only alternative was for the United States to take over the entire country, which was impossible. Such pessimism inflamed the influential China lobby that was mustering in the Senate, Congress and press. It was dismayed by the setbacks in China and feared that the country would slip through the fingers of a defeatist Democrat administration. That instinctive hawk and America's proconsul in occupied Japan General Douglas MacArthur warned that 'The fall of China imperils the United States.'[9] This was good news for Mao, who had correctly guessed that failure in China would open political rifts inside the United States.[10]

*

Britain was a powerless and anxious neutral during the Chinese Civil War. The Japanese occupation had damaged or destroyed British property and factories and terminated the activities of financial agencies. But it was not all gloom. At the end of 1946, a British trade mission reported that 'now there are no longer any foreign concessions left in Shanghai', Hong Kong is the only part of China with 'a system of law and administration on Western lines with political, economic and financial stability'.[11] For this reason, British and foreign businesses made a beeline for the colony, where they were safe from the confiscations that would follow a Communist victory. New businesses were attracted to Hong Kong: nearly 1,000 were registered between 1946 and 1949.

Residual British imperial prestige lingered in the collective imagination of some Chinese. Recently, the artist and human rights activist Ai Weiwei (born in 1957) recalled that when he had been about ten, his poet father described Britain as 'a country on which the sun never sets, because their [sic] colonies are 100 times bigger than the small island'.[12] Britain's reputation for intrigue and cunning also survived. In February 1949 Zhou Enlai and Mikoyan seriously speculated about clandestine British plots to stir up the Muslims in Xinjiang.[13]

On paper at least, and despite wartime depredations, Britain was still a force to be reckoned with in Chinese economic life. In 1945, British assets in China totalled £170 million and represented 68 per cent of all the capital invested in the country.[14] These assets mattered to the government, so the possibility of a Communist takeover was troubling. Paying for the war effort had hit the British economy hard: overseas investments worth £1,229 million had been sold off and annual exports had fallen from £471 million in 1939 to £258 million. Labour's post-war reconstruction policies required that every foreign asset had to be exploited to the full and exports increased to rebuild the economy. For the British people, this was a time of self-denial, rationing, fuel shortages and export drives.

Britain's present and future position seemed jeopardised by an unexpected crisis in April 1949. It began with what seems to have been an accidental exchange of fire between shore batteries of the PLA and the frigate HMS *Amethyst*. The vessel's mission had been to steam up the Yangtze and act as guard ship to the British embassy in Nanjing, assisting with the evacuation of British subjects. Badly damaged by shellfire which killed or wounded over fifty of her crew, including her captain, the *Amethyst* was grounded on a mudbank, where she lay for the next 100 days. Throughout, the Communists treated her as a hostage whose release would require Britain to accept blame for the incident. The *Amethyst*'s plight was exploited by Mao's propaganda machine. The stranded frigate symbolised the death spasm of the old imperialism: foreign warships would no longer enjoy free passage on China's rivers, enforcing alien laws and chastising those who broke them. Mao also demanded the immediate removal of all foreign men-o'-war from China's waters. His defiance struck a chord with his subjects.[15]

The dispute was resolved by a gamble taken by the *Amethyst*'s new captain, Lieutenant-Commander John Kerans. Having replenished his depleted oil stocks from another British warship, he planned a 100-mile night dash downriver past PLA artillery emplacements to Shanghai. Audacity, courage and superb seamanship did the trick and the frigate reached safety. Kerans received a DSO and a Dickin Medal was awarded to Simon, the ship's cat, which, despite its wounds, raised the crew's morale. The press back home had a field day and in 1957 the episode was made into an exciting film, *Yangtze Incident*, in which British pluck and steadiness were to the fore.

But many Chinese in Hong Kong interpreted the *Amethyst* episode as a blow to British prestige at a time when a Communist victory in China seemed without question.[16] The colony's garrison had been raised to 30,000 soldiers supported by artillery, tanks and aircraft in readiness for an expected Communist siege. Many of the troops were national servicemen, eighteen-year-old conscripts who had replaced that old source of imperial power, the Indian army.

In the end, there was no battle for Hong Kong. In October 1949 the PLA was ordered to halt when it reached the border with the colony, a decision that had far-reaching repercussions for Britain's relations with China and the United States. Why had it been taken by a government which had recently interned the *Amethyst* and whose propagandists never missed a chance to vilify the 'British imperialist gold diggers'? The simple answer was that self-interested expediency had prevailed over Communist dogma. Zhou Enlai explained this in a message to Hong Kong's Communist underground, who were waiting hopefully for the arrival of the PLA. They were instructed 'to adjust to Hong Kong's historical situation and reality' and accept 'the mutually beneficial relationship between Hong Kong and China'.[17]

The newly installed People's Republic of China (PRC) faced economic problems that Hong Kong could solve. Henceforward, Hong Kong would serve as a link between China and the outside world. It would be the sole conduit for trade, investment, the transfer of funds from abroad and vital imports from the West such as medicines and industrial machinery. All would be needed for national reconstruction. Hong Kong was already a new home for many companies that had hitherto been based in Shanghai. The cannier entrepreneurs and bankers had anticipated the new status of Hong Kong and were shifting themselves and their firms accordingly. There were other benefits. As Zhou shrewdly remarked, the colony was 'an instrument to divide the British from the Americans in their Asian problems' as well as an entrepôt for China.[18]

Zhou was right. As the civil war approached its end, the British government faced a dilemma. Did it formally recognise the legitimacy and international status of the PRC? Or did it follow America and acknowledge Taiwan as the only legal government of China and treat it as such? Over the past year, Nationalist refugees, including Chiang, had been fleeing to the island, which they took over, ruthlessly crushing local opposition. In 2008 the Taiwanese president, Ma Ying-jeou, publicly apologised for the white terror that had killed tens of thousands of native Taiwanese and anti-Nationalists.[19]

Attlee's Cabinet placed realpolitik before Cold War commitment. On 6 January 1950 Britain recognised the People's Republic as the legitimate government of China. The Opposition concurred: Churchill observed that the decision was made 'not to confer a compliment, but to secure a convenience'. By recognising the PRC, Britain had adopted a new, flexible and pragmatic policy which would be followed until the end of the century. The Americans were displeased.

## *Pax Americana:*
## Conflict and Compromise, 1950–1958

In October 1949 Mao Zedong, the son of a prosperous peasant, and chairman of the Chinese Communist Party, became supreme ruler of China and would remain so until his death in September 1976. Past emperors would have envied his power, which was absolute and overarching; the ancient 'mandate of heaven' had been restored by Mao and the apparatus of the party he dominated.

Resistance and disaffection were ruthlessly crushed. As the civil war ended, the CCP launched the first Great Terror in which 'enemies of the people', principally landlords and the professional and commercial classes, were arraigned before impromptu people's courts. They were de-humanised, harangued, forced to confess their errors and usually executed. At least a million landlords were killed. These purges were undertaken in the name of a new unity whose prime ingredients were social equality and ideological solidarity. Orthodoxy of thought was complemented by uniformity of dress: civilians of both sexes wore dark-blue or drab trousers and jackets and the workman's peaked cloth cap.

Coercion was the cement of national unity and purpose. These were vital, for China was about to play a part in international affairs which she had been denied for the past 100 years. Her global ambitions were also entwined with the promotion of world Communism. One of Mao's first acts was to recognise Ho Chi Minh's Viet Minh as the legitimate government of Indo-China. Arms and Chinese officers followed to equip and train the partisans.[1] Mao also intended to restore China's old frontiers. In 1950, Chinese troops occupied Tibet, which until Indian independence in 1947 had been a de facto British protectorate. As for Britain, Mao was more than content to let it remain in Hong Kong and provide China with a convenient and invaluable connection with the rest of the world. Frictionless relations with Britain mattered, which may be why Mao distanced himself from the mainly Chinese

Communist guerrillas in Malaya who received significantly less aid than their counterparts in Indo-China.[2] By 1954, the British had gained the upper hand and the colony became independent three years later.

China had little to fear from Britain even though the two countries were ideological antagonists. America and the Nationalist regime in Taiwan were another matter. Mao saw both as threats to China's security at a time when she was in the midst of profound, sometimes violent social and economic changes. The United States was actively hostile. She refused to recognise the Communist government, encouraged other countries to do likewise, and initially blocked China's admission to the United Nations (UN), where Taiwan remained the international voice of China. Thanks to America, Communist China had been humiliated and isolated.

Fraternal help was at hand in the form of Russia, which had long been the CCP's patron, guide and armourer. Mao had always regarded Stalin as the supreme leader of the world's Communists. In November 1949, he set off for Moscow to honour his benefactor, seek advice and procure a loan. On his arrival he joined in the extended celebrations of Stalin's seventieth birthday, where he added his voice to the chorus of praise. Afterwards he was settled into a suburban dacha to await his hero's pleasure. A frustrated Mao grumbled: 'I have only three tasks here. The first is to eat; the second is to sleep; the third is to shit.'[3]

More disappointment followed when Mao and Stalin finally met and hammered out an agreement in February 1950. Russian financial assistance in restoring the Chinese economy was sparing and with unfavourable strings attached. A military alliance was agreed, but it would only be activated in the unlikely event of a Japanese attack on China. There was also a humiliating concession by which Russian technicians and advisers would enjoy immunity from Chinese law. Stalin was concentrating on the Cold War in Europe, which took precedence over beefing up his new ally in Asia and spreading Communism there. There was little Russian aid for Ho Chi Minh either.[4]

Soon after Mao's departure, Stalin was visited by Kim Il-sung, the Communist ruler of North Korea, who asked for Russian backing for the invasion and annexation of South Korea, then under American protection. Stalin agreed in principle, calculating that the war would be a swift walkover and that the United States would accept the outcome as a fait accompli. As ever with Stalin, Soviet interests were uppermost in his mind. A war in Korea would suck in American resources and manpower and distract Washington from its Cold War commitments to Western Europe. He therefore took the plunge but hedged his bets. He warned Kim: 'If you should get kicked in the teeth, I shall not lift a finger. You have to ask Mao for help.'[5] Mao gave his blessing to Kim's war. If he won, it would be a warning blow to America and deny her a launching pad for a future invasion of China, a possibility that greatly troubled Mao then and afterwards.

Britain was unperturbed by the prospect of a Communist takeover of Korea. A War Office assessment written in October 1949 predicted that the American-trained South Korean army would not stand its ground. It was, however, more likely that internal subversion would overthrow the ferociously anti-Communist president, Dr Syngman Rhee, and his ramshackle and corrupt regime. This would prove no loss, for a compliant South Korea 'is not essential for Allied strategic plans'.[6]

The first prediction came true. On 25 June 1950 the North Korean army invaded and the South Koreans buckled and retreated. The American reaction was swift and decisive. It called on the UN to intervene to check North Korea's aggression and secured the approval of both the Security Council and the General Assembly. Luck was on America's side, for the Russian delegations had recently stormed out of both bodies in a protest over some lesser matter. The UN resolution created a coalition whose forces, 90 per cent of whom were American, mustered for a counter-attack. Allied sea and air power tipped the balance: an amphibious landing behind North Korean lines was the spearhead for an offensive. It was devastating and by late October UN land forces reached the Yalu River, the frontier with China.

Mao had blundered. His proxy war in Korea had become unstuck and he was faced with a predominantly American army on his doorstep. To make matters worse, the Americans had mastery of the air. Mao's response was to deploy 200,000 Chinese troops in Korea with orders to counter-attack and by sheer numbers overwhelm the UN forces. It was a bold gamble, not least because Mao dreaded an American nuclear response.

Throughout the fighting, Communist armies had been hamstrung by inadequate air cover. In 1950 China possessed about 200 warplanes and only Stalin could make up the deficiency. Early the next year, he agreed to fund a frantic programme of building airfields, training pilots and supplying up-to-date MIG jet fighters. Some were flown by Russians: for the only time in the Cold War did the servicemen of the two big players fight one another, although details of the dogfights over Korea between American and Soviet pilots were kept secret by both sides.

In the meantime, Mao's gambit had paid off. The PLA all but overwhelmed UN forces, which retreated as rapidly as they had advanced a few months before. It seemed that manpower had trumped fire and air power and so the UN commander-in-chief, General MacArthur, turned to atomic power to even the odds. Washington too was thinking along the same lines. On 30 November President Truman told a press conference that his administration would take 'whatever steps were necessary to meet the military situation'. A journalist then asked whether these steps included the use of an atomic bomb. The president answered that there was 'active consideration of its use'.[7] America was well ahead in the nuclear race with 200 atomic bombs, while Russia lagged behind with twenty-five, Britain was about to test its first bomb and China had none at all. There was, therefore, no risk of retaliation in kind. At the end of December, MacArthur drew up a list of twenty-six Chinese targets including cities and military installations.

Truman's statement shocked the British government. Hitherto, Britain had been a willing partner in the war so long as it involved conventional arms and its principal objective remained the restoration of South Korea's autonomy. Britain also questioned whether Syngman Rhee's dictatorship was worth saving and was unconvinced that Mao was Stalin's cat's paw. Washington's hardliners were in the saddle and they saw the conflict in broader terms: a war against Communist China that could reverse the recently ended civil war and deprive Russia of an ally.

In December 1950, an alarmed Attlee flew to Washington to press his government's views and persuade Truman to reject the nuclear option. The president was unmoved but conceded that in future major strategic decisions would only be taken after consultation with America's allies. Churchill also approached Truman with a suggestion to offer a UN seat to China and to protest against the use of that vile battlefield novelty napalm 'in crowded areas'.[8] British pleas for restraint were seen as faint-heartedness and were ignored.

In the next few months Britain and America drifted further apart. In Whitehall, the chiefs of staff shrank from giving 'a blank cheque to the Americans' and Air Marshal Sir John Slessor recoiled from the idea of 'a big war with China'.[9] The brass hats were also fearful that such a conflict would lead to the loss of Hong Kong.[10] America shrugged off these doubts and qualms. Her strategists continued to discuss a nuclear attack on China as a quick way to end the stalemate in a war which was now treated as a contest against China. American prestige was at stake and had to be preserved at all costs. In April 1951 Truman again signalled his resolution by approving the delivery of atom bomb components to the air force base at Guam.

Domestic politics contributed to the president's determination. The recriminations that had followed the 'loss' of China continued to agitate public opinion, which swung behind MacArthur, who was emerging as a stout-hearted patriot willing to use America's nuclear capacity to defeat Communism. He made no secret of his views on how the war should be waged and relations between him and the White House became increasingly fissile. In April 1951 Truman sacked MacArthur because his insubordination had become intolerable – in private he called the general a 'dumb insolent son of a bitch'. His real crime was arrogantly to assume that he had the authority to dictate a grand strategy which at its heart included waging a nuclear war against China.

MacArthur's departure coincided with a calmer, more measured approach in Washington to the war. By mid-1951, it was clear that neither side would secure an outright victory. The upshot was tentative moves towards a negotiated settlement. Exchanges proceeded slowly and were largely about where to draw a demarcation line across the Korean peninsula and the machinery for the exchange of prisoners of war. An armistice was signed in July 1953 which set the boundaries between the independent states of South and North Korea. These still remain in force, for there was no formal peace treaty.

Stalin, who died in March 1953, had been eager for a settlement and pressed China not to launch offensives that could jeopardise the talks. Both Russia and China had been unnerved by America's readiness to use atom bombs and were further alarmed by the election victories of Eisenhower and the hawkish Republicans in November 1952. Nonetheless, Mao had some cause to celebrate. He had thrown the Americans back from China's border and, for the first time in recent history, a Chinese army had inflicted heavy defeats on foreign soldiers. Many of the Chinese soldiers were young, enthusiastic volunteers driven by patriotism rather than Communist dogma.[11]

Mao was, however, dismayed by Stalin's insistence that China foot the bill for Russian assistance. It totalled $650 billion and he sourly observed that the demand 'made the Soviets seem more like arms merchants than genuine Communist internationalists'. Subsidising the Chinese deal was for Russia a business deal rather than a political gesture. Another downside of China's intervention in the Korean War had been a heavy death toll, with estimates varying from 400,000 dead to more than twice that number. During the 1954 Geneva negotiations to end the Indo-China war, Zhou Enlai confessed to Khrushchev, the new Russian premier, that China was unable to take a strong line, for 'we have already lost too many men in Korea – that war cost us dearly'.[12]

The Korean War confirmed a new dispensation of power in the Far East. Two days after America obtained the UN resolution to assist South Korea, President Truman had ordered the 7th Fleet to proceed to the China Sea with orders to prevent a Chinese invasion of Taiwan and ensure that the island did not become a base for Nationalist operations against mainland China. Sir Oliver Franks, Britain's ambassador to the UN, observed that 'the *Pax Americana*' had finally replaced 'the *Pax Britannica*'.[13]

This transferral of power aroused regret and envy among British politicians, diplomats and strategists who had served their apprenticeships during the interwar years, when Britain's global and imperial pretensions had some substance. Comparative decline generated resentment in the corridors of power and in the press.

During and after the Second World War, there had been a strong groundswell of anti-American feeling in Britain. In essence it was jealousy of America's preponderance of economic and military power; this animosity was strongest among Conservative right-wingers, who mourned the loss of imperial power, and the Labour Left, which mistrusted American capitalism.

The British remained proud of their diplomatic finesse based on experience. Even Chiang Kai-shek, no lover of Britain, admitted that she was 'more experienced in world affairs' than the United States.[14] Patience and subtlety distinguished British diplomacy, qualities that were lacking in the State Department and the Pentagon. In the middle of the ruckus about the use of American atomic bombs in Korea, Sir Malcolm Macdonald (commissioner-general for South-East Asia) spoke for many of his colleagues when he suggested that Britain could provide a 'restraining influence' on her ally. Americans possessed a 'fundamental generosity' which was hampered by 'the clumsiness of their efforts'.[15] Such views were seen as patronising in Washington.

Twice, in the summers of 1954 and 1958, Britain again attempted to act as a 'restraining influence' on American diplomats and strategists with respect to China. On each occasion, Chinese batteries had bombarded the defences of the offshore islands Quemoy and Matsu, which had been held by Chinese Nationalist forces since 1949. Mao wanted to recover them, and, in London, there seemed to be no reason why he should not. For Taiwan to cling on to them with American backing was futile and dangerous. Events could get out of hand, as they nearly had in Korea, and a general, possibly nuclear war would follow in which Britain would lose Hong Kong and soon to be independent Malaya.[16]

This outcome was extremely unlikely given Mao's intentions. He was ultimately responsible for Chinese foreign policy, although it was conducted by the more sophisticated and pragmatic Zhou Enlai. Bombarding Nationalist outposts reminded the world of China's long-term intention to secure Taiwan in spite of the United States. Yet, during each crisis, Mao moved cautiously, taking care not to invite American retaliation: during the 1958 crisis he forbade Chinese warships to impede supply convoys escorted by American warships. What Mao wanted was a low-risk gesture of defiance to remind Asia of China's continued and unbending opposition to American 'imperialism'.[17] The 1954 shelling of the islands coincided with the forming of the anti-Communist Southeast Asia Treaty Organization (SEATO), an American creation. Its other members were Britain, Australia, New Zealand, the Philippines, Thailand and Pakistan.

Mao was also addressing the Chinese people: bombarding the fortifications and dugouts of Quemoy and Matsu was intended to inject them with fresh patriotic zeal as they engaged in the opening phases of Mao's 'Great Leap Forward', a vast programme for industrial and agricultural regeneration launched in 1958. The propaganda stunt failed, as did the economic programme, which was the cause of the 1958–61 famine in which 40 to 50 million died.

The Americans treated the Chinese shelling of the offshore islands as a challenge to their prestige. Washington's response was, therefore, adamantine and designed to assure Chiang Kai-shek and other allies in the Far East that America would go to any lengths to protect them. Compromise, as suggested by the British, was out of the question. In 1954 America scuppered a British plan to trade recognition of the islands as part of mainland China in return for Chinese recognition of Taiwan's independence.

American resolution reached a feverish pitch during the 1958 confrontation. In August senior officers discussed how nuclear weapons might be used to browbeat China. General Laurence S. Kuter, commander of the air force in the Pacific, urged dropping atomic bombs on Chinese airfields in the event of an amphibious attack on the islands. Such action 'would forestall some misguided humanitarian's intention to limit a war to obsolete iron bombs and hot lead'.[18] General Nathan F. Twining suggested that if these attacks failed to persuade the Chinese, then nuclear attacks should be launched against targets 'deep into China as far north as Shanghai'. For John Foster Dulles, the secretary of state, handing over the islands would invite 'further aggression'. He added: 'Nothing seems worth a world war until you look at the effect of not standing up to each challenge.' Dulles was correct about a world war, for Khrushchev had warned that an attack in mainland China would be treated as one on the Soviet Union.[19]

The *Dr Strangelove* moment passed and calm prevailed. The status quo of the islands was accepted by the United States to the relief of Britain and her other allies, although their advice and misgivings were brusquely dismissed in an official version of the 1958 episode. Washington 'took British opposition as a sign of widespread dissent from American policy', but it failed to 'have any specific effect on US policy'.[20]

When it came to a potential war with China, British advice was unwelcome if it clashed with decisions already made in Washington and, when it came to China and the Far East, leaned too far towards compromise and appeasement. Nevertheless, Britain had a part to play in American Far Eastern geo-strategy. If China followed Japan and attempted a large-scale advance southwards, Britain's chiefs of staff agreed that the response had to be nuclear.[21] In 1954, British V bombers were stationed at Tengah in Malaya in readiness to launch nuclear strikes against southern China in the event of war.[22] The *Pax Americana* was fragile indeed.

# The East Is Red:
# Mixed Fortunes, 1959–1972

The third quarter of the twentieth century was a period of profound and often painful change for Britain and China. Each country was anxious about its place in the world, economic resurgence and playing a significant part in the Cold War. There were differences: Britain was preoccupied with the search for a new role in the world and remedies for fundamental economic deficiencies, while China was pursuing superpower status and an economy to match, albeit based upon Communist principles. Both powers needed allies to secure their goals. Britain marched in step with the United States, not always willingly. China still required Soviet assistance, particularly in her nuclear programme, but the two socialist states were drifting apart over ideology.

For the Chinese, this period was an extended, tumultuous and often bloody rite of passage into a new age under the guidance of Chairman Mao. He was deified by intense propaganda and hailed as a messiah in 'The East Is Red', China's unofficial national anthem:

> The East is red, the sun is rising,
> From China comes Mao Zedong.
> He strives for the people's happiness
> Hurrah, he is the people's great saviour.

This song, performed by a mass choir with thunderous musical backing, was relayed to earth by China's second orbital satellite in 1970. This achievement was, however, overshadowed by the Americans sending – and safely returning – two astronauts to the moon the previous year. Nevertheless, what counted for Mao was prestige. Ambitious and extravagant space programmes were a yardstick for a superpower's technical and scientific superiority, and they have remained so since.

While China strove to enhance her world status, Britain's wilted. Her former capacity to project her hard power was exposed as a sham in November 1956, when Anglo-French forces invaded Egypt and President Eisenhower ordered his two allies to arrange a ceasefire and go home. Old-style military adventures by declining imperial powers were not a part of America's Cold War strategy. Nor were the old colonial empires whose existence and alleged iniquities were exploited by Soviet and Chinese propagandists.

Urged on by America, Britain began a hurried dismantlement of her empire. One by one, Britain's Asian, African, Caribbean and Far Eastern colonies received their independence. Cold War imperatives dictated that the successor states were democracies and anti-Communist, although some soon adopted socialist policies, and others drifted towards one-party dictatorships. Domestic politics did not stop these new nations from joining and remaining within the Commonwealth, a benevolent association of the old dominions and former colonies whose links were for the most part sentimental.

Terminating the empire was a starkly pragmatic business. As the Labour prime minister Harold Wilson warned the Commons in July 1967, 'One cannot stay in a base where one is not tolerated by the local population.'[1] Hanging on consumed blood and taxes, as the French knew from their long-drawn-out wars in Algeria and Indo-China. Nonetheless, friendly governments occasionally needed assistance. Between 1963 and 1966, British, New Zealand and Malaysian forces successfully repelled Indonesian guerrillas who infiltrated Borneo and Sarawak. Their aim was to destabilise Malaysia and the campaign was masterminded by the Indonesian president, Sukarno. He'd had close connections with the PKI (Indonesian Communist Party) and was seen in Beijing as a sympathetic adversary of 'imperialism'.[2]

Sukarno was unseated by a coup that ushered in a military strongman, General Suharto. His regime instigated a wave of massacres of PKI supporters across the country in which hundreds of thousands were killed. Beijing protested against the 'right-wing hooligans' whose victims included local Chinese Communists, but lacked the naval power necessary to intervene. However, thanks to its land border, China could and did provide military assistance to North Vietnam in its war to take over its southern neighbour. In 1965, while the PKI was being destroyed, China delivered more than 3,000 artillery pieces to Hanoi and 1.8 million shells.[3]

As China pushed her ideology and power in the Far East, Britain moved out. The end of the Malaysian 'confrontation' (as the campaign was euphemistically called) coincided with the early stages of the policy of Britain's military disengagement from the region. In February 1968, the Defence White Paper declared that Britain would no longer take part in 'major military operations' beyond Europe 'except in co-operation with allies'. This, of course, had been the position ever since 1942, although Hong Kong's garrison remained to support the local police against sporadic riots.

Bringing home the soldiers, warships and aircraft raised the hackles of some right-wing Conservatives who felt a strong, atavistic passion for an empire which had for so long been the mainstay of British power in the world. There was, however, compensation in the establishment of the British nuclear deterrent. Atomic weapons and the means to deliver them were the new geopolitical status symbols, even if their development and manufacture relied heavily on American research and development programmes. Post-imperial Britain became the world's third nuclear power with 600 warheads.

The economic background to Britain's imperial eclipse and military retrenchment was marked by fitful growth, intermittent crises and a quest for remedies that would revitalise moribund industries and establish new ones. National productivity figures crept up, stalled and drooped, while levels of unemployment rose steadily with a brief peak of 20 per cent in 1978. Strikes were commonplace, most for higher wages. Conservative and Labour governments devised national plans that promised miracles which proved elusive.

Yet while the national economy sickened, the British people had more money to spend and more to spend it on. Addressing the Commons in March 1979, the Labour MP Eric Heffer noted that 'the mass of ordinary working people' had benefited from what was already being called the consumer revolution. He then explained why:

The television tells the working man 'Go to Majorca for your holi-day. Buy a new car. Get a new bedroom suite. Get new carpets.' His wife is tempted and her husband lets her have her way. 'All right, love. I will go to my Union branch meeting next week and suggest that we have another wage increase.'[4]

While millions enjoyed the novelties of the good life, Britain's educational system was failing to provide the workforce needed for the technologies of a new, computer-led industrial revolution. Thirty-five per cent of school-leavers proceeded to higher education and vocational training. The figures for France were 69 per cent, Japan and Germany 77 per cent, and America 80 per cent.

Britain's economic tribulations were far less traumatic than China's. There were no television sets for China's workers and peasants, who faced decades of hardship as Mao translated Marxist-Leninist dogma into large-scale programmes for economic regeneration. His guidebook was *History of the Communist Party of the Soviet Union (Bolsheviks): Short Course*, a Stalinist text published in 1938.[5] Mao imposed a command economy, allocating resources, deciding production quotas and controlling prices. These, together with the collectivisation of agriculture, were intended to achieve self-sufficiency in food and growth in manufacturing. All were the goals of the 1957 Great Leap Forward which contributed to the 1958–61 famine and a drop in living standards. At the time, Chinese life expectancy was just under forty, roughly equal to that in India and just under half that in America. There was some good news: literacy levels were rising steadily from 28 per cent in 1949 to 65 per cent by the mid-1970s.

Mao's dogmatism hampered economic progress. The Chairman became obsessed with ideological purity, and he convinced himself that the people's faith in Communism was withering and could only be saved through perpetual momentum. The Communist victory of 1949 was just the beginning of a process that required the fervour of the masses to be at a constant fever pitch. Standing still was dangerous, for Mao believed that stasis would erode popular revolutionary zeal and encourage the dormant forces of reaction. This paranoia was the mainspring of Mao's 'Great Proletarian Cultural Revolution' (usually known as the 'Cultural Revolution') which began in May 1966.

The leader directly appealed to the masses to rescue their revolution and provide it with fresh impetus by waging a merciless war against covert heretics who clung to Chinese traditions and capitalism. Myriad enemies within had to be chivvied out, driven to admit their ideological crimes and punished. This was a task for the young: they were called Red Guards, wore uniforms and fulfilled Mao's wishes with fanatical fury.

Events in Beijing University in August 1966 may stand for others across China during the next few years. Students pounced on teachers suspected of being 'anti-Mao' and 'anti-Party' and forced their victims to confess their heresies. All were publicly humiliated, beaten and many were tortured. Some were driven to suicide and others were murdered. Estimates of the death toll run to 1.5 million. In Beijing, one woman teacher was terrified into confessing: 'I am an ox-ghost and snake demon. I am guilty. I committed crimes against the people.'[6] The invocation of spirits suggests that some of the Red Guards had not abandoned deviant superstitions. There were also purges of the ruling elite and the PLA. Everywhere, the tormentors brandished copies of *The Thoughts of Chairman Mao*, a thin volume of mostly commonplace slogans bound in red plastic.

Historic antipathies to imported goods quickly reappeared. Red Guards were urged to root out 'bourgeois rascals' and 'hooligans' addicted to 'Hong Kong clothing' and 'pornographic books and degenerate photos'.[7] In the summer of 1967 Beijing's Red Guards even vented their anger against the enemies of Communism beyond China. They sacked and torched the Indonesian embassy in Beijing in retaliation for the massacres of Communists. What an official news agency called the 'frantic, fascist persecution of patriotic Chinese in Hong Kong' was avenged by a Red Guard assault on the British embassy in August.[8] Its staff had been forewarned by an Eastern European mission and had retired to a safe (i.e. defensible) area inside the embassy.[9] This was broken into by Red Guards, who hustled out officials and their wives who were beaten and sexually molested until rescued by PLA soldiers. The Red Guards then demolished the embassy and massed outside the French and Soviet embassies chanting slogans.

The Cultural Revolution had already spilled over into Hong Kong. The colony had never been quarantined from Chinese political strife. In the winter of 1956–57 there had been clashes between Nationalist and Communist factions which had led to large-scale riots. These in turn had revived older grievances and foreigners had been assaulted, with the Chinese underclass grabbing the opportunity to loot. The authorities had taken a stern line: the police had opened fire on several occasions and thirty rioters had been killed and over 100 wounded.

The disorders in Hong Kong between May and December 1967 were far more serious. Their roots were in the underground Communist cells in the squatter camps and the shanty towns that had expanded as a result of spiralling immigration from China. An underclass, barely surviving on the margins of society, and students and schoolchildren were easily seduced and organised by Communist agitators. Their objective was to paralyse the colonial authorities.

Making Hong Kong ungovernable required a general strike (which petered out), intermittent riots and a campaign of scattering small, handmade and lethal bombs in public places. Eight thousand were manufactured, some by schoolchildren. Historic antipathies were revived when Europeans were accosted and reviled as 'running dogs' and 'white-skinned pigs'. Policemen were 'yellow-skinned dogs'.[10] Europeans gained some protection by waving red bound Hong Kong and Shanghai Bank account books which rioters imagined were copies of Mao's *Little Red Book*.

At the start of the disturbances, the Communists commandeered the Bank of China office block from which loudspeakers blared out Maoist slogans. The authorities replied with high-volume blasts of current pop music, including the latest Beatles hits. Bandaged rioters smeared with fake blood posed before television cameras as victims of imperialist oppression. There were plenty of real casualties: in all, fifty-one were killed and 800 wounded. Among the dead were five policemen, part of a detachment attacked on the border by Chinese militiamen in July. Gurkha reinforcements saved the remaining policemen and afterwards British soldiers manned all frontier posts. Inside China, some hotheads contemplated an invasion and occupation of Hong Kong, but they were warned off by Zhou Enlai. Even in a state of spasmodic anarchy the city remained an economic asset for China. He later apologised for the border incident.

The authority of the Chinese state was wobbling. The Red Guards were running amok. Workers left their factories to strike or join the protests and food production was disrupted by influxes of urban students ordered to learn from the rural peasantry. China's national income fell by nearly 3 per cent, although growth projects somehow continued with imports of factory installations from the West and Japan.[11] Mao also ordered the delivery of rifles to the Red Guards, which led to pitched battles between them and workers and peasants, which, in turn, led to the deployment of the PLA as a peacekeeping force. The PLA turned out to be about the only beneficiary of the Cultural Revolution. Marshal Lin Biao, minister of defence and commander-in-chief of the PLA, who had at first embraced the Cultural

Revolution, adjusted his loyalty and then deployed his troops to suppress the violence in the cities, towns and countryside. Among their achievements was ensuring the safety of China's atomic research and development facility in Xinjiang province.[12]

In April 1969 the Ninth Congress of the CCP officially terminated the Cultural Revolution, although its tremors were felt for several years after. Mao had blundered, but no one dared to say so openly for his cult status was unassailable. There had been muted criticism from Zhou Enlai, who recognised the social and economic perils of fragmentation and violence from below, and, latterly, Lin Biao.

In 1978, two years after Mao's death, Marshal Ye Jianying, a Party veteran who had studied in the Whampoa Military Academy in the 1920s, denounced the Cultural Revolution. He told the CCP's Central Committee Conference that its participants had been 'traitors, spies, ambitious schemers, double-dealing counter-revolutionaries and usurpers' who had wreaked 'havoc' throughout China.[13] Thus, blame was allocated and the past set aside. Ye's invective would join other warnings from China's past of the terrible perils posed by mass populist movements which ran out of control. A direct line of fanaticism connected the Red Guards to the Boxers and the Taiping rebels.

The terminal quivers of the Cultural Revolution overlapped with a Sino-Russian confrontation that brought the two countries to the verge of a nuclear war and a result that had been hitherto unimaginable: a rapprochement between China and the United States. Since Stalin's death in 1953, relations between Moscow and Beijing had veered between co-operation and conflict. Russia had helped China's nuclear research but in 1959 supported India in her border dispute with Pakistan, which was backed by Beijing. In 1964, the CCP's National Congress had accused Russia of 'imperialism' in its occupation of Outer Mongolia (as well as Poland and East Germany) and, four years later, Mao made similar charges after the Soviet invasion of Czechoslovakia in 1968. There was also dismay in Beijing over Russia's tepid approach to assisting the North Vietnamese war effort. Seen from Beijing, the Soviet Union, once the banner bearer of world revolution, was slipping into bad reactionary ways.

Yet it was an old-fashioned land dispute rather than ideological differences which sparked the 1969 crisis. The contested territory was Zhenbao island on the Ussuri River, part of a region occupied by

Russia under an agreement made more than sixty years before when China was still making concessions to minatory foreign powers. These injustices were recalled by Zhou Enlai, who compared Russia's attitude towards his country as reminiscent of the 'unequal treaties' of the nineteenth century.[14]

The crisis began in March, when Chinese and Soviet border troops fought a sequence of engagements on Zhenbao island. There were casualties, and both sides quickly called up reinforcements supported by tanks. Prestige and dogma were now at stake. Beijing boasted that the PLA would prove its 'superiority ... in spirit and intellect' over the 'politically degenerate and morally decadent' Red Army.[15] Beijing's rhetoric throughout the crisis was instructive: the Soviet Union was abandoning its Communist principles and replacing them with a rehashed tsarist imperialism.

As China poured more and more troops into the frontier, Moscow became alarmed. The Soviet leader, Alexei Kosygin, favoured negotiation, but his nervous generals feared a mass Chinese attack across the border in which the Red Army would be outnumbered. An unstoppable Chinese advance could reach as far as Vladivostok. Only nuclear weapons could redress the imbalance. In August, Soviet embassy officials in Washington asked what America's reaction would be to a big, pre-emptive nuclear strike against China's 'nuclear facility'.[16] Aware of this, Mao promised 'terrible revenge'. He placed his faith in numbers: his military philosophy was explained by the PLA's journal, *Liberation News*. The Chinese fighting man, inspired by Mao and the Communist Party, was a 'moral atom bomb' and more than a match for Russian rockets and warheads.[17]

Neither was put to the test, for both sides paused and then negotiated. A boundary was fixed in 1995 and subsequently confirmed in 2008. What was important about this incident was the lengths to which China would go to challenge the territorial status quo imposed on it by foreigners. There was a message here for Hong Kong and Taiwan.

There was a message too for the United States. It was understood and acted upon by Henry Kissinger, a genius of realpolitik and President Nixon's foreign policy adviser. What he called 'a war of nerves' over an island on the Ussuri River had created a rift between Russia and China which, if cultivated, could persuade the latter to 'lean towards America'.[18] Secret negotiations under Kissinger's directions followed which culminated in Nixon's visit to Beijing in February 1972, where he dealt directly with Mao. Their discussions and those of their advisers ended with a historic accord. America lifted her embargo on Chinese membership of the UN and agreed to measures for bridge-building between the two powers which included trade and scientific, technical and cultural exchanges. The joint statement issued after the talks also included references to 'China's integrity' and Mao's insistence that 'Taiwan was a province of China'. The implication for Hong Kong's future was clear.

# Asian Tigers:
# China and Hong Kong, 1972–1989

When Mao took power in 1949 China was a broken and supine nation. When he died in 1976 it was a great world power, respected and feared. His record of international successes was impressive. Chinese troops had held their own against the Americans in Korea; Mao had seen off a challenge from Washington during the offshore islands dispute and firmly told Britain that she remained in Hong Kong as a favour; and he'd faced down Russian threats of a nuclear war. Chinese weaponry and advisers had also secured the defeat of the United States in Vietnam. Mao went on to meet President Nixon as an equal, secured China her rightful place in the UN and began a mutually fruitful economic partnership with her hitherto most implacable adversary.

Outward appearances were, however, deceptive. A stronger and self-assertive China faced the world, but she had conspicuously lagged behind in terms of economic growth and living standards. Her progress had been slow, fitful and punctuated by a major famine and the mayhem of the Cultural Revolution. In terms of growth, production figures and standards of living China was the sick man of the Far East, and the welfare of the people suffered: in 1970 there were thirteen hospital beds for every 10,000 people and 70 million were underfed and impoverished.

Mao's death in September 1976 was followed by a palace coup. The 'Gang of Four', a quartet of senior figures including his widow, Jiang Qing, tried to seize power. Their plot failed and they were arrested, tried for conspiring to install a 'Fascist dictatorship', found guilty and imprisoned. Jiang, who had once advertised her ambitions by appearing in public in the costume of the seventh-century empress Wu Zetian, committed suicide in gaol in 1991.

Supreme rule passed to Deng Xiaoping. Born in 1904, he was a CCP activist from the 1920s who had learned his Communism in

Paris and Moscow. He was both a pragmatist and a man of action. A posthumous encomium described how, in the early 1950s, Deng the soldier had imposed order in Sichuan and Tibet. 'Fleeing bandits and secret agents' were ruthlessly pursued and 'deep-rooted feudal forces' deracinated.[1] He would deploy the same spirit and drive in overcoming the problems of Mao's legacy.

While China languished economically, her versatile, competitive capitalist neighbours were flourishing. From the mid-1960s onwards, Japan, South Korea, Singapore, Taiwan and Hong Kong had enjoyed a spectacular and continuing boom: new industries proliferated, exports expanded and living standards rose. The rest of the world invested in their new enterprises, purchased their products and spoke admiringly (and sometimes enviously) of the 'Asian Tigers'.

China's economic maladies were not, however, incurable. She possessed the human, capital and physical resources to equal if not outmatch the Tigers. Deng understood this and convinced himself and others within the CCP's ruling elite that the source of China's infirmity was allowing Maoist economic dogma to perpetuate failure. Recovery and progress required a profound change of policy at the highest levels and equally deep shifts in habits of mind at the lower. In December 1978, Marshal Ye Jianying told the CCP's Work Committee that their country was on the brink of a 'historic turning point' which would mark the beginning of 'socialist modernising'.

In essence, 'socialist modernising' demanded a total break with the past. Maoist economics were jettisoned and replaced by universal capitalism, while 'the people's dictatorship of the proletariat' remained in the saddle of power and beyond criticism. Henceforward, it would rule a nation in which all individuals were free to fulfil their ambitions, exploit their talents and accumulate wealth, as long as they didn't challenge the ruling orthodoxy. Competition, the free market, individual commercial enterprise and personal enrichment were now encouraged by the state. China would follow the path of Hong Kong.

As Deng famously remarked, it did not matter whether a cat was black or white so long as it caught mice. The capitalist mouser performed its duties well and within years had become a Tiger second to none in its strength and vitality. The statistics chart this metamorphosis. Between 1978 and 2007, China's gross domestic product rose from $214.2 billion to $400.4 billion and average per capita income from $224 to $2,604. During the same period, exports had risen from

$9.8 billion to $1,218 billion and imports from $16.9 billion to $955.5 billion. China ascended the global economic ladder: it overtook Germany in 2000, surpassed Japan in 2010 and analysts predicted that it was on course to supplant America by 2025 to become the world's largest economy.

Deng proceeded cautiously at first, likening China to a man 'crossing a river feeling for stones'. At the end of 1979 he told the Japanese prime minister that he was seeking 'comparative prosperity' for his people and more foreign trade, but China would not become 'too competitive'. Much would depend upon foreign investment which flowed into China once her growth began to gather impetus. By 2019, it totalled $217 billion.

Most important of all was the response of the Chinese people to the new capitalist ethos and the opportunities offered by the free market. Latent entrepreneurial talents and ambitions were released at every level. In many instances the necessary capital was to hand, for the Chinese had always been keen savers and Communism had never smothered their thrifty instincts. The farmer could now sell his eggs where he chose for the best price and accumulate capital from the profits with which he was free to extend his business, diversify, or invest in another venture. The government approved and did whatever was needed to lubricate new growth. One measure was the creation of Special Economic Zones such as Guangdong and Sichuan, where new enterprises were tempted by inducements such as low taxes and light regulations. Hong Kong was the model for these regions.

Hong Kong's future was one of the concerns which preoccupied Britain's new prime minister, Margaret Thatcher, who won the general election of May 1979. She had waged a passionate campaign against a Labour Party which had attempted over the past five years to manage successive economic crises rather than tackle their long-term root causes. Mrs Thatcher's alternative was that of the tree surgeon: dead wood would have to be pared and profitable new growth nurtured. The catalysts for Britain's recovery were strict control of the money supply, reduced taxation and allowing market forces a free rein. Armed with a monetarist creed and a granite willpower, Mrs Thatcher set to work. As with Deng's accession, her victory was a historic and sometimes painful turning point.

Soon after the election, Mrs Thatcher and her Cabinet turned their attention to the problem of Hong Kong's future. They were politicians brought up during the interwar years, when the British Empire had still been a force to be reckoned with, and they had witnessed its recent dissolution. Colonies might have been shed, but old attitudes lingered on. Hong Kong was seen as a glowing example of benevolent imperialism which had provided its subjects with stability, physical and moral progress, and chances for self-betterment. With this in mind, the Cabinet adopted a policy of preserving the colony's status quo under direct British rule. This arrangement would, it was claimed, be in China's best interests.[2]

Geography and history combined to frustrate this plan, and the Chinese would deploy both to reject Britain's demands. Hong Kong island and Kowloon had been annexed in 1842 and 1860 respectively under duress and the mainland New Territories in 1898 under a ninety-nine-year lease which expired in 1997. The last two comprised 92 per cent of the colony's land area and were essential providers of water, food and labour. Deng, meanwhile, insisted that all parts of Hong Kong were an indivisible entity to which China had just historic claims. Regaining all of the colony was a further and major step in erasing the injustices of the 'unequal' treaties and restoring China's former territorial integrity.

In response, British negotiators attempted to trump history with economics. They stressed that Hong Kong's current value to the Chinese economy overrode all other considerations and took some comfort from the fact that China had suffered two brief financial crises during 1980. Sir Percy Cradock, Britain's ambassador in Beijing, warned that 'investor confidence' would crumble once the Chinese took over Hong Kong. In April 1982, when the former prime minister Edward Heath met Deng, he rightly insisted that Britain drew no revenues from Hong Kong. What mattered, he airily insisted, was that 'Britain managed Hong Kong for the benefit of China and mankind'.

Mrs Thatcher repeated this point when she met Deng in September 1982. She was in resolute form, for her personal kudos had grown during the previous four months. In April, the neo-fascist military junta which ruled Argentina had invaded and occupied the Falkland Islands. Mrs Thatcher had risen to the challenge, ordering a British seaborne expeditionary force to retake the islands, which it did by mid-June. This victory owed much to her resolve, and when she met Deng she was in no mood to temporise.

During discussions in Beijing, Mrs Thatcher warned Deng that potential investors prized the 'stability' of Hong Kong and referred to China's 'recent turbulent past' and her still-unfinished 'modernisation programme'. Deng was unmoved, emphasising the issue of Chinese sovereignty over Hong Kong and making a veiled threat of a 'confrontation' if Britain denied it. Deng was not cowed by the prime minister's Palmerstonian posturing. China's sovereignty over the whole of Hong Kong was accepted by Britain and, for the next two years, both countries negotiated the arrangements for the colony's governance under Chinese rule.

The result of the negotiations was an accord reached in Beijing in December 1984 which would give China full sovereignty over Hong Kong in July 1997, when the New Territories lease expired. Britain had no choice in this matter, as Deng had observed when he bluntly told the prime minister that the PLA could take the colony 'in an afternoon'. She riposted that such an invasion would lower China's standing in the world. Nonetheless, Deng was happy to make concessions by agreeing to the principle of 'one country, two systems'. Those for the 'Special Administrative Region' of Hong Kong rested on an agreed 'Basic Law' which permitted a degree of autonomy, capitalism, freedom of expression and an uncensored press. This new regime would remain in place for fifty years. Mrs Thatcher publicly praised Deng's 'vision and foresightedness' and predicted that Hong Kong would become an 'even more flourishing place than it is today'. There was no mention of democracy.

Hong Kong was promised unique freedoms in an authoritarian state which looked askance at any kind of criticism. As inheritors of the 'mandate of heaven', Deng and the CCP were incapable of error and, therefore, above the judgements of their subjects. Yet during 1987, 1988 and the early months of 1989, the Chinese people were becoming restless. They saw the regime as aloof and indifferent to their multiple grievances. Food prices were rising, inflation rates were increasing, and there were mass redundancies among factory workers, and allegations that the CCP was riddled with corruption.

Leadership of another and more responsive kind was on offer. It was provided by university students, who had a historic record of radical political activism stretching back to the May 1919 nationalist agitation. Given the ancient Chinese tradition of respect for learning, they enjoyed public respect. As popular unrest spread, students demonstrated, disseminated radical ideas among the masses and gave inchoate unrest a political agenda. Its prime ingredients were democracy and an end to state censorship.

With success came optimism. In April 1989 an American academic found that students in Beijing were heartened by recent demonstrations in Tiananmen Square, during which protesters had broken through a cordon of unarmed military police. Some likened the present regime to some distant, short-lived dynasty and predicted its imminent downfall and replacement by democracy. Others condemned 'modernisation', although a few possessed its products in the form of high-tech cameras, wireless sets and stereos. There was also a feeling that Deng was favourable towards intellectuals and, therefore, sympathetic.[3]

These young men were soon disappointed. For the past eighteen months, Deng and the CCP's bigwigs had been filled with trepidation about the protests and the remedies they advocated. Two senior officials, the Party's general secretary Hu Yaobang and his successor Zhao Ziyang, were flexible about the need for reforms, but they were isolated among a hostile ruling elite. Hu was toppled and died from a heart attack in April 1989. His funeral witnessed a mass demonstration and he was subsequently hailed by the students as a martyred lost leader. Zhao was more cautious. He kept a foot in both camps and was asked to mediate with the students but finally closed ranks with his diehard colleagues. He was later demoted: the Party would not tolerate wobbling.

By the first week of May 1989, the crisis was running out of control. The growing numbers of the vocal and active opposition were estimated to total 1.5 million across the country and crowds of up to 150,000 were regularly assembling in Tiananmen Square, where they were seen by the Soviet leader Mikhail Gorbachev, then on a state visit. His presence was an uncomfortable reminder that Communism was in retreat in Europe. Moscow's satrapies were being convulsed by popular agitation. Free elections had been held in Poland and throughout the summer and autumn there was unrest in Czechoslovakia, Estonia, Lithuania, Latvia and East Germany. Gorbachev refused to apply the customary Soviet corrective of merciless armed force and instead offered concessions. Seen from Beijing, it appeared that the Communist world was imploding under the pressure from below.

Deng feared that Europe's contagion was spreading to China.[4] He had always believed in the virtue of the masses and had spent the past decade endeavouring to secure their betterment, but he did not believe in their capacity to rule. This was the task of the Party alone, and if it shirked it, the revolution would be undone. His attitude was shared by his elderly advisers who had helped bring about the revolution. Their position would have been understood by the Qing emperors and their servants, for whom the concept of democracy would have been equally abhorrent. On 20 May Deng was overheard to say: 'Two hundred dead could bring twenty years of peace for China.'[5]

Shortly afterwards, units of the PLA earmarked for operations against the Beijing demonstrations undertook a four-day course of 'intense' political indoctrination to insulate them against subversion. It seems to have been successful, for British and Australian embassy intelligence sources revealed that the soldiers deployed in Beijing were 'happy and exalted' when they heard their orders to 'suppress a counter-revolutionary uprising'.[6]

Martial law was declared in Beijing on 3 June and the one-sided battle for the city lasted for two days. According to the information gathered by British and Australian intelligence from participants on both sides, the PLA was ordered to 'spare no one', and some of the soldiers were 'illiterate peasants' from remote upland regions. Nonetheless, there were fears that units might side with the demonstrators. Terror was ruthlessly applied: tanks and armoured personnel carriers drove into crowds which also came under heavy machine-gun fire. The wounded were shot or bayoneted and their corpses burned with flame-throwers. The death toll has been estimated at between 200 and 2,000, with official accounts favouring the smaller number.

Press reporters and newsreel cameramen from across the world recorded many scenes, providing eyewitness narratives and images. One, in which a single protester stood in front of a column of tanks, symbolised the courage of his comrades and the hopelessness of their cause. The commonest reactions to these reports were variations on themes of horror and disgust. In Britain, Left and Right were united in fury: Mrs Thatcher voiced her 'utter revulsion and outrage', while the *Guardian* denounced China's 'bankrupt and geriatric government'.[7] There were similar polemics from states of the European Union and countries such as Hungary which were on the verge of open revolt against Soviet rule. The United States, whose ambassador to Beijing had prophesied a crackdown when the unrest began at the end of 1986, added to the international opprobrium.[8] President George Bush the Elder proposed economic sanctions against China but also expressed a strong wish to maintain contacts with her government. The European Union banned the export of arms to China (which is still in force) and Japan froze its China loans for a brief period.

Deng was unshaken by this outcry. The CCP had survived with its power intact, unlike the Communist parties of Eastern Europe and Russia, all of which succumbed during the next twelve months. Then and later, official propaganda blamed the disturbances on American subversion, including broadcasts by the Voice of America radio station.[9] Beijing also insisted that the crackdown was an internal matter and therefore exempt from foreign criticism. Over the following years, there were intermittent official efforts to justify the actions that had saved China from a civil war and to challenge the details of what had happened.[10]

In the second half of 1989 the world's attention was turned to the end of the Cold War. One by one, the Soviet satellites in Eastern Europe broke free, renounced Communism and embraced democracy and capitalism, a revolution that was symbolised by the fall of the Berlin Wall. In the following year, Gorbachev's Russia followed the same path. Deng thought he was an 'idiot' because he had failed to preserve the supremacy of the Soviet Communist Party. In Hong Kong, the mass exhilaration that had greeted the protest movement turned to dread as to their fate when China took control.

# Number-One Threat:
# Prejudice and Pride, 1990–2022

During this period, Anglo-Chinese relations have swung between a cordial partnership in pursuit of shared profit on the one hand and acidic acrimony on the other. Since 2020 the tone has become more rancorous, even warlike at times. Rishi Sunak, in his campaign to become prime minister in the summer of 2022, spoke for many when he warned that China was the 'number-one threat' to Britain's 'economic and national security'.[1] His opponent Liz Truss agreed, as did much of the media. So too did the heads of Britain's and America's secret services.

At the same time, China has believed that she has been being intimidated and has reacted with chauvinistic fury. A country which has squashed all internal criticism regards external criticism as an insolent affront to its status as a global superpower. This was the message from President Xi Jinping during the centenary celebrations of the CCP in July 2021. 'We will never allow anyone to bully and oppress us, or subjugate China... anyone who dares try to do so will have their heads bashed bloody.'[2] His tirade coincided with the passage through the South China Sea of a British naval flotilla headed by the new aircraft carrier HMS *Queen Elizabeth* in support of the American 7th Fleet. For the Chinese, the appearance of a foreign armada off their coasts was a reminder of a bitterly resented past when such vessels were the enforcers of unequal treaties and exploitation.

For Beijing, the independent state of Taiwan remains a reproachful relic of that era. For as long as it has ruled China, the CCP has been determined to absorb the territories once ruled by the Qings, including Taiwan, which was snatched by the Japanese in 1895 and occupied by the American-supported Chiang Kai-shek fifty-four years later. Having warned the rest of the world of the consequences of any attempt to coerce China, Xi added that 'China will take Taiwan, one way or another'. In March 2022 this message was reinforced by his defence minister, who promised that 'if anyone dares to secede Taiwan from China, we will not hesitate to fight'.

The means were at hand, for a few months previously China's War Ministry had announced a programme for 100 new missile silos for new guided missiles that could hit targets across the world. The profits of fifty years of economic growth had funded an arsenal now as sophisticated and formidable as to pose a viable challenge to that of the United States. If she so wished, China could secure air and naval mastery over the South China Sea and launch an amphibious invasion of Taiwan by a million men. Analysts who theorise about the outcome of such a war have speculated as to whether it would become nuclear, because a preponderance of manpower and weaponry is not always a guarantee of swift and decisive victory.

Such a conflict, like the 2022 Russian invasion of the Ukraine, would have been unimaginable in 1990. The Cold War had just ended and American political scientist Francis Fukuyama foretold 'the end of history' as it had unfolded for the past 4,000 years. Ahead lay an age of perpetual and universal harmony under the aegis of benevolent capitalism and international goodwill.

This did not happen, as Beijing's recent fulminations and America's gunboat diplomacy remind us. The first three decades of the post-Cold War era have been punctuated by wars fought for reasons familiar to our ancestors: religious fanaticism and the acquisition of land and influence. The results have been disappointing: interventions in the Middle East have triggered widespread anarchy; Afghanistan has again revealed its historic capacity to see off invaders; and Russia's hammer blow against Ukraine has turned into a grinding war of attrition.

Britain has been an energetic partner in American-led interventions, although not always wholeheartedly. In 2003 at least 750,000 people gathered in London to demonstrate against Prime Minister Tony Blair's decision to join in the US invasion of Iraq. This gesture was integral to Blair's vision of a post-imperial Britain as a moral knight errant slaying the dragons of tyranny wherever they appeared. His perception has since become part of a wider political debate about the country's future approach to foreign policy.

One potent element in this discussion has been a hankering after a not too distant past when the lion roared and the rest of the world trembled. This nostalgia has blended with memories of Britain's heroic defiance in the summer of 1940. These sentiments have been strongest among those who could remember those times and among the generation that followed.

For those who warmly recalled Britain's era of national greatness, the handover of Hong Kong on 1 July 1997 was the symbolic last post for the British Empire, although the Union Flag still flew over Gibraltar, the Falkland Islands, a scattering of tropical islands and a slice of the Antarctic icecap. For the Chinese, Hong Kong had an equally emotional symbolism: it was a further step towards the restoration of 'one China'.

The pageantry of Hong Kong's transfer of power did not hide the undercurrents of regret and contention on both sides. Sir Christopher Patten, a former Tory minister, who was appointed governor of Hong Kong by Mrs Thatcher in 1992, saw himself as the very model of a modern proconsul. Much to her irritation, he disdained to wear the customary white uniform and plumed helmet. Patten also ruffled some political feathers prior to the handover by doing all in his power to extend the influence of Hong Kong's fledgling elected legislative assembly. This displeased the Chinese, who insisted that these measures were contrary to the terms of the 1984 agreement. Beijing expressed its annoyance with the old, familiar allegations of British perfidy and greed and reviled Patten as a 'viper' and 'prostitute'.[3]

Patten also faced domestic critics, whom he later accused of 'working actively to scupper' his cultivation of democracy. Sir Percy Cradock, then ambassador in Beijing, thought he was being 'too soft', while Sir Edward Heath complained that his policies would hamper future trade deals with China which were dear to his heart. Patten dismissed him as a 'despicable bore'.[4] The governor's diaries, published in 2022, catalogued the obstructions he faced and what he saw as a betrayal of the people of Hong Kong. The truth, as revealed to Mrs Thatcher by Deng in 1984, was that China held the whip hand – for the past thirteen years, her forces could have overrun Hong Kong in a few days had Beijing so wished.

Britain's departure from Hong Kong was marked by parades of British and Chinese soldiers, brass bands playing national anthems, and national flags being lowered and raised. Patten was close to tears by the end. Prince Charles, representing the Queen, attempted a positive line in his formal obituary for imperial rule. Britain, he said, was 'proud and privileged' to have created the 'framework' for Hong Kong's amazing economic success.

China's official view of the affair was bluntly expressed by an old man who told an American reporter: 'It is a good thing, we can finally get rid of the imperialists. This land belongs to China. We are all Chinese. I feel great.' An old woman who had fled to Hong Kong to escape the Japanese invasion fifty-six years before, then living under Japanese rule only to see the British return, reacted with a quietist shrug. 'I've never seen a Communist before... I am so old already, all this change doesn't mean much to me.' Many of Hong Kong's 6.5 million population did not share her insouciance and were troubled by memories of the Tiananmen Square massacre just eight years before.

Prince Charles, who had travelled to Hong Kong on the royal yacht *Britannia* (a veteran of the 1954 royal tour of the empire), was dismayed by what he had seen. He jotted down his reactions in a private memo entitled 'The Handover of Hong Kong or the Great Chinese Takeaway', which also included some grumbles about the shallowness of Blair's entourage. Chinese ministers and officials were likened to 'an appalling old waxwork' and the prince was appalled by the 'awful Soviet display' of 'goose-stepping' Chinese soldiers. Eight years later, his observations were leaked to the *Mail on Sunday* which published them. He sued on the grounds that his comments were private and had been illegally obtained – and won.[5]

At home, the loss of Hong Kong was widely seen as the curtain call of the British Empire; Britain's former greatness would never be revived. She was now a second-rank power and had been treated as such by China throughout the process of transferring authority. Nonetheless, Britain ranked fifth in the world's economic league, and her leaders went to great lengths to stress her moral influence and an abstraction that was labelled 'soft' power.

Politicians of all parties strove to refute suggestions of national decline and offered lifelines of hope for the future. Blair (who held office between 1997 and 2007) set the tone and the goals with his 'vision of New Britain' which, in spirit and aspiration, would be 'a young country' and 'a great country'. His jaunty faith was echoed by his successors Gordon Brown, David Cameron, Theresa May and Boris Johnson. All agreed that Britain had the latent willpower, native inventiveness and energy required to flourish in a world overflowing with new economic opportunities.

One tempting treasure trove of opportunity was waiting in China. It was uncovered in October 2015 when the prime minister, David Cameron, agreed a new trade deal which, he predicted, marked the start of a 'golden age' of Anglo-Chinese relations that would enrich both countries. Its dawn was celebrated when President Xi paid a state visit, dined with the Queen and downed a photo-opportunity pint of beer with Cameron in a Chilterns village pub. Steep rises in trade were forecast and there was an uplifting moral dimension to the new relationship. Philip Hammond, the foreign secretary, looked forward to co-operation between Britain and China 'on global issues such as climate change and tackling poverty'.

But the new era of Anglo-Chinese harmony was brief and within seven years had fallen apart. The reasons were an undercurrent of public hostility towards what was being called 'globalisation', public and media disgust at China's internal policies, and a growing fear of China's long-term international ambitions. In short, China became an enemy, and a dangerous one at that.

Behind this demonisation of China lay popular perceptions of forces imagined to be at large in the world that were working to Britain's disadvantage. As in America, mass anxieties were often the mainspring for conspiracy theories. Within a year of Cameron's pact with Xi, Nigel Farage, the leader of the mushrooming United Kingdom Independence Party, better known as UKIP, warned that 'China is doing and will do more damage to impoverish the British people by their [sic] control of British companies and their creation of unemployment than the Germans did in two world wars'.[6]

This astonishing statement, which linked China with Britain's ancestral adversary, touched raw nerves among those stranded by recent economic changes. Farage expressed the forebodings of the redundant and politically alienated when he predicted that 'the white working class is in danger of becoming an underclass'.[7] His voice became the siren of a new phenomenon, populism, which soon found influential allies in the mass-circulation *Sun*, *Daily Mail* and *Daily Express* newspapers and the Tory European Research Group. Their immediate target was the EU, which was imagined to be the prime source of Britain's woes, and its begetter, 'globalisation'.

Globalisation had many ingredients. It was a loose abstraction created by economic movements that had been gathering momentum for the past forty years and now seemed irreversible. They included the new international capitalism, in which millions of pounds could be transferred across continents at the press of a button, the accelerated diffusion of information and ideas via the Internet, cheap airborne tourism, imported cuisines and mass entertainment and sport. The American-made puppet show *The Muppets* was one of China's most popular TV programmes and Manchester United claimed more than a billion fans worldwide.

Mass transcontinental immigration was also blamed on globalisation by those already hostile towards incomers from the EU, Asia and Africa. Immigrants were blamed by populists as the catalyst for the dissolution of traditional urban communities, turning their inhabitants into what one pundit called 'citizens of nowhere'. Paradoxically, many of those Brits who perceive themselves to have been economically and politically cast adrift habitually took holidays abroad, were addicted to Chinese-manufactured mobile phones and American television programmes, and patronised Indian and Chinese takeaways. There are 11,000 Chinese restaurants in Britain.

At first, apprehensions about globalisation were focused on the EU and the upshot was a referendum held in June 2016. Seventy-two per cent of the electorate voted: 17.4 million chose to leave the EU and 16.1 million to remain. The processes of disengagement dragged on for more than six years and were still under way in 2022, with no obvious end in sight.

Beijing was stunned by these events. China had been in favour of Britain staying in the EU because it suited her investment and marketing strategies. According to the state-controlled media, Britain had succumbed to 'a losing mindset' and had deliberately isolated herself 'from the outside world'. This benefited China, for 'the world's centre no longer lay on the two sides of the Atlantic' and 'the focus has shifted to the Pacific'. No doubt the CCP felt that the referendum result justified its aversion to free elections.

After Brexit, Anglo-Chinese relations rapidly soured. They did so against a background of fractious political rows generated by the complications of disengaging from the EU. This was understood in Beijing, where British hostility was interpreted as being to distract attention from internal tensions. In July 2022, a senior diplomat, Zhao Lijian, protested: 'I do want to inform some UK politicians that they can't solve their own problems by frequently using China and hyping the Chinese threat.'

There was some truth in this. Yet the demonisation of China in the UK was also a moral reaction to China's domestic and foreign policies. The increasingly fierce restrictions imposed on the remaining liberties of the population of Hong Kong and the state terror unleashed on the Muslim Uyghurs horrified the public and the media.

The Uyghurs are an ethno-religious group who live in Xinjiang province, which borders Russia and which has a history of resisting Chinese rule and, in the 1930s, of flirting with Moscow. Obstreperous outsiders, as the Uyghurs were perceived to be, had no place in either the Qing Empire nor its successor the People's Republic. A flurry of Uyghur demonstrations and terror attacks in the early 2000s persuaded Beijing that they needed to be reminded of their loyalty to Party and state, in the form of an official campaign of terror which was outlined by President Xi in August 2014. 'We must be harsh with them and show them absolutely no mercy.' They were 'terrorists' and would be treated 'like rats scurrying across the streets with everybody shouting "beat them"'. One of Xi's satraps promised 'to bury the corpses of the terrorists and terror groups in the sea of the People's war'.[8]* At least a million Uyghurs have been corralled into concentration camps and forced-labour factories and many have been murdered, tortured, sterilised and raped.

These abominations mirror those of Nazi Germany and Soviet Russia and have provoked an international outcry. Britain and forty-two other countries have condemned China for what Washington called 'crimes against humanity and genocide'. Revealingly, nations in receipt of Chinese investment have been silent; they include Pakistan, Egypt, Algeria and Sudan. All have a bad record for human rights.

Britain's official position has been ambivalent. In January 2021, the Commons debated an embargo on Chinese products whose manufacture involved the 'slave labour' of Uyghur prisoners. There was multi-party vilification of Chinese barbarity, yet the foreign secretary, Dominic Raab, while acknowledging Britain's 'moral duty' to protest, shied away from provoking a valued trading partner. It was wiser,

---

* This violent rhetoric was noted by an American journalist Raffi Khatchadourian and was the prelude to a reign of terror which has still to run its course.

he thought, to work in harness with the UN rather than impose a unilateral ban.

Closer to home, there were growing suspicions that China was infiltrating British public life through funding academic programmes such as the Confucius programme and by its financial gifts to universities. The China Centre at Jesus College, Cambridge, was singled out, although its funding represented less than 2 per cent of the college's revenues. Behind these fears was a theory that Beijing was aiming to buy friends and exert undue political influence in intellectual and political circles.

This collective angst had been given substance by China's National Intelligence Law of 2017, which demanded that every Chinese business corporation should work hand in hand with the country's intelligence agencies at home and abroad. The implications of this forced alliance between China's spies and entrepreneurs lay at the root of the Huawei affair of 2020. The Huawei company planned to export mobile phones that had the potential to penetrate existing 5G systems. If adopted in Britain, this would provide the means by which Chinese intelligence agencies could harvest personal, commercial and official data. A media outcry was followed by demands for a ban on the Huawei contract, although the company denied any connection with Chinese intelligence-gathering. The issue was debated in the Commons, where one MP warned that Britain would be at the mercy of Chinese 'espionage, sabotage and cyber-attack'. Iain Duncan Smith, a onetime Tory leader, added a melodramatic touch by likening acceptance of Huawei to government co-operation with Nazi Germany in the development of radar. Such nightmares also disturbed America, which blocked any deal with Huawei, as, in the end, did Britain.

The Uyghur furore in particular was instructive. It revealed a world deeply divided by moral principles in which Britain and the rest of the Western democratic nations reviled China as an outcast. Nevertheless, she could no longer be isolated and coerced as she had been in the past. Now China had a growing circle of friendly states, particularly in Asia and Africa, who had been drawn towards her by the Belt and Road initiative launched in 2013. These links were intended to bind China to national economies through massive investments of her abundant surplus capital. President Xi initially reserved $124 billion for loans for distribution among poorer, under-developed states. Infrastructure was a priority: Kenya, for instance, got a high-speed railway between Mombasa and Nairobi.

The attractions, success and political implications of the Belt and Road proposal caused jitters in London and Washington, for it looked like a master plan for a China-centric world. There were also worrying military implications: modernised Asian, African and Pacific port facilities could become bases for the Chinese navy. But China too faced problems with the Belt and Road initiative, the most troublesome of which were those of borrowers who defaulted. In 2017, Sri Lanka was unable to service a loan made for the new port of Hambantota and was compelled to cede it to China on a ninety-nine-year lease. It is not known whether anyone in Beijing noticed the paradox of China securing a replica of the agreement that had been made in 1898 between her and Britain for Hong Kong's New Territories.

Once a state that could be coerced, cajoled and invaded, China is now a titan on the world stage, free to do as she wishes and indifferent to the values of her critics. Protests about the Uyghurs can be ignored, as can those made by Britain against new laws to tighten Hong Kong's administration and curtail free speech. The drive for a united, monolithic China overrides promises to maintain the 'one state, two systems' regime in Hong Kong. It is now effectively a part of a China which makes its own rules, just as Britain had done in the nineteenth century.

'One China' includes Taiwan, for over seventy years an independent state 100 miles from the Chinese mainland. Since it came to power in 1949, the CCP has repeatedly made it clear that it will secure an island occupied by Japan more than fifty years previously as part of a wider policy to absorb all the territories lost to China during the period of submission. The final objective of Taiwan, with a population of 23.5 million and a per capita income of $36,300, is to become an independent state. Its wealth derives from services and industries that include the manufacture of two-thirds of the world's microchips. Taiwan is, therefore, a desirable prize for China, but it will come at a heavy cost.

Since 1949, the United States has been Taiwan's patron and armourer, and the 7th Fleet her protector from the invasion long promised by China. Over recent years, Beijing has become increasingly hawkish. Threats are backed by naval and aerial demonstrations, often close to Taiwan's territorial waters, and in 2022 Chinese guided missiles were fired over the islands. The American 7th Fleet and that of its ally Japan avoid close confrontation with the Chinese wherever possible. Neither country has an alliance with Taiwan, but both are determined not to allow the South China Sea to become a Chinese lake.

The latest prognosis by Washington's analysts is bleak. An outright war could see the destruction of the American and Japanese fleets, the loss of air supremacy over Taiwan, heavy Chinese losses and the likelihood of a resort to tactical nuclear weapons. In addition, China has just gained an ally of convenience, Russia, which has been isolated by her so far bungled invasion of the Ukraine. How long Moscow can keep the friendship of a traditional rival is not yet clear, nor is the price that Beijing will set for its favour.

Like America, Britain has no alliance with Japan or Taiwan. Nevertheless, since July 2022 Britain has had two warships stationed in Far Eastern waters as an earnest sign of her traditional support for freedom of international navigation. They are, perhaps, the faint afterglow of the long imperial sunset.

# ACKNOWLEDGEMENTS

First, I would like to thank Alan Samson and Andrew Lownie for their encouragement and interest, and Kate Morton and Frances Rooney for their excellent editing and patience. My gratitude also extends to Jonathan Fenby and Andrew Williams for their guidance and sharing with me their knowledge of China. Thanks are also due to my wife Mary, Edward James, Henry James, Andy Joyce, Justin Wells, William Thomas, the late Jeremy Barrett, and the staff of the London Library for morale and technical assistance. Much of the writing of this book coincided with the tribulations of the Covid-19 emergency and I would like to thank the staff of Gloucestershire NHS for their efficiently run and effective programme of vaccinations.

# NOTES

For Chinese provinces, cities and towns, I have used modern names. For other countries, I have used historical names, for example the name of Indo-China for Vietnam before 1954.

## Chapter 1
### Barbarians: The Origins of the First Opium War, 1830–1839

1   Chen, S.G., pp. 2, 17, 166
2   Zhaoguang, pp. 3, 13
3   Fletcher, *The Heyday*, pp. 396–8
4   Perdue, p. 46
5   Dikötter, *Discourse*, pp. 38–9, 43–6
6   Rait, vol. 1, p. 120
7   *China Trade*, ed. Le Pichon, pp. 556, 564, 568–9
8   Ibid., p. 388
9   Cunynghame, vol. 1, p. 202

## Chapter 2
### Energetic Measures: The First Opium War, 1839–1842

1   Bowring, p. 119
2   *China Trade*, ed. Le Pichon, pp. 43, 388
3   Hansard, 5th Series, Lords, 54, 1208
4   *Naval and Nautical Magazine*, 9 (1840), pp. 9, 284
5   Hansard, 5th Series, 52, 1222
6   Lovell, p. 103
7   Hansard, 5th Series, 53, 693, 700, 703, 707, 782
8   Ibid., 53, 717
9   Hansard, 5th Series, Lords, 54, 3
10  *Naval and Nautical Magazine*, 9 (1840), pp. 625, 821
11  Hansard, 5th series, 61, 789
12  Rait, vol. 1, p. 14
13  *Colburn's United Service Magazine*, February 1842, p. 275; Rait, vol. 1, pp. 185–6
14  Rait, vol. 1, p. 168; *Colburn's United Service Magazine*, December 1841, p. 536

[15] Hansard, 5th Series, Lords, 59, 4
[16] Andrade, pp. 240–41
[17] *Colburn's United Service Magazine*, January 1842, pp. 113–14
[18] Hall and Bernard, vol. 1, p. 4
[19] Andrade, p. 184; Hall and Bernard, vol. 1, p. 271; *Chinese Repository*, 10 January 1841, p. 42; Bingham, vol. 2, pp. 69–70
[20] *Colburn's United Service Magazine*, November 1841, pp. 402–3
[21] Ibid., December 1841, p. 530
[22] Rait, vol. 1, pp. 235–6
[23] Lovell, p. 113
[24] Waley, pp. 162–5, 179–80
[25] Lovell, pp. 223–4
[26] Ibid., pp. 141–2
[27] Ibid., p. 185
[28] Ibid., p. 187
[29] Rait, vol. 1, p. 246
[30] Rowe, pp. 173–4; Westad, pp. 1, 45
[31] Lovell, p. 461

## Chapter 3
*Shi Yizhi*: Reactions to the Opium War

[1] S.G. Chen, pp. 127–8
[2] Dikötter, *Things Modern*, pp. 193, 195
[3] Bickers, *Britain and China*, p. 65
[4] *Spectator*, 29 October 1842
[5] Hansard, 5th Series, 68, 322, 374, 391
[6] Wong, p. 82
[7] Young, A.J., p. 40
[8] Ibid., p. 59
[9] TNA, Adm 116/3253
[10] Clowes, vol. 4, pp. 354–5; Fox, pp. 110–11; HMS *Medea*; *Colburn's United Service Magazine*, 1858, 1, pp. 305–6
[11] Preston and Major, p. 46
[12] Veniukov, pp. 327, 444–5, 466
[13] Lindenfeld, p. 337
[14] Andrade, pp. 264–5
[15] Polachek, p. 274
[16] Dikötter, *Discourse*, pp. 48–9
[17] Halsey, *passim*
[18] Bennett, pp. 2, 356, 363
[19] Liu, p. 273
[20] Hall and Bernard, vol. 1, p. 381
[21] Cunynghame, vol. 1, pp. 65, 80, 129
[22] Hill, p. 229

## Chapter 4
## Heavenly Kingdom: Civil War and Foreign Invasion, 1847–1858

[1] Spence, *God's Chinese Son*, p. 161
[2] Smith, *passim*, for the sermon
[3] Bowring, p. 145
[4] Fox, p. 89
[5] Wong, p. 78
[6] Bowring, pp. 131, 133
[7] *Colburn's United Service Magazine*, 1858, 3, pp. 230, 233
[8] Hansard, 3rd Series, 144, 1431, 1541
[9] *Leader*, 27 March 1858
[10] Lane-Poole, p. 163
[11] *Colburn's United Service Magazine*, 1858, 3, pp. 230–33
[12] Ibid., p. 236
[13] Ibid., p. 164

## Chapter 5
## Knuckle Down: More Wars, 1858–1864

[1] Hansard, 5th Series, 776, 810
[2] *La Presse*, 1 March 1860
[3] *Colburn's United Service Magazine*, 1860, 3, p. 585; Wolseley, p. 75
[4] Wolseley, p. 75
[5] Spence, *God's Chinese Son*, p. 273
[6] Elgin, *Letters and Journals*, 22 November 1858, Platt, p. 49
[7] *Nautical Magazine*, vol. 5 (1859), p. 78
[8] Wolseley, pp. 338–9
[9] Ibid., p. 36
[10] *Colburn's United Service Magazine*, 1860, 3, p. 597; Wolseley, p. 101
[11] Bowers, pp. 19, 39, 42
[12] *Colburn's United Service Magazine*, 1859, 1, pp. 102–3
[13] Wolseley, pp. 94, 168
[14] Ibid., p. 90
[15] Loch, p. 67
[16] *Punch*, 5 November 1860
[17] Hill, pp. 232–45
[18] Morse, p. 63
[19] Liu, p. 102

## Chapter 6
## Pure Magic: Machines and Money

[1] Dikötter, *Things Modern*, p. 102
[2] Ibid., pp. 82–4

3   Ibid., p. 90
4   Morse, p. 414
5   Van de Ven, *Breaking with the Past*, pp. 94–5, 98–9
6   Morse, p. 237 note
7   Bickers, 'Infrastructural Globalisation', p. 432
8   Otte, pp. 76–7

## Chapter 7
## Fear of Demons: Missionaries and Their Enemies

1   Wellings, p. 10
2   *Church Missionary Record*, January and December 1878; multiply these figures by 66 to get their modern equivalent.
3   Wellings, p. 10
4   Scully, 'Prostitution', p. 856
5   Esherick, pp. 85, 93
6   Ibid., p. 93
7   *Missionary Herald*, August 1898
8   Young, E.P., p. 101; Lindenfeld, pp. 343–4
9   Hansard, 3rd Series, 195, 131–2
10  *Missionary Herald*, February 1898, p. 57
11  Litzinger, pp. 50–51; Lindenfeld, p. 334
12  Chuan, p. 113
13  Morse, p. 410
14  Esherick, pp. 84–5
15  E.P. Young, pp. 103–4
16  Esherick, pp. 124–5
17  Hanan, p. 338
18  *Missionary Herald*, January 1882

## Chapter 8
## I Always Mistrust a Russian: Power Struggles

1   Otte, p. 95
2   Preston and Major, p. 261
3   Sakowicz, pp. 275, 278, 280
4   Lieven, p. 38
5   Veniukov, pp. 43–4; Lieven, p. 36
6   Marshall, p. 78
7   Ibid., p. 77
8   *Photographic Album of the Japan-China War* (Yokohama, 1895)
9   Andrade, pp. 287–92
10  Dikötter, *Discourse*, p. 113
11  Otte, pp. 30–33, 39
12  Jansen et al., p. 191

13 Martel, p. 363
14 Otte, p. 11
15 Ibid., p. 27
16 Inaba, p. 65
17 Yang, p. 178
18 Otte, pp. 107, 117–18
19 Esherick, pp. 136–7, 163

## Chapter 9
## The Hearts and Minds of the People: The Boxer Uprising, 1898–1900

1 Spence, *Search for Modern China*, p. 232
2 Esherick, pp. 323, 235
3 Van de Ven, *Breaking with the Past*, p. 1466
4 Esherick, p. 183
5 Otte, p. 184
6 Spence, *Search for Modern China*, p. 233
7 *Buffalo Commercial*, 2 September 1901: MacDonald expressed these views to American businessmen.
8 Fleming, p. 77
9 Kočvar, p. 137
10 Ion, pp. 37–8
11 Kočvar, p. 143
12 Ibid., pp. 158–9
13 Lynch, pp. 81–2, 140
14 Cohen, P.A., p. 84
15 Ibid., pp. 97, 103

## Chapter 10
## The Oncoming Awakening: War and Revolution, 1901–1912

1 Marshall, p. 82
2 Otte, pp. 291–2; Neilson, p. 54
3 Neilson, p. 51
4 Ferris, pp. 249–50
5 Chapman, p. 91
6 Inaba, p. 71
7 Marshall, p. 90; Walker, pp. 48–9
8 Otte, p. 98
9 Marshall, p. 101
10 Dickinson, p. 201
11 Marshall, p. 96
12 Dickinson, p. 105

## Chapter 11
## Better Our Condition: The Fortunes of Hong Kong

[1]   Tsai, pp. 243–4, 247
[2]   Sinn, *Pacific Crossing*, pp. 219–21
[3]   Tsai, p. 28
[4]   Sinn, *Pacific Crossing*, p. 228
[5]   Horrocks, p. 12
[6]   Sinn, *Pacific Crossing*, pp. 281–3
[7]   Sinn, 'The Strike and Riot of 1884', p. 78
[8]   Tsai, p. 114
[9]   Man and Lun, pp. 56–8
[10]  Horrocks, p. 41
[11]  Ibid., p. 97
[12]  Poon, *passim*
[13]  Sinn, *Pacific Crossing*, p. 247
[14]  Man and Lun, p. 37
[15]  Tsai, p. 121

## Chapter 12
## No Hope for China, 1912–1927

[1]   Chen, 'Defining Chinese Warlords', p. 563
[2]   Stone, p. 48
[3]   Lowe, p. 167
[4]   TNA, WO 95/83 (4–5 September 1917); WO 95/4018 (25–6 February 1918). Mutinies by Egyptian and African labourers were similarly suppressed.
[5]   Lieutenant Williams recalled this incident to his son Vivian many years later. Like many others, he rarely spoke about his experiences at the front.
[6]   Loh Pinchon, p. 421
[7]   Macmillan, p. 339
[8]   Reid, p. 391
[9]   Van de Ven, *War and Nationalism*, p. 79
[10]  Stone, p. 73
[11]  Horrocks, p. 108
[12]  Ibid., p. 162
[13]  Hansard, 5th Series, 185, 27–26
[14]  Best, 'Our Respective Empires', p. 268
[15]  Bickers and Howlett *Britain and China*, pp. 143–5

## Chapter 13
## A Feeling of Power: The Coming of War, 1927–1937

1   Mitter, *China's War with Japan, 1937–1945: The Struggle for Survival*, pp. 74–5
2   Ikurai, p. 231
3   Thorne, pp. 4–5
4   Best, 'India, Pan-Asianism and the Anglo-Japanese Alliance', p. 241
5   Ferris, p. 232
6   Ibid., pp. 259, 261
7   Dudden, pp. 84–5
8   Kiernan, p. 229
9   Dudden, p. 80
10  *Atlantic*, September 1906
11  Mitter, *China's War*, p. 43
12  Marder, p. 17
13  McMeekin, pp. 62–4
14  Mitter, *China's War*, p. 55
15  Man and Lun, p. 90
16  Ibid., p. 101
17  Marder, p. 7

## Chapter 14
## Japan Is Now Bullying Us: Appeasement in China, 1937–1939

1   Marder, pp. 24–6
2   Ibid., p. 22
3   Bickers and Howlett, *Britain and China*, p. 12
4   Ibid., p. 121
5   Lee, p. 122
6   Hansard, 5th Series, 355, 845
7   Ibid., 338, 1785–6
8   Thorne, p. 30
9   Lee, p. 153
10  Ibid., pp. 162–3
11  Elphick, pp. 77, 87–8
12  YouTube, Pathé newsreels, Sino-Japanese War
13  *Guardian*, 4 October 2002
14  Wilson Center, Digital Archives, China and the Soviet Union in Xinjiang, 1934–49
15  Mitter, *China's War with Japan, 1937-1945* p. 163
16  Lee, p. 195
17  Thorne, p. 38
18  Medvedev, pp. 68–9
19  Braumoeller, pp. 21–2

[20] *Time*, 30 August 1937; 29 November 1937; 27 December 1937; 21 February 1938

## Chapter 15
## We Cannot Risk Another War: The Road to Pearl Harbor

[1] Overy, p. 292
[2] De Vries, p. 4
[3] Amery, pp. 641–4
[4] Thorne, p. 55
[5] McMeekin, pp. 252–4
[6] Ibid., p. 245
[7] Thorne, p. 74
[8] Ibid., p. 3
[9] Overy, p. 179
[10] Chiang Kai-shek, *All We Are*, p. 3

## Chapter 16
## What the Hell Is the Matter?: The World Turned Upside Down, 1942–1943

[1] Stilwell Diaries, 15 February 1942
[2] *Foreign Relations of the United States*, p. 323
[3] Overy, p. 168
[4] I am grateful to the late Colonel Frank Turner for this recollection.
[5] Marder, p. 81
[6] Kershaw, p. 456
[7] Overy, p. 179
[8] Wang, Z., p. 22
[9] Ibid., p. 74
[10] Amery, p. 774
[11] Man and Lun, p. 179, quoting TNA WO 172/1689, 3
[12] *The War against Japan*, vol. 1, p. 31
[13] Man and Lun, p. 213
[14] TNA, WO 208/1529
[15] TNA, WO 206/2357C, 1A
[16] TNA, Adm 199/622A, 628B
[17] Historic Hansard: House of Representatives, 20 February 1942
[18] Amery, pp. 823, 826, 829
[19] Hansard, 5th Series, 366, 399
[20] *Foreign Relations of the United States*, pp. 323–7
[21] Ibid., pp. 343–4
[22] Alanbrooke, pp. 477–9
[23] Moran, p. 151
[24] Mitter, *China's War with Japan, 1937-1945*, pp. 311, 313

Chapter 17
Territorial Ambitions: Victory and Rewards, 1944–1945

1 Bickers and Howlett, *Britain and China*, p. 74
2 Thorne, p. 552
3 Kit-ching, pp. 76, 82
4 Thorne, p. 552
5 Ibid., p. 495
6 Kit-ching, p. 87
7 Thorne, p. 498
8 Ibid., pp. 392–3
9 Ibid., p. 539
10 Ibid., p. 577
11 O'Toole, 17 May 1942, 27 March 1943 and *passim*
12 Hong Kong's War Crimes Trials Collections, *passim*
13 Hong Kong's Resistance: The British Army Aid Group, 1942–1945, *passim*
14 Wang, Z., p. 100
15 Walker, p. 17
16 McMeekin, p. 646
17 Wang, Z., p. 105
18 Ibid., p. 103
19 Hansard, 6th Series, 413, 792–3
20 Wang, Z., p. 104

Chapter 18
The Fall of China: New Realities, 1946–1950

1 Sutton, pp. 84–5
2 Ibid., pp. 90, 98–9
3 Walker, p. 37
4 Mitter, *China's War*, p. 353
5 Loh Pinchon, p. 412
6 Howlett, pp. 130–32
7 Dikötter, *The Tragedy of Liberation*, pp. 52–3
8 McMeekin, p. 653
9 Walker, p. 66
10 Cohen, N., p. 282
11 Bickers and Howlett, *Britain and China*, p. 239
12 *Guardian*, 20 January 2022
13 Memorial of Convention between Anastas Mikoyan and Zhou Enlai, Wilson Center
14 Howlett, p. 227
15 Dikötter, *Tragedy of Liberation*, p. 43
16 Wang, Z., pp. 136–7
17 Sutton, p. 163

[18] Wang, Z., p. 138; Sutton, *Sino-British Relations*, p. 142
[19] BBC News, 16 July 2008

## Chapter 19
### *Pax Americana*: Conflict and Compromise, 1950–1958

[1] Zhai, *China and the Vietnam War, 1950-1975*, pp. 18–19
[2] Ibid., p. 64
[3] Fenby, p. 364
[4] Zhai, *China and the Vietnam War, 1950-1975*, p. 13
[5] Dikötter, *Tragedy of Liberation*, p. 129
[6] Hastings, p. 47
[7] Ibid., pp. 257–8
[8] Gilbert, vol. 8, p. 928
[9] TNA, Defe 4/41, 14
[10] TNA, Defe 14/58
[11] Dikötter, *Tragedy of Liberation*, p. 141
[12] Zhai, 'China's Evolving Role', p. 63
[13] Sutton, p. 141
[14] Tsang, pp. 30–31
[15] Sutton, p. 141
[16] Tsang, pp. 113, 133
[17] Halperin, p. ix.
[18] Ibid., pp. 141–2; *New York Times*, 3 November 2021
[19] Halperin, p. 315
[20] Ibid., p. 444
[21] TNA, Defe 13/228, 15
[22] Moore, *passim*

## Chapter 20
### The East Is Red: Mixed Fortunes, 1959–1972

[1] Hansard, 5th Series, 750, 2473
[2] Zhai, 'China's Evolving Role', p. 119
[3] Ibid., p. 136
[4] Hansard, 5th Series, 969, 511
[5] Hobsbawm, p. 467
[6] Wang, Y., *passim*
[7] CIA Report on the Role of Red Guards (1968), www.cia.gov
[8] Fenby, p. 479
[9] *Independent*, 17 August 1997
[10] *South China Post*, Magazine Section, 24 January 2021
[11] Lüthi and Jian, p. 148
[12] Ibid., pp. 153–4

13 Speeches at the Closing Session of the CCP Central Committee Conference, Wilson Center, www.wilsoncenter.org

14 Kuisong, p. 27

15 Ibid.

16 Ibid., p. 34

17 Gerson, pp. 28, 30

18 Ibid., p. 50

## Chapter 21
## Asian Tigers: China and Hong Kong, 1972–1989

1 *China Daily*, 21 April 2022

2 Hurst, *passim*: this article draws on unpublished papers from the Thatcher Archive

3 Calhoun, pp. 44, 48–9

4 Sarotte, *passim*

5 This comment was picked up by the Foreign Office and conveyed to Washington (UKE Peking to FO: PROTESTS PREM 19-2597.148).

6 Bevan and Mitchell, np.

7 *Guardian*, 5 June 1989

8 Richardson and Lewis, Document 4

9 Ibid., Document 28

10 E.g. *China Daily*, 7 July 2011, BBC News, 2 June 2019

## Chapter 22
## Number-One Threat: Prejudice and Pride, 1990–2022

1 *The Times*, 25 July 2022

2 Quoted in 'The UK and China's Security and Trade Relationship', pp. 24, 41

3 BBC News Online, 4 April 2002, news.bbc.co.uk

4 Cradock, in *Prospect*, 20 April, 1997

5 *Guardian*, 19, 21 November 2005

6 Esparraga, np

7 *Daily Mail*, 2 April 2014

8 Khatchadourian, *passim*, for these quotations and much that follows.

# BIBLIOGRAPHY

Unpublished:
National Archives, Kew (TNA), Adm 116 and 119; Defe 4 and 14; WO 95, 172, 206, 208.

All published in London except where stated otherwise:
Field Marshal Lord Alanbrooke (A. Danchev and D. Todman eds), *War Diaries 1939–1945* (2002 edn).

G. Alexander, 'Reminiscences of a Visit to the Celestial Empire and Rough Notes on the Chinese', *Colburn's United Service Magazine*, January 1859.

L. Amery, *The Empire at Bay: The Leo Amery Diaries, 1919–1945* (1983).

J.L. Anderson, 'Piracy in World History: An Economic Perspective on Maritime Predation', *Journal of World History*, 8(2) (1995).

T. Andrade, *The Gunpowder Age: China, Military Innovation and the Rise of the West in World History* (Princeton, NJ, 2016).

Anon., 'Japan and China', *World Affairs*, 100(2), September 1937.

D.H. Bays (ed.), *Christianity in China from the Eighteenth Century to the Present* (Stanford, CA, 1996).

I. Bellér-Hann, *Community Matters in Xinjiang, 1880–1949* (Leiden, 2008).

T. Bennett, *History of Photography in China: Chinese Photographers, 1844–1870* (2013).

A. Best, 'India, Pan-Asianism and the Anglo-Japanese Alliance', in O'Brien (ed.), *The Anglo-Japanese Alliance*.

A. Best, '"Our Respective Empires Should Stand Together": The Royal Dimension in Anglo-Japanese Relations, 1911–1941', *Diplomacy and Statecraft*, 16(2) (2005).

M.B. Bevan and S. Mitchell, 'Australian Broadcasting Corporation Previously Classified Cables Reveal What PM Bob Hawke

thought he knew about the Tiananmen Massacre' (2021).
www.abc.net.au

R. Bickers, *Britain and China: Community, Culture and Colonialism 1900–1949* (Manchester, 1999).

R. Bickers, 'Infrastructural Globalisation: Lighting the China Coasts, 1860s–1930s', *Historical Journal*, 56(2) (2013).

R. Bickers, 'Britain and China, and India, 1830s–1940s', in Bickers and Howlett (eds), *Britain and China*.

R. Bickers and J. Howlett (eds), *Britain and China, 1840–1970: Empire, Finance and War* (2015).

J.E. Bingham, *Narrative of the Expedition to China from the Commencement of the War to Its Termination in 1842; with Sketches of the Manners and Customs of the Singular and Hitherto Almost Unknown Country* (2 vols, 1842).

R. Bowers, 'Lieutenant Charles Cameron's Opium Diary', *Journal of the Royal Asiatic Society, Hong Kong Branch*, 52 (2012).

P. Bowring, *Free Trade's First Missionary: Sir John Bowring and Asia* (Hong Kong, 2014).

B.F. Braumoeller, 'The Myth of American Isolationism', *Foreign Policy Analysis* (2010). https://doi.org/10.1111/j.1743-8594.2010.00117.x

P. Cain, 'China, Globalisation and the West: A British Debate'. www.historyandpolicy.org

C. Calhoun, 'Revolution and Repression in Tiananmen Square', *Society*, 26 June 1989.

J.M. Carnoll, '"The Usual Intercourse of Nations": The British in Pre-Opium War China', in Bickers and Howlett (eds), *Britain and China*.

J. Chapman, 'The Secret Dimension of the Anglo-Japanese Alliance', in O'Brien (ed.), *The Anglo-Japanese Alliance*.

J.T. Chen, 'Defining Chinese Warlords and Factions', *Bulletin of the School of Oriental and African Studies University of London*, 31(3) (1968).

J.T. Chen, 'The May Fourth Movement Redefined', *Modern Asian Studies*, 4(1) (1976).

S.G. Chen, *Merchants of Peace and War: British Knowledge of China in the Making of the Opium War* (Hong Kong, 2017).

Chiang Kai-shek, *All We Are and All We Have* (1943).

W.M. Chow, E. Han and X. Li, 'Brexit Identities and British Public Opinion on China' (2019). Internet.

W. Clowes, *A History of the Royal Navy from Earliest Times to 1900* (7 vols, 1897–1903).

N.I. Cohen. 'Conversations with Chinese Friends: Zhou Enlai Reflects on Chinese-American Relations in the 1940s and the Korean War', *Diplomatic History*, 11(3) (1987).

P.A. Cohen, 'The Boxers in History and Myth', *Journal of Asian Studies*, 51(1) (1992).

A. Cunynghame, *China and the Chinese: Being an Aide-de-Camp's Reflections of Service in China, a Residence in Hong Kong and Visits to Other Islands in the China Seas* (2 vols, 1844).

R. Davenport-Hines (ed.), *Hugh Trevor-Roper: The China Journals, Ideology and Intrigue in the 1960s* (2021).

A. Davydov, 'Radical Right Ideologies and Foreign Policy Preference: Attitudes towards Russia, China and the USA in EU Member States', *Révue Transatlantique sur l'Europe Politique* (2021).

B. de Vries, 'The Battle for Oil in the Dutch East Indies', *International Planning History Society Proceedings*, 18(1) (2018).

F. Dickinson, 'Japan Debates the Anglo-Japanese Alliance: The Second Revision of 1911', in O'Brien (ed.), *The Anglo-Japanese Alliance*.

F. Dikötter, *The Discourse of Race in China* (1992).

F. Dikötter, *Things Modern: Material Culture and Everyday Life in China* (2006).

F. Dikötter, *The Tragedy of Liberation: A History of the Chinese Revolution, 1947–1957* (2013).

J.A. Dolliver, 'The Significance of the Anglo-Japanese Alliance', in O'Brien (ed.), *The Anglo-Japanese Alliance*.

L. Duan, 'Between Social Control and Popular Power: The Circulation of Private Guns and Gun Control', *American Journal of Chinese Studies*, 24(2) (2017).

A.P. Dudden, *The American Pacific: From the China Trade to the Present Day* (Oxford, 1992).

*Letters and Journals of James, Eighth Earl of Elgin* (2012 edn).

P. Elphick, *Far Eastern File: The Intelligence War in the Far East* (1997).

J.W. Esherick, *The Origins of the Boxer Rising* (Berkeley, CA, 1987).

F. Esparraga, 'Rhetoric of the Right: European Populist's View of China', policy brief no. 205, 27 September 2017, Institute for Security and Development Policy.

J. Fenby, *The Penguin History of Modern China: The Rise and Fall of a Great Power 1850–2008* (2008).

J. Ferris, 'Armaments and Allies: The Anglo-Japanese Strategic Relationship', in O'Brien (ed.), *The Anglo-Japanese Alliance*.

P. Fleming, *The Siege at Peking* (1951).

J. Fletcher, 'Sino-Russian Relations, 1800–1862', in *The Cambridge History of China*, vol. 10 (1978).

J. Fletcher, 'The Heyday of the Chiang Order in Mongolia', in D. Twitchen and J.K. Fairbank (eds), *Sino-Russian Relations 1800–1863* (1978).

*Foreign Relations of the United States: Diplomatic Papers, the Conferences at Cairo and Tehran, 1943* (Washington DC, 1961).

R.G. Forman, 'Hong Kong, 1898', in *Victorian Review*, 36(1) (2010).

G.E. Fox, *British Admirals and Chinese Pirates* (1940).

S. Fröhlich, 'Pictures of the Sino-Japanese War of 1894–1895', *War in History*, 21(2) (2014).

E.S.K. Fung, 'Military Subversion in the Chinese Revolution of 1911', *Modern Asian Studies*, 9(1) (1975).

M. Gerson (ed.), 'The Sino-Soviet Border Conflict: Deterrence, Escalation, and the Threat of Nuclear War in 1969', CNA (2010).

M. Gilbert, *Winston S. Churchill: Never Despair 1945–1965* (1988).

R. Grace, *Opium and Empire: The Lives and Careers of William Jardine and James Matheson* (Montreal, 2014).

W.H. Hall and W.D. Bernard, *Narrative of the Voyages and Services of the Nemesis from 1940 to 1843 and the Combined Naval Operations in China* (2 vols, 1845).

H. Halperin, 'The 1958 Taiwan Straits Crisis: A Documented History', RAND Corporation (1966).

S.A. Halsey, 'Sovereignty, Self-Strengthening, and Steamships in Late Imperial China', *Journal of Asian History*, 48(1) (2014).

D. Hanan, 'The Missionary Novels of Nineteenth Century China', *Harvard Journal of Asiatic Studies*, 60(2) (2000).

Hansard, 1803–2019: Parliamentary Debates.

M. Hastings, *The Korean War* (1987 edn).

K. Hill, 'Collecting on Campaign: British Soldiers in China during the Opium Wars', *Journal of the History of Collections*, 25(2) (2013).

K. Hirata, 'Sino-British Relations on Railway Construction: State Imperialism and Local Elites, 1905–1911', in Bickers and Howlett (eds), *Britain and China*.

E. Hobsbawm, *The Age of Extremes: The Short Twentieth Century* (1996 edn).

Hong Kong Resistance: The British Army Aid Group, 1942–1945. https://digital.lib.hkbu.edu.hk

Hong Kong's War Crimes Trials Collection. https://hkwctc.lib.hku.hk

N. Horesh, 'From Mudflats to Cyber-Hub? The Shanghai Experience, 1842–2009', *American Journal of Asian Studies*, 16(2) (2009).

R.J. Horrocks, 'The Guangzhou-Hong Kong Strike', 1925–1926: Hong Kong Workers in an Anti-Imperialist Movement (1994). Internet.

J.J. Howlett, 'Decolonisation in China 1949–1950', in Bickers and Howlett (eds), *Britain and China*.

M. Hurst, 'Britain's Approach to the Negotiations over the Future of Hong Kong, 1979–1982', *The International History Review*, (2002).


A. Ikura, 'The Anglo-Japanese Alliance and the Question of Race', in O'Brien (ed.), *The Anglo-Japanese Alliance*.

C. Inaba, 'Military Co-operation under the First Japanese Alliance', in O'Brien (ed.), *The Anglo-Japanese Alliance*.

H. Ion, 'Towards a Naval Alliance: Some Naval Antecedents to the Anglo-Japanese Alliance', in O'Brien (ed.), *The Anglo-Japanese Alliance*.


I. Jackson, 'Expansion and Defence in the International Settlement in Shanghai', in Bickers and Howlett (eds), *Britain and China*.

M.B. Jansen, S.C. Chu, S. Okamoto and B. Oh, 'The Historiography of the Sino-Japanese War', *Journal of International History*, 1(2) (1979).

R. Khatchadourian, 'Surviving the Crackdown in Xinjiang', *New Yorker*, 12 April 2021.

I. Kershaw, *Hitler 1936–1945: Nemesis* (2000).

V.G. Kiernan, *European Empires from Conquest to Collapse, 1815–1960* (1982).

S. Kirby, *The War against Japan* (1957).

C.L. Kit-ching, 'Symbolism as Diplomacy: The United States and Britain's China Policy during the First Year of the Pacific War', *Diplomacy and Statecraft*, 16(1) (2005).

J. Kočvar, 'Germany and the Boxer Uprising in China', *West Bohemian Historical Review*, 5(2) (2015).

Y. Kuisong, 'The Sino-Soviet Border Clash of 1969: From Zhenbao Island to Sino-American Rapprochement', *Cold War History*, 1(1) (2010).

S. Lane-Poole (ed.), *Sir Harry Parkes and China* (1903).

B.A. Lee, *Britain and the Sino-Japanese War 1937–39: A Study in the Dilemmas of British Decline* (Stanford, CA, 1973).

A. Le Pichon (ed.), *China Trade and Empire: Jardine Matheson and the Origins of British Rule in Hong Kong* (Oxford, 2008).

D. Lieven, 'Pro-Germans and Russian Foreign Policy 1890–1914', *International History Review*, 2(1) (1980).

D. Lindenfeld, 'Indigenous Encounters with Christian Missionaries in China and West Africa, 1800–1920: A Comparative Study', *Journal of World History*, 16(3) (2005).

C.A. Litzinger, 'Rural and Village Organisation in North China: The Catholic Challenge in the Late Nineteenth Century', in Bays (ed.), *Christianity in China*.

L.H. Liu, *The Clash of Empires: The Invention of China in Modern World Making* (2004).

H.B. Loch, *Personal Narrative of Occurrences during Lord Elgin's Second Embassy to China* (1864).

P.Y. Loh Pinchon, 'The Politics of Chiang Kai-shek: A Reappraisal', *Journal of Asian Studies*, 25(3) (1966).

J. Lovell, *The Opium War* (2011 edn).

P. Lowe, 'War and War Plans in the Far East', *International History Review*, 21(1) (1999).

L.M. Lüthi (ed.), *The Regional Cold Wars in Europe, East Asia and the Middle East* (Washington DC, 2015).

L.M. Lüthi and C. Jian, 'China's Turn in the World', in L.M. Lüthi (ed.), *The Regional Cold Wars*.

G. Lynch, *The War of Civilisations: Being a Record of a 'Foreign Devil's' Experience with the Allies in Peking* (1901).

M. Macmillan, *Peacemakers: Six Months That Changed the World* (2002 edn).

*The Maisky Diaries: The Wartime Revelations of Stalin's Ambassador in London*, ed. G. Gorodetsky (2016 edn).

K.C. Man and T.Y. Lun, *Eastern Fortress: A Military History of Hong Kong, 1840–1970* (Hong Kong, 2010).

A.J. Marder, *Old Friends, New Enemies: The Royal Navy and the Imperial Japanese Navy: Strategic Illusions 1936–1941* (1981).

A. Marshall, *The Russian General Staff and Asia, 1800–1917* (2006).

G. Martel, 'Documenting the Great Game: "World Policy" and the "Turbulent Frontier" in the 1890s', *International History Review*, 2(2) (1980).

S. McMeekin, *Stalin's War: A New History of World War Two* (2021).

R. Medvedev, *China and the Superpowers* (Oxford, 1956).

C. Meissner and J.P. Tang, 'Upstart Industrialization and Exports: Evidence from Japan, 1880–1910', *Journal of Economic History*, 78(4) (2018).

T. Mingteh, 'Christian Missionary and Christian Intellectual, Gilbert Reid (1857–1927)', in Bays (ed.), *Christianity in China*.

*The Missionary Herald*, 1894 and 1898.

R. Mitter, '1911: The Unanchored Chinese Revolution', *China Quarterly*, 208 (2011).

R. Mitter, *China's War with Japan, 1937–1945: The Struggle for Survival* (2013).

R.J. Moore, 'Where Her Majesty's Nuclear Weapons Were', *Bulletin of the Atomic Scientists*, 57(1) (2001).

Lord Moran, *Winston Churchill: The Struggle for Survival, 1940–1965* (1968).

H.B. Morse, *The International Relations of the Chinese and Europe: The Period of Submission* (1918).

A.E. Moule, *The Glorious Land: Short Chapters on China, and the Missionary Work There* (1891).

K. Neilson, 'The Anglo-Japanese Alliance and British Strategic Policy', in O'Brien (ed.), *The Anglo-Japanese Alliance*.

P.P. O'Brien (ed.), *The Anglo-Japanese Alliance, 1902–1922* (2003).

J. O'Toole, 'The Prisoner of War Diary of Staff Sergeant James O'Toole, RAOC'. Internet.

T.G. Otte, *The China Question: Great Power Rivalry and British Isolation, 1894–1905* (Oxford, 2007).

*Our National Relationship with China: Being Speeches delivered at Exeter Hall by the Bishop of Victoria* (1857).

R. Overy, *Blood and Ruins: The Great Imperial War, 1931–1945* (2021).

C. Patten, *The Hong Kong Diaries* (2022).

P.P. Perdue, 'Culture, History, and Imperial Chinese Strategy: Legacies of the Qing Conquests', in Van de Ven (ed.), *Warfare in Chinese History*.

S.R. Platt, 'British Intervention in the Taiping Rebellion', in Bickers and Howlett (eds), *Britain and China*.

J.M. Polachek, *The Inner Opium War* (Cambridge, MA, 1992).

S.W. Poon, 'Dogs and British Colonialism: The Contested Ban on Eating Dogs in Colonial Hong Kong', *Journal of Imperial and Commonwealth History*, 42(2) (2014).

V. Popov, *Mixed Fortunes: An Economic History of China, Russia and the West* (Oxford, 2014).

A. Preston and J. Major, *Send a Gunboat! A Study of the Gunboat and Its Role in British Policy, 1854–1904* (1967).

C. Qianping, 'Foreign Investment in Modern China: An Analysis with a Focus on British Interests', in Bickers and Howlett (eds), *Britain and China*.

R.S. Rait, *The Life and Campaigns of Hugh, First Viscount Gough* (2 vols., 1902).

G. Reid, 'Japan and China', *The Journal of Race Development*, 8(3) (1918).

P. Richards, 'British Policy towards China with Special Reference to the Shantung Question', PhD Thesis, London School of Economics, 1970. www.lse.ac.uk

J.T. Richardson and M. Lewis, 'Tiananmen Square: Declassified History: National Security Archive Briefing, no.16 (June 1993)'. Internet.

W.T. Rowe, *China's Last Empire: The Great Qing* (2009).

O. Sahin and B. Ianosev, 'UK: Between Managed Moderation and Far-Right Conspiracy Theories', in Giuliano Bobba and Nicolas Hubé (eds), *Populism and the Politicization of the COVID-19 Crisis in Europe* (2021).

I. Sakowicz, 'Russia and the Russians: Opinions of the British Press during the Reign of Alexander II (Dailies and Weeklies)', *Journal of European Studies*, 35(3) (2005).

M. Sarotte, 'China's Fear of Contagion: Tiananmen Square and the Power of the European Example', *International Security*, 37(2) (2012).

E.P. Scully, 'Taking the Low Road to Sino-American Relations: "Open Door" Expansionists and the Two China Markets', *Journal of American History*, 82(1) (1995).

E.P. Scully, 'Prostitution as Privilege: The "American Girl" of Treaty Port Shanghai, 1860–1937', *International History Review*, 20(4) (1998).

D. Shum, *Red Roulette: An Insider's Story of Wealth, Power, Corruption and Vengeance in Today's China* (2021).

E. Sinn, 'The Strike and Riot of 1884: A Hong Kong Perspective', *Journal of the Hong Kong Branch of the Royal Asiatic Society*, 22 (1982).

E. Sinn, *Pacific Crossing: California Gold, Chinese Migration, and the Making of Hong Kong* (Hong Kong, 2013).

G. Smith, *Our National Relations with China: Being Two Speeches Delivered in Exeter Hall and in the Free-Trade Hall, Manchester* (1857).

Speeches at the Closing Session of the CCP Central Committee Work Conference, 1978, Wilson Center. www.wilsoncenter.org

J.D. Spence, *The Search for Modern China* (1990).

J.D. Spence, *God's Chinese Son: The Taiping Heavenly Kingdom of Hong Xiuquan* (1996).

Stilwell Diaries, Hoover Institute Archives. www.hoover.org

D.R. Stone, 'Soviet Arms Exports in the 1920s', *Journal of Contemporary History*, 48(1) (2013).

T. Summers, H.M. Chan, P. Gries and R. Turcsany, 'Worsening British Views of China in 2020: Evidence from Public Opinion, Parliament, and the Media', *Asia Europe Journal*, 20 (2022).

C. Sutton, *Britain's Cold War in Cyprus and Hong Kong: A Conflict of Empires* (2017).

J.E. Taylor, 'The Production of the Chiang Kai-shek Personality Cult, 1929–1975', *China Quarterly*, 185 (2006).

C. Thorne, *Allies of a Kind: The United States, Britain and the War against Japan 1941–1945* (Oxford, 1978).

J.-F. Tsai, *Hong Kong in Chinese History: Community and Social Unrest in the British Colony, 1842–1913* (New York, 1992).

S. Tsang, *The Cold War's Odd Couple: The Unintended Partnership between the Republic of China and the UK, 1950–1958* (2006).

'The UK and China's Security and Trade Relationship: A Strategic Void', House of Lords International Relations and Defence Committee, 1st Report of Session 2021–22. https://publications.parliament.uk

'United States Nuclear Target List', National Security Archives (George Washington University). www.gwu.edu

'United States Strikes against Chinese Nuclear Facilities', 1964, Wilson Center. www.wilsoncenter.org

C. Vance Yeh, 'The Life-Style of Four *Wenren* in Late Qing Shanghai', *Harvard Journal of Asiatic Studies*, 57(2) (1997).

H. Van de Ven (ed.), *Warfare in Chinese History* (Leiden, 2000).

H. Van de Ven, *War and Nationalism in China, 1925–1945* (2003).

H. Van de Ven, *Breaking with the Past: The Maritime Customs Service and the Global Origins of Modernity in China* (New York, 2014).

V.M. Veniukov (trans. J.R. Mitchell), *The Russians in Central Asia* (1865).

D.W. Walder, *Short Victorious War: Russo-Japanese Conflict, 1904–5* (1974).

A. Waley, *The Opium War through Chinese Eyes* (1958).

M. Walker, *The Cold War: And the Making of the Modern World* (1993).

Y. Wang, 'Student attacks Against Teachers: The Revolution of 1966', *Issues and Studies*, 2 (2001).

Z. Wang, *Sino-British Negotiations and the Search for a Post-War Settlement 1942–1949: Treaties, Hong Kong and Tibet* (Berlin and Boston, MA, 2022).

M. Wellings, 'Methodist Missions and Popular Literature' (2014). www.methodistheritage.org.uk

O.A. Westad, *Restless Empire: China and the World since 1750* (2012).

G. Wolesley, *Narrative of the War with China in 1860: To Which is added the Account of a Short Residence with the Taiping Rebels in Nanking and a Voyage from There to Hankow* (1862).

J.Y. Wong, *Deadly Dreams: Opium, Imperialism and the Arrow War (1856–1860) in China* (1998).

A. Wyle, *Memorials of Protestant Missions to the Chinese* (Shanghai, 1867).

D. Yang, *Technology of Empire: Telecommunications and Japanese Expansion in Asia, 1883–1945* (Cambridge, MA, 2010).

A.J. Young, 'Roots of Contemporary Maritime "Piracy" in Southeast Asia', MA Thesis, University of Hawaii at Manoa, 2004.

E.P. Young, 'The Politics of Evangelism at the End of the Qing: Nanchang 1906', in Bays (ed.), *Christianity in China*.

Q. Zhai, *China and the Vietnam Wars, 1950–1975* (Chapel Hill, NC, 2000).

Q. Zhai, 'China's Evolving Role on the World Stage', in Lüthi (ed.), *The Regional Cold Wars in Europe*.

G. Zhaoguang, *What Is China? Territory, Ethnicity, Culture, and History* (Cambridge, MA, 2018).

# INDEX